The Female Pen

* *

By the same Author:

THE PSYCHOLOGY OF GENIUS: STUDIES IN BROWNING. University of London Press, 4s. 6d.

WOMEN WRITERS: Their Contribution to the English Novel, 1621-1744. (The Female Pen, Vol 1). 3rd. Impression, 1946. Cork University Press, 10s. 6d.

THE LATER WOMEN NOVELISTS *1744-1818*

BY

B. G. MacCARTHY, M.A., Ph.D.

CORK UNIVERSITY PRESS
NEW YORK: WILLIAM SALLOCH
1948

Dublin Agents: The Standard (1938), Ltd.,
Pearse Street, Dublin, C.5.

Printed in Ireland
By The Kerryman Ltd., Tralee.

Foreword

This book is the second part of a work which was originally intended to be published in one volume entitled *The Female Pen.* The reader who has delved in English literature of the seventeenth and eighteenth centuries will not question the appositeness of the name, since he will recall that such was the term by which a woman writer was designated. The exigencies of war-time made publication in a single volume impossible. In 1944 appeared the first volume under the title: *Women Writers, their Contribution to the English Novel*, 1621—1744. Later impressions of this volume have the sub-title: *The Female Pen* — a sub-title which may now be taken to indicate both volumes.

I wish gratefully to acknowledge my indebtedness to Dr. E. J. Thomas of Cambridge not merely for his generous advice and valuable criticism during the preparation of *The Female Pen*, but also for his faith and encouragement during long years of friendship. I am very much obliged to the Editor of the *Dublin Magazine* for his kind permission to include in this volume some pages (on the Irish Regional Novel and Maria Edgeworth), which had already appeared in the *Dublin Magazine*.

I desire also to express my gratitude to the Senate of the National University of Ireland for the grant made towards the cost of publishing this work.

B. G. MacCarthy.

For
Anne Quinlan

Contents

Chapter I

THE ORIENTAL NOVEL

To Persia and Arabia and all the gorgeous East I owed a pilgrimage for the sake of their magic tales.

(Nathaniel Hawthorne)

From France had come the classicism which closed like a vice on literary England during the eighteenth century. From France, cramped by its own restrictions, came a way of escape. It was not a full release; the prisoner did not throw off his fetters, leave his narrow cell, expand his lungs with fresh air, gaze his fill at the sky, and mingle with the common people. No, he found freedom in imagination, wild, colourful, romantic, fantastic, impossible, as far from reality as might be, yet satisfying. A magic carpet plied from the gorgeous East to fairyland. France turned from Boileau to Ali Baba and Mother Goose.

This dawning of Romanticism in France came from the East, and the first finger of light was seen in 1684, when Marana published his *L'Espion turc*. This was merely a pseudo-Oriental translation in letter form, wherein a disguised Oriental observes European society and politics, and comments thereon from an Eastern point of view. But the sun arose in all its splendour with Galland's translation: *Les mille et une Nuits*, *Contes Arabes*.[1] Thereafter the Oriental novel took its place among the recognised genres of French fiction. The reading public demanded more and more of these astonishing tales, and there at once appeared the translations by Pétis de la Croix: *L'histoire de la Sultane de Perse et des Vizirs*, *Contes turcs* (1707); and *Les mille et*

[1] *Les mille et une Nuits, Contes arabes traduits en français par M. Galland* (Paris, 1704-1717).

un Jours, Contes persans (1710-1712). Galland and Pétis de la Croix had been to the East, and knew Oriental languages. Their translations were authentic, if bare. But soon many pseudo-translators tried their hand at Eastern tales, the most facile and prolific being Thomas Simon Gueullette.[2] Thenceforward four main streams are observable in the flood of Oriental fiction which flowed from French pens, i.e. imaginative, moralistic, philosophic, and satiric.[3]

The English movement in Oriental fiction echoed the French movement, with certain notable variations, due, no doubt, to differing national characteristics. Galland's *Mille et une Nuits* was translated into English between 1704 and 1712, and it took even the most conservative English writers by storm. Johnson, Addison and Steele were enthusiastic, and their experiments gave to this new genre the necessary prestige. Whether they would have given the *Arabian Nights* so hearty a welcome if it had not come via France, is a question. Because, after all, this was not the first Oriental invasion of England, and previous borrowings, although they produced notable results, had never led to a literary movement.

Oriental influences in England go as far back as the eleventh century. We find descriptions of the wonders of India in Anglo-Saxon translations of legends concerning Alexander the Great. During the Middle Ages merchant-travellers like Marco Polo, missionaries, pilgrims and crusaders established a link with the East, and many Oriental tales came to England in this way, or else indirectly by way of Syria, Bizantium, Italy and Spain. In addition four great collections of Oriental tales were translated into Latin, the *lingua franca*

2 Four of his collections were translated into English under the following titles: *Chinese Tales, or The Wonderful Adventures of the Mandarin Fum-Hoam* . . . (1725); *Mogul Tales, or The Dreams of Men Awake*; *being Stories Told to Divert the Sultanas of Guzarat, for the Supposed Death of the Sultan* (1736); *Tartarian Tales, or a Thousand and One Quarters of Hours* (1759); and *Peruvian Tales Related in One Thousand and One Hours by One of the Select Virgins of Cuzco, to the Inca of Peru* . . . (1764, 4th ed.?). The last named collection is worthless.

3 This is the classification made by Miss M. P. Conant in her distinguished treatise, *The Oriental Tale in England in the Eighteenth Century* (Columbia Univ. Press, 1908).

of Europe: *Sendebar*; *Kalila and Dimna, or the Fables of Bidpai*; *Disciplina Clericalis*; and *Barlaam and Josaphat*. These influences produced in England such works as the fabliau of *Dame Sirez*, *The Proces of the Sevyn Sages*, Mandeville's *Voiage*, and Chaucer's *Squire's Tale*. In the sixteenth century, which was characterised by its eagerness for translations, there appeared the first English edition of the *Gesta Romanorum*, and the *Fables of Bidpai*. The earliest English translation of the *Fables* was entitled: *The Moral Philosophie of Doni . . . englished out of the Italian, by Thomas North* (1570). Other factors contributed towards intercourse with and interest in the Orient, e.g. Elizabethan voyages, the fall of Constantinople (1453), and the westward incursions of the Turks. In Painter's *Palace of Pleasure* we find several Oriental tales, and the drama also reflects this influence, as for example, *Tamburlaine*, *Soliman and Perseda*, and even, perhaps, the induction to *The Taming of The Shrew*. In the seventeenth century the translation of French Heroic Romances (many of which had Oriental heroes) and the activities of playwrights and Oriental scholars maintained some interest in the East.

Then came Sir Roger L'Estrange's version of *The Fables of Bidpai*, and the Latin translation by Edward Pococke of the Arabian philosophical romance, *Hai Ebn Yockdhan* (1671). The first English translation of *L'Espion turc*, by William Bradshaw, slightly edited by Robert Midgley, appeared 1687-1693.[4] There were other Oriental stirrings, such as Defoe's *System of Magic* (1726).

It is clear, therefore, that there was some precedent for the Oriental tale in England, and, no doubt, the eighteenth century impetus was due in England, as in France, to the fact that the *Arabian Nights* came at the psychological moment. In both countries the Oriental novel met with opposition as well as enthusiasm, and

[4] Mary Manley maintained that the English version was written by her father (Sir Roger Manley). J. M. Rigg, in D.N.B., says it is 'practically certain that the first volume of the letters was composed not by Manley, but by Marana; and it is at least very probable that the Italian was the author of the remainder of the work.' See D.N.B. Life of Robert Midgley.

it was evident that classicism was making its last stand, and that Romanticism had determined to break away. 'The history of the Oriental tale in England in the eighteenth century might be called an episode in the development of English Romanticism.'[5]

Since the pseudo-Oriental novels showed varying characteristics, it may be as well to glance for a moment at the parent stem. The structure of the *Arabian Nights* is typically Oriental, consisting as it does in a great number of apologues, romances, fables and anecdotes intricately fitted into a loose framework. There is a rich confusion of life and colour, great diversity in events, detailed and vivid descriptions of Eastern customs, and the charm of Oriental names. All the interest is centred on the action, and the appeal to the imagination is unlimited, since magic may at any moment intervene.

In this wonderland fishes talk, hideous slaves become in a twinkling beautiful maidens, and terrible jinn appear from nowhere. Caverns contain gold, silver and rubies beyond the dreams of men. Sharkheaded monsters and alluring mermaids arise from the sea, and one may encounter dwarfs, and 'tremendous black giants, one-eyed and as high as a palm-tree,' or be caught up in an earthly convulsion when lightning tears the sky, 'followed by most tremendous thunder . . . hideous darkness . . . a dreadful cry . . . and an earthquake such as Asrayel is to cause on the day of judgment.' These descriptions and this use of magic give an effect of naïveté, and despite the appeal to the impossible, there is a sense of reality. The *Arabian Nights* really shows Eastern life as it might have been if freed from the limitations of physical laws. The characterisation is very thin, generally a mere representation of stock-types, but by mysterious incidents, dramatic touches and the piling up of adventures the reader's interest is maintained. There is the charm of the story for the story's sake. A sententious element is apparent and yet, on the other hand, there is coarseness in many of the tales.

5 M. P. Conant, *The Oriental Tale in England in the Eighteenth Century* (Columbia Univ. Press, 1908), Intro., p. viii.

The period of the Oriental tale in England was roughly from the first English version of the *Arabian Nights* until about the year 1786. The English Oriental tales may, like the French, be classified according to imaginative, moralistic, philosophic and satiric types, but there is, nevertheless, a difference between the development of this Oriental movement in France and in England. Due, perhaps, to the fact that the fairy tales of Perrault reinforced the magic of the *Arabian Nights*, the movement began in France with great imaginative impetus, which soon gave way to the satirising of human life and manners. This satiric school was the most powerful in the development of the Oriental tale in France. The moralistic tendency (set on foot by Marmontel) was less powerful, and its didacticism, as well as the *Contes licencieux* of such writers as Crébillon fils, hastened the decay of Oriental fiction.

In England, on the contrary, although the Oriental period began with imaginative stories, they were poor in quality and output,[6] and it was not until the very end that *Vathek* appeared to close the history of the Eastern tale in England with a blaze of glory. In the meanwhile, Dr. Johnson, Hawkesworth, Addison and Steele saw in Oriental fiction a very good medium for philosophic and didactic purposes, and these were the predominant trends of the Oriental novel in England. Indeed, it was felt by the Johnsonian circle that only by such uses could such wild and exaggerated tales justify their existence. As for satire, it was in quality of a much narrower and slighter type than in France. It was concerned chiefly with conduct, and found its best expression in Goldsmith's *Citizen of the World*. Save for Horace Walpole's *Hieroglyphic Tales*, there is no original English parody in the Oriental medium.

With one notable exception, women cannot be said to have made any notable contribution to Oriental fiction in England, although they attempted to follow three of the trends which we have enumerated. To the

6 It may be cogent to observe that Perrault's *Contes de ma mère l'oye* was not Englished until 1729.

imaginative group belong Mrs. Aubin, Mrs. Pilkington and, in a sense, Clara Reeve. Mrs. Aubin did not write an Oriental story. Her *Noble Slaves, or the Lives and Adventures of Two Lords and Two Ladies* (1722?) has a Spanish background and Spanish characters, but there are minor people in the story—Asiatics, who recount their adventures. Mrs. Pilkington also, although her principal character was Asiatic, did not attempt an Eastern background. In *The Asiatic Princess* (1800) the heroine is Princess Merjee of Siam. Under the guardianship of an English lady and her husband, the Princess travels so that she may be more thoroughly educated. Her mentors moralise on the difference between Eastern and English customs, and seldom lose an opportunity to improve her mind with moral tales. There are references to the Eastern treatment of slaves and to suttee (the Indian custom which made the greatest appeal to English readers).

Although Clara Reeve did not make any original contribution to the Oriental genre, she had the judgment to publish in *The Progress of Romance*, a slightly modernised version of *Charoba*[7] which had been translated by Davies in 1672. This was one of the most interesting of all the imaginative Oriental tales and the direct source of Landor's poem *Gebir* (1798).

The only woman who attempted the satiric genre was Eliza Haywood, and as her satire was directed against people, her work is merely an *histoire scandaleuse* with a pseudo-Oriental background. In 1736 she published *The Adventures of Eovaai, Princess of Ijaveo. A Pre-Adamitical History. Interspersed with a great Number of Remarkable Occurrences, which happened, and may again happen, to several Empires, Kingdoms, Republics, and particular Great Men . . . Written originally in the Language of Nature (of later Years but little understood).*

7 *The History of Charoba* extracted from *The History of Ancient Egypt, translated by J. Davies,* 1672, *from the French of Monsieur Vattier, written originally in the Arabian tongue by Murtadi.*

First translated into Chinese . . . and now retranslated into English, by the son of a Mandarin, residing in London. It was revised later as *The Unfortunate Princess, or the Ambitious Statesman* (1741). This tale was servilely dedicated to the Dowager Duchess of Marlborough: 'O most illustrious Wife, and Parent of the Greatest, Best and Loveliest! it was not sufficient for you to adorn Posterity with the amiableness of every virtue . . .' One may well wonder how the Duchess swallowed such flattery from the woman who, some twelve years before, had pilloried her in *Memoirs of a Certain Island adjacent to the Kingdom of Utopia.*

In *Eovaai* Mrs. Haywood happily sets herself to flay Walpole under the name of Ochihtou, Prime Minister of Hypotofa:

> This great Man was born of a mean Extraction, and so deformed in his Person, that not even his own Parents cou'd look upon him with Satisfaction . . . As he was extremely amorous, and had so little in him to inspire the tender passion, the first proof he gave of his Art was to . . . cast such a Delusion before the Eyes of all who saw him, that he appeared to them such as he wished to be, a most comely and graceful man . . .

She goes on to describe the hypocritical methods by which he won to power and encompassed 'the almost total ruin of both King and People.'

Eovaai begins with a fantastic account of the Pre-Adamitical world, and a very laboured description of how the book came to be written. The story at first is rather in the nature of a moral allegory, but Mrs. Haywood finds this impossible to maintain, and soon draws upon her répertoire of scurrilous anecdotes, erotic situations and melodramatic adventures. In her key-novels she had, like Mrs. Manley, frequently introduced some personified abstraction to act as *deus ex machina.* Now it was merely going a step further to employ the magical devices which the Oriental tale placed at her disposal. In *Eovaai* her use of magic was greatly exaggerated. As a writer, Mrs. Haywood never learned the value of moderation.

The story of *Eovaai* is briefly as follows: the King

of Ijaveo leaves to his daughter Eovaai a magical jewel on the keeping of which her happiness depends. One day, as she is admiring it in the palace garden, it is carried off by a little bird. Immediately misfortunes fall thick and fast upon Eovaai. Her quarrelsome subjects forsake her and her suitors turn away. The wicked Ochihtou, Prime Minister of the neighbouring kingdom of Hypotofa, has the worst designs upon Eovaai. By black magic he has gained ascendancy over his king and has instigated the banishment of the young prince. Now he uses the same means to satisfy his own desire for power and for the possession of Eovaai. By infernal agencies he conveys her to the court of Hypotofa, corrupts her mind, and is about to complete his domination of her, when a political crisis calls for his immediate attention. The Princess is saved by her good Genius, who enables her to see Ochihtou as he really is and to escape to the kingdom of Oozaff, where his evil spells cannot pursue her. He kidnaps her, and again she escapes his evil intentions by substituting one of his former mistresses, who has been languishing under the shape of a monkey and whom she changes back into human shape. While Ochihtou is amorously employed, the populace storm the palace. Ochihtou is so enraged at the trick played upon him that he now changes his wretched mistress into a rat, and seizing Eovaai, carries her through the air to a neighbouring kingdom, which he intends to use as his base of attack against the rebels. He discovers by magic that the King of Hypotofa is now free from his evil spells, and he persuades Eovaai to return to Ijaveo with him so as to regain her kingdom. He transforms himself into a vulture and Eovaai into a dove, and flies with her to a wood where he again tries to complete his designs. She manages to break his wand, and just as he is about to scourge her, she is rescued by a splendid stranger. Ochihtou dashes out his brains against an oak, and Eovaai and the banished Prince of Hypotofa[8] (for such he is) are married, and rule happily their united kingdoms.

8 Possibly a reference to the Young Pretender.

Mrs. Haywood's story is not important in itself, because the background is weak even as a pseudo-Oriental effort, but chiefly because everything is subordinated to the purpose of a lampoon. The story is a political allegory hotly spiced with scandal and unrelieved by any philosophic or indeed moralising purpose. Mrs. Haywood was merely scavenging again—this time in a turban.

Women's best contribution to the Oriental tale was moralistic. In 1767 Mrs. Frances Sheridan published *Nourjahad*, one of the best moralising stories of the period. Her education had been limited to the ability to read and write, and, as we have already seen, this instruction was given in secret by her brother, very much against her father's wishes. By the time she wrote *Nourjahad*, her success as a novelist was already established by *Miss Sydney Bidulph* (1761), which won the warm admiration of Dr. Johnson, and which was translated by Prévost under the title of *Mémoires d'une jeune dame*.[9]

Nourjahad[10] was meant for the first of a series of instructive moral tales which the author meant to dedicate to the Prince of Wales. Translations from Marmontel[11] and Thomas Parnell's poem, *The Hermit*, had already shown that didactic purpose and imaginative treatment could be fused with excellent results. With Marmontel the word *moral* referred chiefly to manners, but Addison, Steele and Hawkesworth were concerned with questions of conduct. It is in this latter sense that *Nourjahad* is a moral tale.

When Schemzeddin, the wise young prince, mounted the throne of Persia, it was necessary for him to appoint a new ministry. He strongly wished to advance to the office of 'First Minister' a young man of about his own age, who had been bred up with him from infancy, and

9 Part of it was also dramatised under the title: *L'habitant de la Gaudaloupe.*
10 Dramatised by Sophia Lee.
11 e.g. *The Watermen of Besons*, and *Friendship put to the Test.*

whom he loved. But Schemzeddin had a sense of responsibility towards his people and, before taking any decisive step, he consulted the aged councillors of the late Sultan. With one voice they vetoed the appointment of Nourjahad, advancing as their various reasons that he was too young, too avaricious, too pleasure-loving, and was, moreover, irreligious. Schemzeddin requires proofs, but they retort that these faults, though not yet obvious, are in Nourjahad's nature and need only an opportunity to show themselves. Schemzeddin turns in displeasure from these advisers, but their words linger in his mind. He determines to test Nourjahad and, choosing a moment of friendly relaxation, he asks him what he would wish for, if he could have anything he desired. Nourjahad replies that he would wish for inexhaustible riches and everlasting life in which to enjoy them. His doubts thus confirmed, the Sultan angrily upbraids him, but Nourjahad, now seeing his hopes of advancement vanishing, tries to persuade him that he merely spoke in jest. Schemzeddin accepts this explanation without enthusiasm, and Nourjahad retires, cursing his unguarded tongue. He spends the remainder of the night and all the next day torturing himself with regrets and despair. Night falls again, and Nourjahad falls into an exhausted sleep. He awakens to behold a vision. It is his guardian Genius, who offers him anything he may wish for. Nourjahad repeats the wish he had expressed to Schemzeddin. The Genius warns him that happiness may not follow, and says that if he should grievously offend the Prophet, he will be punished by falling into a sleep that may last even for a hundred years. Nourjahad persists in his wish despite the warning of the Genius, who yields at last. Nourjahad is now immortal and rich beyond the dreams of men. He is so stunned at his good fortune that he spends days in planning glorious schemes of living and neglects to make his peace with Schemzeddin, who enraged casts him off, but permits him to keep his house as a gift. Nourjahad rejoices at permission to keep the house because all his treasure is stored in a vault in the garden. He surrounds himself with splendour and with every possible means of gratifying the senses and, sunk in this luxurious existence, remains for some months indifferent to the outside world. He is particularly happy in loving and being loved by Mandana, the most beautiful and gentle in all his seraglio. Then one evening, carried beyond all reason by excessive pleasures, Nourjahad so far forgets the law of the Prophet that he drinks to excess. When he awakens from sleep, it is only to discover that he has been asleep for over four years and that Mandana has died in giving birth to his infant son. Nourjahad is overwhelmed with grief at the loss of Mandana, and the possession of a son does not greatly comfort him. But he has to face an eternity of life so he must forget, if he is to avoid an eternity of sorrow. He wishes to travel, but the Sultan decrees that, though he may remove to a house in the country, he shall be a prisoner within his own grounds. Thus doomed to narrow limits of life, Nourjahad plunges into more complete debauchery than before. Finally, having exhausted every pleasure, he casts about for some new diversion, and decides on playing at being Mahomet in Paradise surrounded by the houris. The ladies of his seraglio are as unfit for this rôle as he is for that of the Prophet, but he does not shrink from the final impiety. All is prepared, and he retires to rest a little before the excesses to come. When he awakes it is to find that he has slept for forty years. His beautiful slaves are withered hags. His trusted major-domo is dead. His son has robbed him of all the money in his coffers and stolen away out of Persia forever. The Sultan, now very old, still is bent on Nourjahad's captivity, but he is permitted to return to his house at Ormiz. This Nourjahad does, and so embittered and disillusioned is he that now he can find amusement only in cruelty. Finally he stabs an old slave and laughs while she welters in her blood. After a night's debauch he goes to rest. When he awakens he finds that he has been asleep for twenty years. The Sultan has just died. His son rules in his stead. The city is in mourning for twenty days. Nourjahad is now so overwhelmed by the nothingness of earthly pleasure, so weary of losing everyone whom he has ever known or loved, that his heart changes and he repents. He bids his servant to go about the city giving alms. But this is contrary to the commands for public mourning, and his servant is condemned to death. He himself is given a chance to escape the death sentence by bribery, but he is tired of the power of money and he cries to Mahomet to take back his gift. No blow falls. Instead, he learns that he has been the victim of a benevolent hoax. Schemzeddin, during the short space of fourteen months, has made him imagine that he has experienced the joys and sufferings of a hundred years. His sleeps were due to soporifics, not magic; his wealth, his slaves were merely lent by Schemzeddin. The Genius was the gentle Mandana who was happy to have a share in redeeming him. Now, purified and wise, he has his reward in Mandana, and in the office of First Minister to Schemzeddin who loves and trusts him.

This charming story is excellently constructed, and the magical effects are most ingeniously and convincingly suggested and reasonably explained. The moralising is not in the least overdone. Indeed, throughout the action the reader is left to gather the moral for himself, and it is only stated explicitly at the end. The background is like the background of all these pseudo-Oriental tales, an Eastern setting as imagined by an eighteenth-century mind—without glamour, but illuminated by the serene light of reason. The conversation is spirited; the interest is very well sustained. All the time we remain in suspense as to the impending punishment of Nourjahad's evil deeds—either by the deep slumbers into which he falls, or by the displeasure of Schemzeddin. There is a satisfying sense of justness in the course of events. The style is graceful, dignified and flexible. The moral is expressed in Schemzeddin's final speech to Nourjahad:

> I now discovered with joy, that thou hadst entirely divested thyself of that insatiable love of pleasure to which thou hadst before addicted thyself, and that thou no longer didst regard wealth, but as it enabled

thee to do good. Only one trial more remained. 'If,' said I, 'his repentance be sincere, and he has that heroism of mind which is inseparable from the truly virtuous, he will not shrink at death, but, on the contrary, will look upon it as the only means by which he can obtain those refined enjoyments suited to the divine part of his nature, and which are as much superior in their essence as they are in their duration, to all the pleasures of the sense.

I made the trial—the glorious victory, O Nourjahad, is thine! By thy contempt of riches, thou hast proved how well thou deservest them; and thy readiness to die, shows how fit thou art to live.

Very much inferior to *Nourjahad* is *Dinarbas* by Ellis Cornelia Knight (1790). Miss Knight, a companion to the Princess Charlotte, had the temerity to attempt a continuation of Johnson's *Rasselas*, a task in which she failed, not merely in degree but in conception. *Rasselas*, as the finest philosophic novel of the English Oriental School, would have been very difficult indeed to equal, even if it lent itself to continuation, which it did not. But Miss Knight, apparently not understanding its philosophic content, continued *Rasselas* in moralistic vein. *Rasselas* had for its subject the vanity of human wishes, the impossibility of happiness except through serenity and patience, which Johnson thought could be attained only by integrity and knowledge. Rasselas reared in the Happy Valley is the optimist brought up in unreality. In contact with actual life he finds that 'human life is everywhere a state in which much is to be endured and little enjoyed.' There is no free choice of one's lot in life. We are enmeshed in circumstances. Rasselas finds that nobody is happy—neither the simple shepherd, nor those who make pleasure their pursuit, nor hermits, nor sages. Even the illusion of happiness found in the past is a source of misery. One can endure life only by inner harmony of spirit. Indeed 'the choice of life is become less important. I hope hereafter to think only on the choice of eternity.' Though differing in treatment, *Rasselas* and *Candide* (which were published almost simultaneously) have much the same philosophic content.

Of the return of Rasselas to Abyssinia Johnson said: 'It is a conclusion in which nothing is concluded.' No doubt, he referred to the impossibility of making some final pronouncement on the riddle of life, but Ellis Cornelia Knight may have found in this remark the germ of her intention to write a sequel. At any rate, her purpose sprang into being when she read in Sir John Hawkins's life of Dr. Johnson: 'The writer had an intention of marrying his hero, and placing him in a state of permanent felicity.' She says: 'This passage suggested the idea of the continuation now offered with the greatest diffidence, to the reader, and without any thought of a vain and presumptuous comparison; as every attempt to imitate the energetic stile, strong imagery, and profound knowledge of the author of *Rasselas*, would be equally rash with that of the suitors to bend the bow of Ulysses.'

She begins at the point where the returning travellers reach Abyssinia. They are held up on the frontier, as war has been declared between Egypt and Abyssinia, and their approach from Egypt is regarded with suspicion. Rasselas with his sister Nekayah, her attendant Pekuah, and Imlac, the poet and philosopher, are taken to a nearby fortress by Dinarbas, the young warrior in charge of the frontier guard. The Governor of the fortress (Amalphus, father of Dinarbas) entertains the party and listens with belief and interest to an account of their travels. The travellers do not acknowledge their identity, but suggest that they are known at the Abyssinian court. A messenger is sent to verify this statement, and meanwhile Rasselas determines to try a military life, partly as an experiment in living, and partly to avoid the company of Zilia, the daughter of Amalphus, who is too charming, too wise and altogether too perfect for his peace of mind. He departs with Dinarbas on a military expedition, and returns after some weeks, having acquitted himself so well that his friendship with Dinarbas is firmly established.

If Rasselas is in danger of loving Zilia, Dinarbas is already in love with Nekayah, who unknown to herself returns his affection. But all is thrown into confusion when the Egyptians attack the fortress. Rasselas is captured and Dinarbas left for dead. He is not dead, however. In the midst of the funeral oration he gives signs of life, and is soon restored. He pays court to Nekayah, who discloses to him that she is the daughter of the Emperor of Abyssinia, and that Rasselas is his fourth son. Nekayah says that, although she loves him, their fates must remain apart.

All this time Rasselas has remained a prisoner in the hands of the Egyptians. He is rescued and brought back to the fortress, where a command awaits him from his father. He is bidden to succeed the Emperor, who is now too old to rule, but first he must subdue his rebellious brothers. This he does. Eventually he marries Zilia. Nekayah marries Dinarbas and all live happily ever after in the Happy Valley.

But did Johnson consider marriage 'a state of permanent felicity', as Sir John Hawkins seems to aver? Johnson said in *Rasselas*: 'Marriage has many pains, but celibacy has no pleasures.' That is the extent of his claim for marriage in an imperfect world. Miss Knight evidently felt that two marriages would produce a greater amount of happiness than one, and gracefully ignored the question of ratio. She ignored also, or she did not understand, that the return to the Happy Valley might be regarded as a return to unreality, and consequently as a defeat. Or is it, after all, the happiest philosophy to cultivate one's garden and to shut one's ears to the still sad music of humanity? Miss Knight was not preoccupied with reflections on mankind as a whole. She moralised about the life of an individual, and she believed that the sum of good outweighs the sum of evil: 'Youth will vanish, health will decay, beauty fade, and strength sink into imbecility: but if we have enjoyed their advantages, let us not say there is no good because the good in this world is not permanent.'

The philosophic theme in Johnson's novel prevents one from dwelling on the slightness of the characterisation and the lack of a convincing Oriental atmosphere.

Dinarbas brings us down to earth, and since we are asked to interest ourselves in the lives of certain individuals, we are entitled to expect that they should be convincingly characterised. One can rise to the personifying of symbols, but one cannot sink to the marriage of cyphers. It is true that none of the Oriental tales of eighteenth century England had more than a shadowy background and thin characterisation; but when, as in *Dinarbas*, love is the main subject described, then we have the final unreality—the love-making of abstractions. Miss Conant says that the value of *Dinarbas* is not literary but historical, that it is an evidence of the desire to moralise everything, even the philosophical tales.[12] But we do not know that Miss Knight deliberately chose to moralise. Indeed it seems that she wrote a moralistic tale because philosophy was beyond her scope.

An example of the persistence into the nineteenth century of the moralising, pseudo-Oriental tale is Maria Edgeworth's *Murad the Unlucky* (1804). This story is sheer edification from beginning to end, and lacks the more imaginative touches of *Nourjahad*, but it is well told. The Sultan of Constantinople debates with his vizier whether fortune or prudence does more for men. The Sultan believes that human success depends on luck, but the vizier is of opinion that there is no such thing as luck, and that success is always the result of prudence, and misfortune merely the natural punishment of imprudence. Wandering one night through the moonlit city, as in the days of Haroun Alraschid, the Sultan and his vizier observe the life around them, and the vizier suggests that the solution of their argument may be found in listening to the stories of two brothers whose fortunes have been so different that one is called Saladin the Lucky and the other Murad the Unlucky. Murad is convinced that he was born under an unlucky star, and by many instances endeavours to show that he has always been dogged by an evil fate, but Miss Edgeworth

12 M. P. Conant, *op. cit*, p. 104.

ingeniously words his narrative in such a fashion as to show that prudence has always offered him a way of escape, which he was always too blind to see. Murad's imprudence is not a reckless disregard for the sensible course, but a stupid inability to recognise it. To mark the moral Maria Edgeworth provides the contrast of Saladin's prudent management of his opportunities, and she even shows how differently each brother acted in the self-same predicament. Murad is fooled by a crafty Jew into buying a chest of second-hand clothes which really come from plague-ridden Smyrna. Murad sells the clothes at a profit, and thus unwittingly spreads the plague throughout Grand Cairo. But Saladin, to whom the Jew previously offered the chest, recognised the suspicious circumstances, and positively refused to have anything to do with so doubtful a bargain. Saladin's prudence wins him respect, honours, riches and true love. Murad's imprudence renders him destitute and miserable—a pariah abandoned by men who fear his ill-luck as a contagion. The moral is summed up thus:

> Had Murad possessed his brother's discretion, he would not have been on the point of losing his head, for selling rolls which he did not bake: he would not have been kicked by a mule, or bastinadoed for finding a ring: he would not have been robbed by one party of soldiers, or shot by another: he would not have been lost in a desert, or cheated by a Jew: he would not have set a ship on fire: nor would he have caught the plague, and spread it through Grand Cairo . . .

The catalogue of folly continues, and long before it ends we are quite convinced of the lesson Maria Edgeworth wishes to convey. She not only hits the nail on the head, but keeps on hitting it long after it is driven home, so eager is she to penetrate our human ignorance with her moral point.

The story is well told in clear, economical prose, but it suffers from its extreme didacticism. English novelists had not yet learnt that, though art may teach obliquely by its own symbolism, it must never be subordinated to mere pedagogy. It was a just retribution that the nearer fiction came to direct teaching, the farther it was from developing its own particular technique and from realising its own destiny.

With the exception of *Vathek*, the pseudo-Oriental novel in England was a peculiar phenomenon of that age. It was the dawning of Romanticism, which might have been expected to stimulate and enrich the imagination. Instead, its light was, for the most part, diverted into the school-room to aid the teaching of pious copy-book maxims. This moralistic genre, despite its obvious limitations, was a safe medium for the female pens, who could not fall into disrepute by such activity. The women who thus moralised had the satisfaction of being in the main stream of the pseudo-Oriental movement in fiction, and one of them, at least, held her own with the best of such writings. *Nourjahad* is a definite achievement in an interesting phase of the English novel.

Chapter II

THE NOVEL OF SENTIMENT AND OF SENSIBILITY

A sufficient quantity of Slobbering and Blessing, and White Handkerchief Work.

(G. L. Way, Learning at a Loss, 1778)

Certain striking features of the novels of eighteenth century women may be said to be due to the general characteristics of the time. The fiction of this century was a curious reflection and denial of contemporary life and thought. It was a reflection of the conventions which a certain level of society chose as the framework of its human and artistic existence, but this framework not only excluded, but tacitly denied all that lay outside its deliberate limitations. It was an age of paradoxes: a period of apparent hypocrisy, but of actual self-deception; a period of earnest ethics divorced from moral principles; a period of philosophic sententiousness which took no thought of social conditions; a period of complacent sensibility, but of the most callous obduracy. It was an England of salons and illiteracy; of thundering divines and pluralism; of languid beaux and highwaymen. The upper stratum of society prided itself on an exquisite sensibility which, however, was invulnerable to the sufferings of the less fortunate. Ladies whose hearts were wrung by the beauty of a snowdrop or the indisposition of a pet bird were unmoved by social injustices, by the iniquitous law which hanged children for theft, or by the squalid horrors of the prison system. Class distinctions in England at that period were completely rigid. The middle class scorned the lower class and was in turn scorned by the privileged class. It was a ladder of condescension which one climbed feverishly for the pleasure of looking down. That Christianity did not bridge the gulf is well seen in the letter of the Duchess of Buckingham to Selina, Countess of Huntingdon. Speaking of the Wesleyan preachers, her Grace says: 'Their doctrines are most repulsive and strongly tinctured with impertinence and disrespect towards their superiors, in perpetually endeavouring to level all ranks and to do away with all distinctions. It is monstrous to be told you have a heart as sinful as the common wretches that crawl on the earth. This is highly offensive and insulting, and I cannot but wonder that your Ladyship should relish any sentiments so much at variance with high rank and good-breeding.' Such, in brief, was the social background which the novel ignored, transmuted or partly revealed.

In considering the Oriental novel and the growth of the epistolary genre we have already touched on certain aspects of eighteenth century fiction. It would be profitable to take a cursory glance at the factors which chiefly influenced the women writers.

In the first place, one cannot fail to be struck by the extraordinary popularity of the novel during the eighteenth century. For some time the growing wealth and power of the middle classes had made it possible for them to share more fully in the amusements of the leisured, and had therefore resulted in a great increase in the reading public. The predilections of so large a class of readers were obviously worth considering, and soon in the greater output of novels we observe a deliberate effort to give the middle classes the sort of pabulum they preferred. But it happened that this economic factor was reinforced by an unpredictable circumstance—by a spontaneous flowering in fiction. When Fielding, Richardson, Sterne and Smollett, for one reason or another, chose the novel as their medium, a new era opened for English fiction, for these men by their genius not only set it firmly on its feet, but raised it to a new level and showed its claim to be recognised as a branch of literary art. This achievement led to great fictional activity but, for a considerable time, had no effect on the quality of subsequent novels. A ceaseless tide of fiction flowed from the printing presses, but the vast majority of these works was worthless and had very little relation to the aims of the Great Four. A number of causes contributed to this lack of succession. It would scarcely be wise to assert that, after Fielding and Richardson, no writer of equal calibre was left to carry their ideas into effect, but it is certain that if such existed they were unwilling to express themselves in fiction. This is easily understood because, though the great novelists had shown that fiction was a branch of literary art, this claim was far from being admitted, and the novel continued to be the pariah of the arts even at the beginning of the nineteenth century. Those who did write fiction seemed unable to grasp the conception and the technique of such works as *Tom Jones* and *Clarissa Harlowe*. This was partly due to their lack of ability, and partly to the difficulty of analysing the artistic subtlety which produces a great literary work. It is true that Fielding, the finest novelist of his age, not content with embodying his artistic principles in his novels, actually enunciated them in his prefaces, but if they were not beyond the comprehension, they were quite beyond the power of the average writer. Fielding was the first to conceive that all of life, focussed with benevolent irony, might be made to live through the personality and behaviour of characters involved in a carefully woven plot. In vision, in perspective, in construction and in characterisation this differed so much from the old desultory aims and methods that a mediocre novelist could not be expected to take so great a leap. A further deterrent was that readers considered Fielding 'low'. Smollett more justly earned the same judgment. Sterne's fictional aim and his subtle sensuality eluded them, but they delighted in his sensibility. Goldsmith's classic simplicity had too fine a flavour for their palates. It was Richardson who really went home to their hearts—not because they realised his greatness as an artist, but because he had so much in common with their outlook and again because, in a general sense, he was more easily imitable.

To understand eighteenth century tastes in fiction one must remember that the reading public was composed of people who had never relinquished the old romantic tradition. It was a middle class public, three quarters of which were women. Thus the bourgeois and the feminine outlook reinforced each other in the reaction against coarseness, in the preoccupation with conventional morality and in a strong bent towards emotionalism. By the second half of the century these were the strongest traits in fiction. They found in Richardson their greatest exponent, and gained from his works an added impetus. But Richardson, the master craftsman, succeeded in manipulating these tendencies in conformity with artistic proportion; his followers, for the most part mere apprentices, sadly lacked this ability. Consequently the influence of Richardson, of Marivaux, and partly of Sterne gave rise to a great accumulation of futility with only an occasional contribution of value. This was the school of sentiment and sensibility, and we shall see later that sensibility also found expression in the Gothic novel. But it was a real sensitiveness to human sufferings, with a determined effort towards amelioration, which gave rise to the *tendenz* group of novelists.

Sensibility, the peculiar boast of the eighteenth century, had many aspects. It differed from sentiment mainly in degree. Sentiment is, in a sense, the norm of feeling. Sensibility was an excessive vulnerability to feeling. It arose from an idealisation of spiritual delicacy. It eventually perished of its own falsity. In its career it exhausted every variety of aim, form and degree. Sensibility did not merely value emotion in itself as a proof of the sensitive nature. It substituted emotion for thought and laid great stress on arriving at a truth instinctively. Mary Wollstonecraft says: 'It is the result of acute senses, finely fashioned nerves, which vibrate at the slightest touch, and convey such clear intelligence to the brain, that it does not require to be arranged by the judgment.'[1] This was sensibility at its healthiest—an exquisite susceptibility to emotion by which one felt one's way through life, by which one lived at the highest possible level. Sensibility made one 'tremblingly alive'; without it one merely existed in 'a vegetative state'.[2] It was the great ideal of eighteenth century novelists and an essential characteristic of all heroines and heroes. Every opportunity for a display of sensibility was seized upon with avidity, and the plot was even deliberately framed so as to involve the characters in the greatest possible number of tribulations. Joy and happiness were at once felt to offer little scope for sensibility. Suffering was a bottomless abyss in which a human being might fall forever—or an eternal winepress in which the victim might forever yield the essence of his soul. This explains the popularity of novels which, like *Sydney Bidulph*, earned the reproach that they caused their readers too much suffering. 'Whether it be that the mind abhors nothing like a state of inaction, or from whatever cause, I know not, but grief itself is more agreeable to us than indifference; nay, if not too exquisite, is in the highest degree delightful; of which the pleasure we take in tragedy, or in the talking of our dead friends, is a striking proof. We wish not to be cured of what we feel on these occasions; the tears we shed are charming—we even indulge in them.'[3] And again: 'Pleased with the tender sorrow which possessed all my soul, I determined to indulge it to the utmost.'[4] This cult of suffering was the inevitable result of the deification of sensibility, and however it may have been strengthened or developed by the influence of Marivaux, Prévost, Madame Riccoboni and others,[5] it seems logical to suppose that the English

1 Mary Wollstonecraft, *Posthumous Works*, i, *The Cave of Fancy*, p. 135 f.
2 Mrs. Frances Brooke, *The History of Emily Montague* (ed. 1784), i, p. 83. Sir George Clayton is a dreadful example of this insensitive nature.
3 Mrs. Frances Brooke, *The History of Lady Julia Mandeville* (*British Novelists* ed., 1820, xxvii, p. 35.).
4 *Ibid.*, p. 201.
5 Mr. James Foster (in 'The Abbé Prévost and the English Novel', *Publications of the Modern Language Assoc. of America*, vol. xlii, no. 2, June, 1927) states definitely that at this period French fiction exerted a strong influence on English fiction. He says that Mmes de la Fayette, d'Aulnoy, de Tencin, Riccoboni and de Genlis, and particularly Marivaux and Prévost, all animated by sensibility,

novel of sensibility, like the French novel of sensibility, would have arrived by much the same path at similar plots of endurance and trial.

Sensibility, however, has other aspects than those of suffering. It may be aroused not only by affection but by love, romantic or dutiful, and also by the poor and the unfortunate. Few of these novels are without at least one incident of charitable succour. Albany in Fanny Burney's *Cecilia* is the incarnation of this philanthropic impulse. Yet there is never a direct reference to the actual conditions of social neglect and injustice. Poverty is a sentimentalised circumstance introduced to give sensibility another outlet; and the poor are always presented from the standpoint of patronage—humbly submissive to their fate and fulsomely grateful for the life-giving crust. There was need for a Mary Wollstonecraft to tell with stark abruptness the sordid story of a servant girl.

Beauty was another delightful irritant of sensibility—whether of a face, a book, or a scene. In *Camilla* the Oxford student reading Thomson's *Seasons* in a bookshop exclaims, cries out, beats his forehead and finally bursts into tears. He is not insane, but commendably sensitive. Nature became, with the growth of the century, an increasing source of sensibility, but it was rarely nature unadorned. Scenery and the elements were

had a most powerful and far-reaching effect on the English novelists. He claims that Prévost and his disciples (of whom Baculard d'Arnaud was one) prolonged the epoch of sensibility in the English novel, and showed that, when the Richardsonian gamut of domestic sufferings was exhausted, a wider field of sensibility was to be found in adventurous perils, this aspect of sensibility finding cumulative expression in the Gothic romance. In addition to a detailed exposition of these views, Mr. Foster gives an account of the numerous English translations of the French writers mentioned and traces the influence of Prévost and his followers on individual English novelists of this period. As against Mr. Foster's opinion there is the opinion of George Saintsbury (Introduction to H. Waddell's translation of *Manon Lescaut*, 1934, p. xxviii):

'Mr. James Foster . . . has collected a mighty list of translations and suggested a mightier one of imitations, inspirations and the like. I confess that I think he has altogether over-rated the Abbé's influence on individuals . . . Prévost influenced those who influenced nobody. I can myself see very little resemblance to him in Mrs. Sheridan's *Sydney Bidulph* and still less in Mrs. Radcliffe anywhere, while he certainly may have any share in Miss Lee's rubbishy *Recess* that anybody chooses to assign to him. I desire not to be in the least impolite to Mr. Foster, but I think that he and all his school are much too fond of assuming direct "imitation", "influence", "origin", etc., when there is merely coincidence or at most similar influence of period and fashion.'

sentimentalised, stage-managed and used romantically to echo a mood or to arouse retrospective emotion. This is an aspect of sensibility which we find most fully exploited in the Gothic novel.

Even morality was only sensibility in another guise—sensibility in this sense meaning moral sensitiveness, roughly the equivalent of conscience. In the words of Mrs. Brooke:

> Women are religious as they are virtuous, less from principles founded upon reasoning and argument, than from elegance of mind, delicacy of moral taste, and a certain perception of the beautiful and becoming in everything. This instinct, however, for such it is, is worth all the tedious reasoning of the men.[6]

This is a view which Hannah More also expresses in her poem on *Sensibility*.[7]

But apart from the enervating waste of emotion and the lack of balanced judgment, apart from the hair-splitting fastidiousness which, says Mrs. Arlbery in *Camilla*, 'refines away' its own happiness, sensibility was damned by its egoism. Even if it had given rise to greater artistry in fiction, it would not have been possible to forgive its complacence at its own capacity for feeling—this subordination of all things to that exquisitely sensitive soul whose sensibility it is their only function to arouse.

> Of this danger the majority of eighteenth-century writers cannot have been much aware: they give themselves away too handsomely. Again and again we find that enormity of self-gratulation with which the weeper at once luxuriates in the beguiling softness of tears and compliments himself on his capacity for shedding them, seeing in his mind's eye not only the object of his attention, but himself in a suitable attitude in front of it.[8]

The modern reader of eighteenth century fiction sometimes feels caught in a nightmare in which seduced girls, dying parents, families starving in garrets, begging

6 Mrs. Frances Brooke, *Emily Montague* (1769), i, p. 225.
7 Prefixed to her *Sacred Dramas* (1782).
8 J. M. S. Tompkins, *The Popular Novel in England*, 1770-1800 (1932), p. 101.

negroes, unctuously repentant sinners, white-haired clergymen and innocently prattling children clutch with their pale fingers a naked heart from which they wring streams of—tears. It is a world in which intensely cultivated emotion finds unrestrained expression. Speech becomes rhodomontade, and action, passing rapidly through every phase of convulsive behaviour, reaches the limit of human endurance and is intermitted. Thus the characters sob, groan, scream, beat their breasts, tear their hair, fall into a frenzy, rave and become insensible. Tears are the only safety valve, and never did the 'vater-vorks', scorned by Sam Weller senior, operate with such torrential force. The slightest tremor of feeling opens the floodgates. Indeed Mackenzie's *Man of Feeling* was a dam of which the sluice gates were never shut. The liquidity of Mr. Villars in Thomas Bridges's *Adventures of a Banknote* shows the extent to which fiction lacked a sense of humour. We read that 'tears cours'd one another down his manly cheeks and form'd a rapid current o'er his garments.'

Implicit in sensibility there appears to have been some notion of focussing the attention on the inner man. But writers, lacking insight or unable to cope with the minutiæ of character and motive, found it easier to enlarge everything to many times its natural size. Yet even such an explanation is too merciful, because the falsity is not merely of scale, but of kind. Even allowing for extreme exaggeration, the fiction of sensibility has little or no relation to reality. Prior to 1740, writers had concerned themselves with external life and padded their narratives with a multiplicity of exciting adventures. Now, since it had been demonstrated that fiction could be written from within, the lesser novelists of the eighteenth century could not be deterred from what they fondly believed to be an internal treatment. The result was unreal and inartistic to the last degree. False notions of nobility and villainy precluded characterisation; orgies of melodrama in plot and style completed the artificiality. It was an unnatural, an hysterical and even a morbid school of fiction. It died of exhaustion accelerated, no doubt, by continuous cardiac hæmorrhage. Jane Austen laughed heartlessly over its corpse.

This period of the English novel was marked by a great influx of women writers. Indeed their proportion was almost equal to that of the women readers. Many reasons co-operated to cause this determined invasion of the lists. In the first place, the epistolary form was easy, and the domestic novel brought fiction into the field of feminine experience. The cult of sentiment and sensibility was so effeminate and the trend of moral earnestness so decorous, that women, without relinquishing their delicacy, could compete with the men writers. As a matter of fact, the supposed feminine pre-eminence of imagination and feeling gave the women such an advantage that some of the male hacks wrote under the pretence of being women. 'We suspect,' wrote the *Critical* (in April, 1778) of the *Memoirs of the Countess D'Anois*, 'that Madame la Comtesse may be found in some British garret, without breeches, perhaps, but yet not in petticoats.'[9]

Another factor which encouraged many women was that the general standard of fiction was low, and was rendered still lower by the money-making devices of the publishers, the book-sellers, and the circulating libraries, which were generally either in league, or actually under the same ownership. The libraries brought novel-reading within the competency of a far greater number of people, the majority of whom were quite uncritical, and it became a very profitable business to cater deliberately for this easily satisfied public. The ready market for rubbish had naturally a debasing effect on fiction, which was still further prostituted by the popularising of the many-volume novel. This mercenary scheme involved novelists in a despairing effort to fill three, four or even five volumes. So gullible and so unfailing was the public that libraries frequently changed the name of a novel and put it into circulation again,

9 Dr. J. M. S. Tompkins makes this point and adds that 'there is evidence that eight years earlier the fraud was already an old and paying one.' See *The Popular Novel in England*, 1770-1800, p. 120.

while publishers brought the faking of editions to a fine art. There is no doubt that the book trade had, at that time, a grievous effect on fictional development, since it made it possible for the merest scribblers to make a living out of their wretched effusions. This was a benefit to the untalented woman writer, but was far from aiding women's contribution to the novel, which must be judged only by sifting the good grain from the chaff.

The standard of criticism applied to the novel in the eighteenth century was a further encouragement to the female pen. Didacticism was regarded as the only justification of the novel; moral teaching was indispensable, and if the novel could also be made the vehicle for general information (such as history or geography), it would then serve the added purpose of sugar-coating the pill of education, which readers, especially females, would otherwise find unpalatable. It was essential that the novel should be both interesting and probable so that it might be able to teach convincingly. General information was, no doubt, beyond the scope of women novelists, but earnest morality was their forte, and their refined imaginations already disposed the critics in their favour. Indeed the critics were much inclined to be indulgent to the 'British fair', so long as she wrote from a legitimate motive and was sufficiently humble. To venture safely into print a woman should be either morally didactic, dilettante or distressed. Any such reason, explained with extreme diffidence and self-depreciation, would win the critic not to soften, but to abstain from applying, the canons of criticism. This uncritical indulgence came particularly into play if the writer penned her tale at the bedside of a bedridden mother, or was the sole support of an invalid husband and nine children. But the superficiality of such chivalry became apparent at the slightest deviation from the apologetic code. Literary ambition in a woman was regarded as an impertinence and led to terrible scourgings. It was considered indelicate for a woman to write her name on the title page—a taboo which was carefully observed, although sometimes we find that a signed preface is not considered inconsistent with a title page that admits nothing. Clara Reeve, that spirited spinster, wrote her first book at forty, and withheld her full signature until she was in her sixtieth year. Very often authorship was an open secret, but it was supposed to remain unacknowledged nevertheless. No reader of Fanny Burney's diary can ever forget her acute sensibility on the subject of her authorship. She was entertained and fêted by the great only because she was the writer of *Evelina*. It was her passport to the most learned and aristocratic circles, yet if anyone mentioned *Evelina* in her presence she was overwhelmed by the indelicacy. Congratulations on her achievement she regarded as a most shocking display of coarseness. This was the attitude sanctioned by the critics. They were not kind to women novelists because they were women—only because they were humble, which, it was hoped, they would continue to remain. Reviewers were ever on the alert for the slightest sign of female self-importance. If a woman, to remain anonymous, put 'Author of—' on the title page she was withered. But there was a worse offence: the innocent use of the editorial plural once drew upon a woman novelist the jeer: 'We suppose the lady is pregnant, and her unborn child shares her emotions.' Still, there must have been women even then who in their hearts resented, more than scoffings, the insulting magnanimity which forgave them their novels in view of their sex. It was an attitude which encouraged mediocrity and crushed real worth.

Although the influx of women into the field of fiction during the eighteenth century happened, for the reasons we have noted, to produce little that was of value nevertheless even the trashy level of their work has a certain interest. It is interesting because it enables us to trace their conception of womanhood and their attitude to life. What emerges is a dead level of conventionality with occasional outbursts of the feminine point of view. Women's conventions were prudential, narrow and superficial. They provided for every contingency of behaviour with the most minute forethought, and absolved women from any need of understanding or reflection. The 'principling' which was the great essential of women's upbringing had little to do with fundamentals, and consisted merely of a set of intricate rules for the preservation of chastity. These taboos appear to have induced a rather distasteful sex-consciousness; womanly delicacy seems chiefly to have implied a complete absence of respect and confidence between the sexes and a defensive rampart of hypocrisy on the part of the women. But it is represented as intuitive integrity and a watchful and scrupulous virtue. Women who were so unfortunate as to fall from virtue always died, generally from a decline, bitterly repentant. Sometimes they are allowed to live long enough to show the earnestness of their reformation, but generally not, in case they should contaminate the community. A modest young woman never loves until the man has declared himself. She should never aim at learning, which would only unsex her and ruin her chances of a husband. All women should have an exquisite fineness of perception and feeling. They should be meek, compassionate, patient and forgiving, particularly wives, who owe the deepest submission to their husbands whether or not such submission is deserved. This is a very brief summary of the women novelists' views. It is at once apparent that they are masculine views. They are to be found in the men's novels. The women novelists who expressed them had, in any case, been reared according to such beliefs. It would be a nice point to determine how much of this ideal of womanhood was imposed on them by men, and how much was a web of high-flown theory which women had been spinning for ages in an unconscious effort to build up a self-respecting pattern of life despite the arbitrary, contradictory and sometimes humiliating circumstances which limited them. No doubt they had listened so long to soporific pronouncements that they really believed them. Effective propaganda does achieve such results; and certainly, at that period, men's comfort and supremacy depended on the credibility of this pseudo-philosophy for soft feminine brains. Now and then, in these women's novels, a spark leaps up for a moment to throw light on the untouched question of the women *per se*. Sometimes there is even a tiny blaze. Then we return again to women echoing the masculine ideal of women. Even the very air of physical delicacy (which gave men of that period a feeling of superior strength) was made by female novelists the essential of every heroine. But it must be said that women took an unintended revenge by evolving a hero who was most elegantly delicate in every way. He was as pure as the driven snow; had perfect manners; dressed charmingly; wrote beautiful verse and frequently swooned.

Still, despite the valueless flotsam that lay thick upon the stream of female fiction during the eighteenth century, the current flowed on and gathered force. Passing from Addison's England to that of Johnson, we note a definite change in women's prestige. In Addison's time it was a fact that: 'in the female world, any acquaintance with books was distinguished only to be censured.'[10] Those were the days 'when a woman who could spell a common letter was regarded as all-accomplished. Now [said Johnson] they vie with the men in everything.'[11] When Richardson was in his glory it was for women the greatest privilege to be admitted to the circle at Northend. By the time *Evelina* appeared women had their own salons. Johnson's broadminded encouragement of female talents had no small share in developing this new attitude. Richardson had surrounded himself with women because they 'listened to him implicitly and did not venture to contradict his opinions.'[12] Johnson's circle consisted of men and women, and the women enjoyed something bordering on equality. But now there were circles where women reigned supreme, either for learning, wit, elegance, or individuality. Of these the greatest was Mrs. Montagu, 'Queen of the Blues'. Other stars in this firmament were

10 *Boswell's Life of Johnson* (ed. Hill), vii, p. 107.
11 *Diary of Madame d'Arblay*, i, p. 160.
12 *Boswell's Life of Johnson* (ed. Hill), v, p. 395 f.

the bookish Mrs. Carter; the ugly and good-natured Mrs. Chapone; the flighty and fashionable Mrs. Vesey; the elegant Mrs. Crewe and Mrs. Boscawen; Mrs. Thrale, the vivacious bourgeoise; Mrs. Cholmondeley and Mrs. Walsingham, both great wits; the social Mrs. Ord and others of less note. Uniquely apart, not competing in learning, wit, fashion, or hospitality, was the ageless Mrs. Delany. In the last quarter of the century these were names to conjure with, so that Fanny Burney well might say: 'Now that I am invited to Mrs. Montagu's, I think the measure of my glory is full.'

Before the great army of female novelists had entered the field of sentiment and sensibility, while yet they were only sharpening their pens for conquest, a woman novelist scored a spectacular triumph. It was the happy fate of Charlotte Lennox, at the beginning of her career, to be publicly crowned with laurels by Dr. Johnson himself. The scene has been well preserved for us in the vinegar of one Hawkins, a pompous gentleman whose powers of revelry were precluded by a 'raging tooth'. One spring evening in the year 1751, a merry party assembled at the Devil Tavern near Temple Bar. It consisted of sixteen members of the Ivy Lane Club, who came at the bidding of Johnson to honour Charlotte Lennox's first novel, then either just published or issuing from the press. The authoress was kept in countenance by the presence of her husband and a lady-friend, and by the wish of the genial lexicographer it was an 'all night sitting'. First there was an 'elegant' supper, of which the pièce de résistance was a 'magnificent hot apple-pye' stuck with bay-leaves—a graceful reference to the volume of poetry that Mrs. Lennox had already published. Then, after a suitable invocation, the coronation took place, and thereafter the company made merry until morning with talk and laughter which flourished, for the most part, on no stronger liquids than tea and coffee. Some few backsliders there were from this plan of non-alcoholic high spirits; but Johnson needed no intoxicant but the exuberance of his own verbosity, and at five o'clock his face still shone with meridian splendour. When St. Dunstan's clock was striking eight, the literary revellers, weary and dishevelled, issued forth into Fleet Street. Mr. Hawkins withdrew to nurse his tooth and his disapproval, and the queen of the evening went home, her brain reeling with exhaustion and fame.

Charlotte Lennox was the daughter of Colonel James Ramsay, reputed to be the Lieutenant-Governor of New York. When she was fifteen she was sent to England to live with an aunt who, when she arrived, was either dead or mad. Then her father died and she had to support herself. She was befriended by Lady Rockingham, was turned away for some supposed love affair, and was taken up for a while by the Duchess of Newcastle. She attempted the stage and was (says Walpole) a 'deplorable actress'. An unfortunate marriage caused her to commence author as a means of support. For over forty-three years she continued to write poems, novels, plays and translations but, despite her outstanding success at one period, she ended her days in penury. Latterly she was supported partly by the Literary Fund and partly by the Hon. George Rose who also paid her funeral expenses. It was a strange declension from the triumph at the Devil Tavern to that poor and lonely death-bed in Dean's Yard, Westminster—a life of effort ending merely in a defeated sigh.

Charlotte Lennox's first novel was *The Life of Harriot Stuart*, which was published in December, 1750. This was a tale centring on the flight of the heroine from marriage with a hated suitor. There are hairbreadth 'scapes from redskins, pirates, ravishment and other perils; and there are the usual misunderstandings between the true lovers who are finally united. In this novel (as in her last novel, *Euphemia*) Mrs. Lennox drew on her memories of American life, but the background also changes to England and France. *Harriot Stuart* scarcely merited Johnson's celebrations, and indeed it brought its author at least as much notoriety as fame, since in it she pilloried Lady Isabella Finch[13] in a manner so obvious that it aroused much resentment in society.

But however opinion may have varied about Charlotte Lennox's first novel, with her second she took the reading public by storm. *The Female Quixote*, which appeared in 1752, is this writer's strongest claim to literary remembrance. Not only Johnson, but Richardson and more especially Fielding were loud in their praises. The book ran into a second edition in three months, and continued to be published up to 1820. It was translated into German, French and Spanish.[14] *The Female Quixote* is an imitation of *Don Quixote*, that is to say that Charlotte Lennox, like Cervantes, satirised the old style of romantic fiction. Charlotte Lennox had chiefly in mind the novels of Mlle. de Scudéry and her followers.

Lady Arabella, the Female Quixote, is the daughter of a nobleman who, through disgust at the injustice of the court, quitted it for a life of complete retirement in the country. Absence of human companionship and endless reading of Heroic Romances have caused her to create for herself a fantastic world peopled with characters who live according to an astonishing code. In this realm of heroic romanticism all the heroines are young, beautiful and virtuous, and time is powerless to impair these qualities. The men are of two kinds: heroes who are generally princes in disguise, and who in every vicissitude remain princely; and villains who devote themselves to foul emprises with an astounding assiduity. They never cease to plot against the heroines, and are everlastingly carrying them off, but this they must do so as to give the heroes an opportunity of rescuing the distressed fair ones, generally in the nick of time. Nothing could be more selfless than these

13 For full details see Miriam R. Small, *Charlotte Ramsay Lennox* (Yale Univ. Press, 1935). Lady Mary Wortley Montagu's letter to the Countess of Bute expresses 'great surprise and indignation'.

14 The earliest translation was into German: *Don Quixote im Reifrocke* (1754), published at Hamburg and Leipzig. The French translation appeared in 1773, second ed. 1801; the Spanish translation (by Don Bernardo Maria de Calzada) appeared in 1808.

services. The heroines live on a system of payment deferred. If the hero is sufficiently valorous, sufficiently devoted, and sufficiently pure-souled, he may with luck win his lady at the end of a quarter of a century. Meanwhile the most he can hope for is her negative toleration. At the slightest offence she will immediately wish his death, whereupon it is understood that he will at once be stricken down. To live in disobedience to such a command would be an unthinkable impertinence, and if the human frame does not spontaneously dissolve, then the hero must deliberately destroy it. If, however, at the last moment, when the hero is actually expiring, the lady should change her mind and command him to live, his physical system will immediately respond, and make it possible for him to return to his duties there and then. There are no duties in this Never-Never country save those connected with love and beauty; adoring beauty, serving beauty, rescuing beauty. As to love, it is the direct antithesis of eroticism; it is known chiefly as a lack:

> It is to be all made of sighs and tears . . .
> It is to be all made of faith and service . . .
> All made of passion and all made of wishes;
> All adoration, duty and obedience,
> All humbleness, all patience, and impatience,
> All purity, all trial, all observance.

The hero may (indeed he must) love, but he must never dare to insult the heroine by a declaration. In fact, that he should centre his affections on a lady is considered so gross in its implications that twenty years of purgatory are all too little as a preface to elysium. If the goddess so served were not infallible and perfect, then the whole code of chivalry would fall to the ground; but she *is* infallible and, as a consequence, completely autocratic.

Such are the fantasies with which Arabella is obsessed, but her father's death and his wish that she should marry her cousin, Charles Glanville, force her to face reality, or rather force her to decide between two possible realities: the actual world of men and women, and the world of the Heroic Romance. She must either abandon the world of the Heroic Romance or force others to share it with her. Her efforts to impose its code on the outer world are the subject of the novel.

It is to be expected that all sorts of absurdities would result from Arabella's obstinacy, and one of Mrs. Lennox's first problems was how best to explain Arabella's persistence in quixotism. She had to choose between making Arabella an idiot or an autocrat. She made her an autocrat. One questions her decision, because it is necessary for a heroine to be lovable, and, on the whole, idiots are more lovable than autocrats. Still, Arabella's high-handedness is relieved by an unconscious childishness, and by her complete innocence, generosity and lack of affectation. These qualities in her are marked by contrast with the sophisticated, envious, husband-hunting flirts with whom she is brought into contact.

The strongest chain of continuity in the story is the love of Charles Glanville which, though tried almost to breaking, still holds firm. Arabella alighting on the *terra firma* of everyday life interprets everything by the standards of romance. The gardener lurking about suspiciously because he plans a theft, the idle gallant staring curiously at Arabella's antique style of dress, are to her disguised noblemen with the worst intentions, awaiting only the opportunity to carry her off. She believes that every male cherishes a secret passion for her and this induces in her such active resentment that several of them are forced to tell her the simple truth: that they never for a moment thought of loving her. She leaves her country estate and goes to Bath and then to London, but the life around her never impinges on her consciousness. Her beauty, social position and riches win a certain amount of tolerance for her eccentricity, and therefore her *idée fixe* is not dislodged. Finally, after she has thrown herself into the river to escape being ravished by some men who have never even noticed her existence, Charles Glanville believes that the time has come for drastic action. He sends a learned clergyman to reason with her, and this logical appeal to her common-sense effects what no amount of ridicule could achieve. All ends happily with her marriage to Glanville.

The humour of *The Female Quixote* arises from the conflict of the romantic and the everyday code of behaviour, and it is very well sustained throughout. For example, there are the conversations between Miss Glanville, the vapid, sophisticated and calculating flirt, and Arabella the intelligent, the unspoiled, but the bizarre. Highly amusing indeed is their interview after Arabella has (as she thinks) barely escaped abduction by a disguised nobleman (who is really the gardener).[15] But still better are the cross-purposes between this ill-assorted pair on the subject of the adventures which beautiful ladies cannot escape, and of the favours which they may grant to their adorers. A favour to Arabella means not actually wishing the death of a presumptuous lover or, at the very most, a ribbon from the lady's sleeve. By the word favour Miss Glanville understands what Mrs. Manley's school politely termed 'the last favour'. Arabella, thinking to compliment Miss Glanville, says that she is sure she must have had many adventures, by which she means being carried off by men of 'unbridled passions' and, of course, always being rescued opportunely by honest princes in disguise. Unfortunately, to Miss Glanville the word adventure connotes the exploits of the adventuress:

> 'Whence comes it, cousin [says Arabella] being so young and lovely as you are that though you questionless, have been engaged in many adventures, you have never reposed trust enough in me to favour me with a recital of them?' 'Engaged in many adventures, Madam!' returned Miss Glanville, not liking the phrase: 'I believe I have been engaged in as few as your ladyship.'
>
> 'You are too obliging,' returned Arabella, who mistook what she said for a compliment; 'for, since you have more beauty than I, and have also had more opportunities of making yourself beloved, questionless you have had a greater number of admirers.' 'As for admirers,' said Miss Charlotte, bridling, 'I fancy I have had my share! Thank God, I never found myself neglected; but, I assure

15 *The Female Quixote* (*Novelists Mag.*) p. 64 f.

you, Madam, I have had no adventures, as you call them, with any of them.'

'No, really,' interrupted Arabella, innocently.

'No, really, Madam!' retorted Miss Glanville, 'and I am surprised you should think so.'

Arabella then cites the case of Mandana who had thousands of adventures, and who so enslaved the great Cyrus that he could refuse nothing she asked, even to the freeing of great number of Jews whom he had taken captive.

'Well,' said Miss Glanville, 'and I suppose she denied *him* nothing he asked; and so they were even.'

'Indeed but she did though,' resumed Arabella; 'for she refused to give him a glorious scarf which she wore, though he begged for it on his knees.'

'And she was very much in the right,' said Miss Glanville; 'for I see no reason why a lover should expect a gift of any value from his mistress.'

'Doubtless,' said Arabella, 'such a gift was worth millions of services; and had he obtained it, it would have been a glorious distinction for him: however, Mandana refused it; and severely virtuous as you are, I am persuaded you can't help thinking that she was a little too rigorous in denying a favour to a lover like him.'

'Severely virtuous, Lady Bella!' said Miss Glanville, reddening with anger. 'Pray what do you mean by that? Have you any reason to imagine I would grant any favour to a lover?'

'Why, if I did, cousin,' said Arabella, 'would it derogate so much from your glory, think you, to bestow a favour upon a lover worthy of your esteem, from whom you had received a thousand marks of a most pure and faithful passion, and also a great number of very singular services?'

'I hope, Madam,' said Miss Glanville, 'it will never be my fate to be so much obliged to any lover, as to be under a necessity of granting him favours in requital.'

'I vow, cousin,' interrupted Arabella, 'you put me in mind of the fair and virtuous Antonia, who was so rigid and austere, that she thought all expressions of love were criminal, and was so far from granting any person permission to love her that she thought it a mortal offence to be adored even in private.'

Miss Glanville, who could not imagine Arabella spoke this seriously, but that it was designed to sneer at her great eagerness to make conquests, and the liberties she allowed herself in, which had probably come to her knowledge, was so extremely vexed at the malicious jest, as she thought it, that, not being able to revenge herself, she burst into tears.

Arabella is overcome by amazement and solicitude, and begs to know how she has offended: 'You have made no scruple,' answered Miss Glanville, 'that you think me capable of granting favours to lovers: when Heaven knows, I never granted a kiss without a great deal of confusion!'[16] A kiss! Arabella is appalled—a kiss, when the chaste Mandana, the virtuous Statira, the wise Antonia felt themselves compromised if, after having been served in humility and with terrific feats of derringdo for long years, they went so far as not to wish the death of their faithful knights!

Arabella reads the erring one a long lecture with Mandana as her text, and points the moral with insulting comparisons to the 'inconsiderate Julia, who would receive a declaration of love without anger from anyone, and was not over-shy any more than yourself, of granting favours almost as considerable as that you have mentioned.' We are not surprised to learn that Miss Glanville, having dried her tears, sits silently swelling with rage, and is restrained only by the hope of revenging herself later—a vain dream, because Arabella's beauty and fortune centre on her all the masculine attention. Nor is there even any hope that Arabella's peculiar views may lead her into humiliating situations as, though she is constantly involved in misunderstandings, that haughty visionary either fails to observe any cause of embarrassment, or else autocratically considers that she is unfortunate in encountering people who lack nobility of spirit.

It has been suggested that Mrs. Lennox attributed Arabella's conversion to her interview with the learned divine simply to compliment Dr. Johnson, who is supposed to have written that chapter;[17] and it has been

16 Ibid., (*Novelists Mag.*) bk. 2, chap. ix, p. 52 f.

17 See Miss M. R. Small, *Charlotte Ramsay Lennox* (Yale Univ. Press, 1935) for a detailed discussion of Johnson's supposed authorship of chapter eleven (book 9), the penultimate chapter of *The Female Quixote*. This point was first raised by Rev. J. Mitford in the *Gentleman's Mag.*, August, 1843.

said[18] that it would have been more natural if Arabella's experiences had forced her gradually to realise that her views were fantastic. This would indeed have been more reasonable, but Arabella is modelled on Don Quixote, and he also was characterised by invulnerability to the opinion of others. When the Knight of the Silver Moon has him at his mercy, the prostrate Quixote still asserts that Dulcinea del Toboso is the finest lady in the world. It is true, however, that Arabella's whims are carried too far; that her declamations, peppered with examples from the French romances, are altogether too long-winded, and that there are too many improbable incidents. These are criticisms which, at first glance, might be supposed to apply also to *Don Quixote*, but in Cervantes' book such points are merely superficial, whereas in Mrs. Lennox's they are the essential matter of the novel. It may be said in Mrs. Lennox's defence that there were special difficulties in satirising a female Quixote. Cervantes' knight could wander where he would in search of adventure: Arabella was forced to find her adventures wherever she happened to be and, although the scene changes, her immediate circumstances do not, because the conventions require that she should be accompanied everywhere by an entourage of her nearest relatives. Don Quixote could initiate romantic emprises as the spirit moved him. Arabella could merely give romantic interpretations to the actions of others (the one exception being when, to escape imaginary ravishers, she jumps into the river—an incident which seriously jars one's ideas of probability). This is one of the points made by Fielding in his long and favourable review of *The Female Quixote*.[19] The surprising thing is not merely that, in some minor respects, he should find *The Female Quixote* better than *Don Quixote*, but that he should seriously compare these works. It is true that he stresses the superiority of Cervantes, but even with Fielding as a precedent, no sensible person could think

18 *Ibid.*, p. 82.

19 *Covent Garden Journal*, March 24, 1752. Johnson may also have written a review of *The Female Quixote* in the *Gentleman's Mag.*, March, 1752, xxii, 146. So, at any rate, suggests Dr. Birbeck Hill in his *Life of Johnson* (1887), i, p. 367.

of comparing Cervantes and Charlotte Lennox. One was a genius. The other was a clever wit. One, intending to write a satire, achieved an immortal work of art: the other, intending to write a burlesque—wrote a burlesque. The greatness of Cervantes (as Heine so finely suggests) lies in the symbolism of the haggard knight and his serving-man who 'so constantly burlesque and yet so wonderfully complement each other, so that together they form the one true hero of romance,—these two figures give evidence of the poet's artistic taste and of his intellectual profundity.' They represent the spiritual and the material—both aspects of life, in short; and they represent also the fusion of the ideal and the common, of the aristocratic and of the popular element, from which sprang the modern novel.[20]

Clara Reeve[21] made the point that the romances satirised in *The Female Quixote* had ceased to be read about forty years before Charlotte Lennox wrote. Fielding[22] also supports this view. But he finds Glanville a very well-drawn character, whereas really no claim can be made for the characterisation in this novel. Austin Dobson[23] stresses this opinion, and says, in addition, that the tale has not lived on because of the absence of real background. Macaulay's words in this regard are worth quoting: '[*The Female Quixote*] has undoubtedly great merit when considered as a wild, satirical harlequinade; but, if we consider it as a picture of life and manners, we must pronounce it more absurd than any of the romances which it was designed to ridicule.'[24] It is as a satirical harlequinade that we must consider it, and it was this aspect which attracted a great train of imitators.

Spurred on by the success of *The Female Quixote*, Mrs. Lennox published a third novel in 1758. *Henrietta* begins by securing our interest at once:

20 *Prose Writings of Heinrich Heine* (1887), p. 264 f.
21 Clara Reeve, *The Progress of Romance* (Colchester, 1785), part 2, p. 6.
22 *Covent Garden Journal*, March 24, 1752.
23 Austin Dobson, *Eighteenth Century Vignettes* (Nelson), p. 89 f.
24 Macaulay, *Critical and Historical Essays*, 'Diary and Letters of Madame d'Arblay'.

> About the middle of July, 17—, when the Windsor stage-coach with the accustomed number of passengers was proceeding on its way to London, a young woman genteely dressed, with a small parcel tied up in her handkerchief, hastily bolted from the shelter of a large tree near the road; and calling to the coachman to stop for a moment, asked him if he could let her have a place.

This is Henrietta Courteney, running away to London from her aunt's house.

Henrietta is the daughter of an earl's younger son who has married beneath him. Her mother was the child of an officer's widow. Hence Henrietta is poor and proud, and most obtrusively honest. She is befriended by her aunt who, however, is estranged by Henrietta's refusal to marry an aged peer, or alternatively to enter a convent. She refuses the peer on sentimental grounds, and the convent on religious grounds, since she is not a Catholic. She believes that she will be either married or immured against her will—hence her flight. Through a confusion of address, she takes lodgings in London at a questionable house, and attracts the attentions of the dangerous Lord B— whose passion and worldliness are foiled by her purity and poverty. Seduction and marriage being both out of the question, he still longs, but continues to negotiate for the daughter of a wealthy parvenu merchant. Henrietta, like Pamela, becomes a servant. She refuses to be a companion, and extols the dignity of honest service compared to dependence. But her real reason is that she wishes to spite her rich relatives who have ignored her. ('What a triumph would be mine if any of my relations should happen . . . to behold me in the character of Miss Cordwain's servant!'[25]) As few mistresses could live up to the beauty, the exalted sentiments and the open superiority of this unusual lady's maid, she is passed from one to another, still refusing to be parted from coronet or apron. Lord B—'s endeavours to make her his mistress are repulsed with fluent scorn. Henrietta goes to Paris with Miss Bellmour who employs her as a maid, but at once promotes her to the position of companion and confidante. Miss

25 Charlotte Lennox, *Henrietta* (*Novelists Mag.*, vol. xxiii), bk. 3, chap. vi, p. 88.

Bellmour is toying with the notion of yielding to her love for a married man. The journey to Paris is in the nature of a virtuous retreat, but it needs Henrietta's most didactic moralising to keep her mistress firm in this attitude. Meanwhile two young men attach themselves to Miss Bellmour and Henrietta, Melvil (really a duke's son) and Freeman (really Henrietta's long-absent brother). Melvil adores Henrietta and she truly loves him, but holds back because of her inferior position. Melvil is so prostrated by his love that the doctors take a serious view, and, to help his recovery, Courteney comes to his sister, whom he has not recognised, and suggests that she yield to Melvil. He discovers whom it is that he is trying to ruin and is horrified. Miss Bellmour, tired of virtuous isolation, summons her lover. Henrietta accompanies her brother and Melvil to England. Her aunt repents of her injustice and gives Henrietta a dowry. Henrietta and Melvil are married.

The Richardsonian touches in this story are apparent[26] but it is to be observed that, unlike Richardson, Charlotte Lennox does not make her heroine forgive all her enemies. On the contrary, Rousseauistic punishment is rigorously assigned to every culprit. Lord B— marries his wealthy plebeian and is miserable. 'The sight of the charming Henrietta renewed his passion. Tortured with remorse, disappointment, and despair, he had recourse to the bottle, and fell an easy sacrifice to intemperance.' Miss Bellmour is forsaken by her lover and enters a convent, where she dies of 'grief, remorse and disappointment.' The younger Mr. Damer (a married man who had been attracted by Henrietta) 'found in the incessant clamours of a jealous wife a sufficient punishment for his treacherous designs on Henrietta.' 'Every branch of the Courteney family made frequent advances towards a reconciliation with the *marchioness* and her brother: but, generous as they were, they had too just a sense of the indignities they

26 Dr. E. A. Baker says that this is not a Richardsonian novel. He says it is rather in the spirit of Fielding, but that the model was not Fielding, but Marivaux's *Marianne*. This may be so, but since *Henrietta* reflects so many influences, and none with fidelity, it is a point beyond proof.

had suffered from them to admit of it; and in this steady resentment they had, as it usually happens with successful persons, the world on their side.' These are the last words of the novel, and it is easy to recognise in them the stifled wishes of Charlotte Lennox herself. She had endured slights from the rich and noble, and it had left in her a steady resentment without hope of outlet.

Henrietta is not merely righteous and oppressed. She is a minx. Witness, for example, her interview with the foolish old baronet whom her aunt wishes her to marry.

> In Sir Isaac Darby, age was contemptible as well as unlovely; he wanted to be young, in spite of time; he talked and laughed aloud; he strutted about the room; he adjusted his bag [-wig], for he was dressed up to five and twenty; he hummed a tune; I sat staring with astonishment at him . . . Since I was obliged to stay, I would draw some amusement from the ridiculous scene before me. I know not whether it was from any particular archness in my looks just then, (for I had composed my countenance to a kind of forced gravity) or whether the old man was at a loss in what manner he should form his address, but it is certain that all his confidence seemed now for the first time to forsake him, and he sat silent during several minutes, stealing a glance at me every now and then; while I with a formal air, played my fan and increased his confusion by my silence.[27]

Finally the unfortunate man summons up a little courage and attempts to take her hand, 'which I withdrew as hastily as if a snake had touched it.' So the scene progresses, Henrietta mercilessly playing with her aged suitor as a cat with a mouse.

The characters in *Henrietta* are types, not individuals. There is much energy, vividness and acute observation. There is no humour, but rather an attitude of acid criticism, chiefly exerted on the *nouveaux riches* and on the nobility who are shown as haughty and heartless, willing to lower their pride only for money. Still, despite its superficiality and its crudities, this is an interesting novel—immensely superior to *Harriot Stuart*, Mrs. Lennox's first attempt at this kind of fiction. The

27 *Op. cit.*, ch. 3, p. 39 f.

Monthly and the *Critical* both hailed it as the best novel that had appeared for some time.

Thereafter Mrs. Lennox published two more novels: *Sophia* which first appeared in *The Lady's Museum* (1760-1) and *Euphemia* (1790). Sophia is a great reader, very reflective and very pious. Her effect on men is startling: '"Angelic creature!" exclaimed Sir Charles, with his eyes swimming in tears.' Mrs. Gibbon, in this novel, is worth mentioning for her resemblance to Mrs. Malaprop. ('She declared she would never have any *collection* with such vulgar creatures . . . ' 'You see, Madam, what affluence your commands have over me.') *Sophia* is a sorry failure. *Euphemia* is little better. This latter novel is in epistolary form. In its efforts at sentimentalising scenery and its complications as to the identity of a lost child, it suggests the influence of Mrs. Radcliffe's *The Castles of Athlin and Dunbayne* which had appeared one year previously.

The difference between sentimentalism and sensibility in fiction is chiefly one of degree and, since many writers are, in their various works, now sentimental and now deliberately emotional, it would be impossible to group them according to the amount of feeling expressed. The most one can say is that, with the growth of the century, sensibility became more exaggerated. This was probably due to the fact that French sensibility gradually reinforced English sensibility. In Richardson's novels sensibility was merely incidental, the aim being to inculcate morality through stories of domestic life and manners. With Sterne, sensibility was little more than an unctuous camouflage for sensuality As time went on, the idea of sensibility for its own sake became predominant on both sides of the Channel, and French writers appear to have given greater scope to the cult of feeling by stressing themes of adventure rather than of domesticity. A flood of French and English translations soon made it difficult to distinguish indebtedness either in regard to national characteristics or particular individuals, and it is perilous to claim that a novelist deliberately modelled his work on that of some French or English writer, since he might possibly be influenced simply by general tendencies which it would be difficult to trace to their true source. For these reasons it seems best, in discussing the principal women writers of this period, not to attempt to group them according to sentiment or sensibility, or to claim definitely that they were influenced by specified authors. It would appear more advisable to consider their works in roughly chronological order. On the whole, the mid-century novels are sentimental and the crescendo of sensibility grows with the years, but even this guide is merely rule of thumb.

The Miss Minifies (to use the contemporary plural) were well-known writers in their day, particularly Susannah Minifie (?1740-1800) who married John Gunning, brother of the famous Gunning sisters. Before her marriage she had written novels in collaboration with her sister Margaret (author of *The Count de Poland*, 1780). These first novels, including *The Picture*, *Family Pictures* and *The Cottage*, are in letter-form, poor in construction and unduly sentimental. In 1763 appeared *The Histories of Lady Frances S— and Lady Caroline S—*, similar to the works above mentioned in form, structure and tone. The epistolary medium is clumsily used. Sometimes the principal characters do not describe their own experiences, which fall to the pen of a third party. This may have the advantage of giving a more objective view but, were that the author's intention, it would have been better to drop the epistolary form altogether. There is the familiar double-barrelled plot in which two stories are forced disjointedly into one dénouement. The story of Lady Frances S— is the better. Lady Frances suffers keenly at the hands of her jealous mother and her weak father. She is befriended by her uncle, at whose house she meets Worthley, a devoted but impecunious lover. Refused her parents' consent, Lady Frances secretly marries the man of her choice. Her marriage is discovered and she is banished from her parents' house. The other story concerns Lady Caroline S—. We are told at first that she is dead, but we do not believe this, and look forward confidently to the final identification by means of a strawberry mark. We see the humble Miss Dalton, daughter of the Duchess of S—'s waiting-woman, living with her grandfather, a Somersetshire parson. We see her pursued by Lord Ormsby who is making his first experiment in seduction. Ormsby abducts Miss Dalton, is confounded by her shining virtue, repents and thoroughly enjoys his repentance even to the extent of taking his sister and a friend to visit Miss Dalton, who is on the verge of brain-fever and a decline through the delicacy of her situation. The visiting ladies are charmed with the beauty, humility and magnanimity of Miss Dalton. Indeed she refuses to marry Lord Ormsby because it would demean him. But virtue has its reward. The Duchess's waiting-woman confesses on her death-bed that she substituted her own infant for the infant Caroline. Caroline lives yet as Miss Dalton and may be identified not indeed by a strawberry mark, but by a cherry mark which is equally convincing. Lord Ormsby now woos Miss Dalton in a garnet suit, 'the coat richly laced with a gold point d'Espagne, the waistcoat entirely covered with a net of gold thread.' She yields. The Duchess, after an attack of small-pox, sees the vanity of maternal jealousy and, happy at recovering one daughter, forgives the other.

Despite its obvious faults, there are points of interest in this novel. Miss Dalton is one of those prodigies so beloved by the newer school of women novelists: she combines much learning with a decent humility. The feminine point of view is also evident in the description of Mr. Martin, the sporting lout. This character who, through Lord Newminster (in Mrs. Smith's *Desmond*) develops into John Thorpe in *Northanger Abbey*, deserves a closer scrutiny. Miss Hamilton (whom he hopes to marry) describes him thus:

a person you have often remark'd, for a bluntness, which tho' he

> does not say anything to offend, yet his boisterous manner keeps you in continual dread.—He enters a lady's drawing-room with the same ease he would his kennel; and seems to consider it as no other, being always attended by a number of his four-footed friends, whom he familiarly introduces to you; and indeed appears more conversant in their language, than that of any intelligent Being . . . This gentleman has lately honour'd me with an offer to be at the head of his pack; but I should have so many rivals that upon my word I cannot accept it. At present there is a Pointer and Greyhound, that he says tenderer things to, than to me, tho' not his wife.—This unaccountable creature tells me, whenever I reject him, that he can follow a chase twenty years, and will not pay me a worse compliment than he should to a fox or a stag.[28]

The brutality of Mr. Martin can only be realised in relation to the feminine ideal of a hero at that period—such a man, for example, as Mr. Worthley shows himself when pleading with the uncle of Lady Frances to help him obtain the consent of her parents. Mr. Worthley throws himself on his knees in soul-piercing agony. When he succeeds in speaking, his words are 'hardly articulate, his manly eyes full of tears, full of imploring sweetness, lifted up to my uncle, as to his judge, whose mercy he petitioned.'[29]

But however much women novelists might subscribe to the sentimentalised conception of hero and heroine, they are very frank as to the minor women characters. In particular they dislike a gathering of women, and are adepts at describing the pettiness and the complacent spitefulness of women's gossip. Miss Hamilton's account of such a séance[30] is the most realistic part of this novel. Fanny Burney herself could not have been more acute.

Susannah Gunning's best work[31] is *The Memoirs of Mary* which was published in 1793. In the interval

28 *The Histories of Lady Frances S—— and Lady Caroline S——* (1763), ii, p. 120 f.

29 *Ibid.*, ii, p. 7 f.

30 *Ibid.*, i, p. 67.

31 The following is a list of Susannah Gunning's novels:
- (a) *The Histories of Lady Frances S——, and Lady Caroline S——* (4 vols. 1763). In collaboration with her sister Margaret.
- (b) *Barford Abbey*, a novel in a series of letters (2 vols., 1768). anon.
- (c) *Anecdotes of the Delborough Family* (5 vols., 1792).
- (d) *Memoirs of Mary* (5 vols., 1793).
- (e) *Delves; a Welch Tale* (2 vols., 1796).

between this novel and *The Histories of Lady Frances S— and Lady Caroline S—*, she had published two novels: *Barford Abbey* in 1768, and *Anecdotes of the Delborough Family* in 1792. *Barford Abbey* is a pleasing story, dealing with the misunderstandings and final happiness of true love. Her marriage in 1798 interrupted the composition of *Anecdotes of the Delborough Family*, which she completed after her separation from her worthless husband, John Gunning. When Gunning turned his daughter out of the house for plotting to marry the man she loved, Mrs. Gunning followed her. Soon afterwards his intrigue with Mrs. Duberly led to litigation. He was obliged to pay the injured husband £5,000 damages. Thereafter he and his mistress retired to Naples where he died in 1797. These events (called by Walpole the 'Gunningiad') are recounted obliquely in *The Memoirs of Mary*. It may have been the sincerity of Mrs. Gunning's feeling which made this her best novel. It has received scant praise, but in the opinion of the present writer, at any rate, it is one of the best of the lesser novels of this period. It is narrated in a spirited, graceful, and effortless style. There is no straining after elegance—almost an entire absence of sentimentality, and no sensibility at all. Compared to Mrs. Brooke, for example, Mrs. Gunning is a strong-minded writer.

Mary Montague is the beloved grand-daughter of Lady Auberry who rears her in the seclusion of her country estate. At the age of eighteen, according to the will of her father, she goes to live with the Duke and Duchess of Cleveland, who are connections of hers. She is beautiful, amiable and ingenuous. She soon has scores of suitors and becomes the toast of the season, but she is enmeshed in a deep-laid conspiracy to deprive her of her legitimacy and of her fortune. Mary Pleydell,

(f) *Love at First Sight; a novel from the French*, with alterations and additions (5 vols., 1797).
(g) *Fashionable Involvements* (3 vols., 1800).
(h) *The Heir Apparent*, revised and augmented by her daughter, Miss Gunning (3 vols., 1802). In association with her sister she also wrote *The Picture*, *Family Pictures* and *The Cottage*.

the daughter of Lady Auberry, had married secretly to avoid her father's anger. Her husband had been obliged to sail at once with his regiment for America, and fell in battle shortly afterwards. Mary Montague is the fruit of this marriage. Her mother died a few days after the birth, and Lady Auberry has the child brought up secretly until Lord Auberry dies, when she brings her home and openly acknowledges her. By her father's will, Mary Montague is to inherit her father's property, but a relative, Sir Ashton Montague, conspires to disinherit her. Her cousin, the young Lord Auberry, had been engaged to her a few years before she came to London, but he was parted from her by a letter purporting to be in her handwriting, she remaining in entire ignorance of the reason for his withdrawal, and supposing that he had jilted her. These are the cross-currents which undermine the happiness of her life in London society. Mary knows nothing except that Sir Ashton Montague is always at her elbow, sinister and cryptic, with veiled allusions to her past engagement to Lord Auberry; and that Lord Auberry, studiously rude, and flaunting in her face his flirtations with such women as the loose Mrs. Oxburn, yet hisses in her ear that he will never renounce his claim to her.

Meanwhile Mary is wooed by Henry Lexington, the nephew and heir of the Duke of Cleveland. She returns his love. They become engaged, but they are parted by the jealous scheming of Lord Auberry. Lexington goes abroad, and the plot against Mary culminates when her parents' marriage certificate and her father's will, carefully preserved by Mary's grandmother, are stolen through the machinations of Sir Ashton Montague. Nameless and penniless, Mary is scoffed at by those who envied her triumphs. But, at that moment, Lexington returns, discovers the plot which parted him from Mary and renews his addresses. By a great stroke of fortune, Sir Ashton Montague meets with a fatal accident and makes a death-bed confession. At a ball given by the Duchess of Cleveland the radiant Mary enters on her husband's arm. The Duchess announces their marriage, and all the ill-wishers are forced to feed on their own bitterness.

Lady Auberry's words to the friend who weeps at Mary's loss of name and fortune, sum up the attitude towards sensibility which this book expresses:

> These emotions, my child . . . are a sort of cannibals, that will feed on our own vitals, if we do not contend against them; let us then . . . conquer these enemies, that will otherwise conquer *us*, and leave us neither sense nor reflection to baffle our misfortunes, or fortitude to support them.[32]

Speaking of Lord Auberry, who appears to resent the fact that his termination of their engagement has not sent her into a decline, Mary says:

> I have no doubt that he expected I should exhaust my whole life in performing funeral obsequies to the memory of his departed vows. Perhaps too, his vanity is piqued and himself injured, in his opinion, in finding me a rational woman rather than a despairing, forsaken heroine. There are mistakes which might easily be adjusted, whenever his Lordship condescends to bestow a moment's serious reflection on what he was, what he is, and what I am.[33]

And she goes on to say that she has had the good fortune not merely to be taught how to sing, draw, paint, and speak languages, but also 'how to distinguish between honour and dishonour; how to be firm as well as yielding; how to be the guardian of my own repose.' 'To be the guardian of my own repose'! This is precisely the attitude of Jane Austen's rational heroines.

The Memoirs of Mary is the least sentimental work of this group of women novelists. Elizabeth Bonhote[34] seems to have patterned her *Rambles of Mr. Frankley*

32 *The Memoirs of Mary* (3rd ed., 1794), iv, p. 146 f.

33 *Ibid.*, iii, p. 43 f.

34 Elizabeth Bonhote (1744-1818), wife of Daniel Bonhote, solicitor of Bungay, wrote the following:

(a) *Rambles of Mr. Frankley, by his Sister* (1773); published anonymously; translated into German at Leipzig, (1773). It describes the characters seen during rambles in Hyde Park.

on Sterne's *Sentimental Journey* and her other novels adhere to the accepted view of feminine behaviour. *Olivia, or the Deserted Bride* shows a dutiful and long-suffering wife freed by her husband's death to make a happier second marriage. In *Darnley Vale*, Mrs. Bonhote works out the theory that a woman parted by treachery from her first lover can be entirely happy in a second attachment, even when she realises how she has been tricked. In *Bungay Castle* some Gothic touches are blended with descriptions of Mrs. Bonhote's own neighbourhood. Another writer intent on depicting domestic morality was Maria Susannah Cooper, author of *Letters between Emilia and Harriet* (1762); *The School for Wives* (1763); and *The Exemplary Mother, or Letters between Mrs. Villars and her Family* (1769). Mrs. Woodfin's *The History of Sally Sable* (1758) introduces the theme of incest, which may have owed some of its popularity to Prévost's literary influence. It transpires that Sally Sable is the natural daughter of one of the rakes who pursue her. This is the best of Mrs. Woodfin's novels,[35] the rest of which do not merit particular mention.

By far the best writer of the school of sensibility was Mrs. Frances Sheridan whose *Miss Sydney Bidulph* (1761) is in the direct line of succession from Richardson. Richardson, indeed, encouraged Mrs. Sheridan as a writer, and he it was who arranged for the publication of this novel. Its reception amply justified the enthusiasm which Richardson had expressed when he first read it in

(b) *The Parental Monitor* (1788). A series of moral essays written for her children's guidance.
(c) *Olivia, or the Deserted Bride* (1787).
(d) *Darnley Vale, or Amelia Fitzroy* (1789).
(e) *Ellen Woodley* (1790).
(f) *Bungay Castle* (Minerva Press, 1797).
(g) *Feeling, or Sketches from Life, a Desultory Poem* (Edinburgh, 1810); anon.

35 Mrs. Woodfin's other novels are:
(a) *The Auction* (1759).
(b) *The History of Miss Harriot Watson* (1763).
(c) *The Discovery, or Memoirs of Miss Marianne Middleton* (1764).

manuscript. It was highly praised by reviewers, and received the warmest commendations from such people as Dr. Johnson, Lord North and Charles James Fox. In the year following its appearance, an adaptation of *Miss Sydney Bidulph* was made into French by Prévost and published under the title: *Mémoires pour servir à l'histoire de la vertu. Extraits du Journal d'une Dame.* In 1762 a German translation appeared, and later it was again translated into French by René Robinet.

Sydney Bidulph is on the point of marrying her brother's friend, Faulkland, when it is discovered that he has seduced and deserted a young girl named Miss Burchell. Sydney and her mother at once break off the match, and shortly afterwards Sydney marries a Mr. Arnold. She is an exemplary wife and devotes herself to rearing her two children, but the happiness she manages to derive from her married life is destroyed when she learns that her husband is intriguing with an adventuress named Mrs. Gerrarde. This woman is actually Miss Burchell's aunt, and she it is who bargained with Faulkland for delivering up her niece to him. Arnold not only refuses to part with Mrs. Gerrarde, but turns Sydney out of his house under the pretence of believing that she is encouraging Faulkland. Griselda that she is, Sydney agrees to give up her claim to her children, and goes to live with her mother. Faulkland concocts a pretty scheme for clearing Sydney's name and making it possible for her to be with her children again. He kidnaps Mrs. Gerrarde under the pretence that he is smitten with her charms. Arnold is therefore forced to believe that Faulkland, so far from thinking of Sydney, is determined to win Mrs. Gerrarde. This point is driven home by a letter which Faulkland cleverly induces Mrs. Gerrarde to write to Arnold, explaining that Sydney is innocent. Arnold repents, and his repentance is the deeper because he is now penniless as a result of Mrs. Gerrarde's extravagances. The magnanimous Sydney forgives her husband, who dies shortly afterwards, leaving her to bring up her children on £50 a year. She again refuses to marry Faulkland and persuades him to marry Miss

Burchell, who actually had not been innocent, but already all too experienced, when he was drawn in by her aunt and herself. This Faulkland later discovers to his cost.

Meanwhile Sydney and her children are pitifully poor. Her brother, Sir George, disgusted with her obduracy towards Faulkland, and under the influence of his selfish wife, ignores her. She is rescued from her distress by a West Indian relative who proves her good genius. This kinsman, because he appears to be destitute, is badly treated by Sir George. Sydney, on the contrary, treats him with all the generosity her poor circumstances permit. He is fabulously wealthy, showers money on her and makes her his heiress. Finally comes the day when Faulkland, who has been living with his wife in Ireland, bursts into Sydney's house to tell her that he has found his wife in adultery, and that, in shooting her lover, he has accidentally killed her also. He begs Sydney to marry him, threatening to commit suicide if she refuses. Her brother and her benefactor both support his entreaties, and Sydney yields. They marry and flee to the Continent. Then it transpires that Faulkland's erring wife is not dead, after all. Faulkland dies, and Sydney, worn out by misfortune and hoping for death, quietly resigns herself to the task of bringing up her daughters and Faulkland's son by his irregular union with Miss Burchell.

The second part of *Miss Sydney Bidulph* describes the romantic complications which arise between these young people, chiefly through the scheming of Audley, a cynical villain.

This brief outline of Mrs. Sheridan's novel testifies to the appositeness of Dr. Johnson's famous criticism that he doubted if the author should have made her readers suffer so much. The *motif* of endless misfortunes suggests the influence of Madame Riccoboni; and the many-volume convention was an added reason for the undue protraction of the story. Indeed the necessity for spinning out the plot appears to have been chiefly responsible for the divagation and discursiveness which are too apparent in this novel. Condensed, it would have gained greatly in strength. Mrs. Sheridan could have omitted her adventitious stories and shortened her sub-stories. She frequently made the mistake of concentrating interest on what should have been merely incidental. For example, when Sydney repeats the account given her by Sir George of Faulkland's deed in Ireland, her narrative is far too detailed. Mrs. Sheridan ignored the fact that Faulkland's past adventures are far less exciting than his present distracted state.

There are many interesting aspects in *Miss Sydney Bidulph.* There is a stressing of sensibility and endurance. Each of these qualities increases the other, and both unite to wring the heart of the heroine. Still, Sydney neither goes mad nor falls into a decline, but survives until her daughters are of marriageable age. Another point worth noting is that, in general, Mrs. Sheridan subscribes to the accepted standards of feminine status and behaviour, and yet, in some respects, most strikingly presents the feminine point of view. In fact, the pivotal point of this story essentially represents a woman's judgment on an issue which, until that time, had not been raised in fiction. Before Mrs. Sheridan, women writers had not required that the hero should be guiltless of seducing innocence. In *Miss Sydney Bidulph* this claim is made, but a single standard of morality is not applied. Faulkland is exonerated when it is discovered that Miss Burchell was guilty before she met him. Mrs. Sheridan does not judge immorality *per se*, but only in relation to its victim. Nevertheless, it was an advance on the code of gallantry and on the code of casual sexual adventure which sheltered women were supposed to take for granted in their men-folk.

But it was not merely in moral outlook that Mrs. Sheridan struck a feminine note. In her presentation of a woman's mind, with its characteristic moods and impulses, there is much that indicates a woman's insight. When the excellent Lord V— pays court to Sydney's daughter, Cecilia, she will have none of him, and makes short work of every argument which a family friend makes in his favour. Yes, he is handsome, very accomplished, extremely well-bred and perfectly good-tempered: his morals are unexceptionable.

> She turned her eyes at me with so arch a look, that I could scarce refrain from laughing. 'I know nothing to the contrary, Madam,' —'Has he not a fine estate?'—'I do not want money, Mrs. B—.'— 'Of a considerable family, and noble rank?'—'I desire not titles either.' —'What then *do* you desire, Cecilia?'—'Only to please myself;' and she shook her little head so, that all the powder and the curls in her hair fell about her face . . . And yet she has her hours of sadness. 'For what, my dear?'—'Oh, you'll know all in time,' in a low voice, as she curtseyed to take her leave; and down she flew like a lapwing.[36]

Cecilia has vivacity, charm and depth; she is a 'bewitching little gypsy,' in marked contrast to her sister Dolly who is a young woman of the greatest sensibility. Dolly is far too full of maidenly delicacy. She is too grave, too prone to tears and swoons. Both sisters love young Faulkland. Dolly feeds on her emotions which so rend her that, when Faulkland's dislocated shoulder is being set, she faints away twice although she is in a distant part of the house. On the contrary, Cecilia candidly avows her love to Faulkland—surely the first woman in fiction thus to take the initiative. '"I always thought you loved me," said she, "yet, Faulkland, you should have spoken first, and spared me the pains of extorting a confession from you."' Faulkland comments:

> What a noble frankness was here! how unlike a *woman*! no affected confusion, no pretty coyness, after such a declaration! Amazed, overwhelmed, and penetrated to the soul, I fell at her feet, and grasping her knees, with the action of a madman—'Oh, Cecilia' cried I, 'dare I believe my senses?'[37]

But Faulkland, in a moment of pity for Dolly, has already given her his vows. Now he engages himself to Cecilia whom he really loves. Their marriage ceremony is interrupted by Dolly's distraught reproaches, and Faulkland fights and kills the man who has played on his weakness and used him as a catspaw. This is the end of

36 *Miss Sydney Bidulph* (*Novelists Mag.*, xxii), p. 298.
37 *Ibid.*, p. 323.

Audley, a most interesting villain with a sense of humour. Audley is determined to marry either Cecilia or Dolly, because both have splendid fortunes. Personally he prefers Cecilia because she is spirited. Dolly, he says (with an echo of *The Female Quixote*):

> would do mighty well to be the mistress of a Don Bellianis, or a Sir Launcelot, who could afford to waste seven years in strolling up and down the world, without either meat or drink, in order to prove his constancy; and after that, would think himself fully paid, if he were allowed to brush his beard (which he had vowed never to shave till he saw her again) on her lily-white hand through the grated window of some enchanted tower.[38]

But Cecilia loves Faulkland, so Audley concentrates his energies on winning this bread-and-butter miss, undeterred by the fact that he has a wife already. He kidnaps her and releases her unharmed, hoping that the compromising circumstances will force her to marry him. His death cuts the tangle he has so cunningly devised.

Audley's philosophy of evil is summed up in the declaration:

> Of all devils, I hate a penitent devil: What a noble figure does Satan himself make, as he is described in the sixth book of Milton, where he boldly defies the whole artillery of Heaven! And what a sneaking rascal does he appear in the fourth book, where just like Faulkland, he recapitulates his woes, and bemoans his lost estate.

Truly excellent is the hypocritical account which he gives Dolly of his efforts to persuade her relatives that she was constrained by illness to spend the night in his house. Poor Dolly is innocent, but he has spread too clever a net. His arguments, his deceptions, his sophistries, his deliberate forcing of her into a corner until there appears no possibility of escape except through lies and a patched-up marriage with him—here is a fine crescendo of subtle and cynical villainy. At the thought of the coil of falsehood to which she must lend herself, Dolly stopped short, striking her forehead with her hand. 'Oh, Lear, Lear!' whispered

38 *Ibid.*, p. 325.

the sardonic Audley, 'beat at this gate that lets the folly in, etc.'[39]

Though Mrs. Sheridan owed much to Richardson's influence and something to French sensibility, these debts are merely incidental—not more than any author owes to the literary atmosphere of his period. *Sydney Bidulph* is an original, vivid, and charming book. It is, above all, human. Mrs. Sheridan never forgets that she is dealing with people of flesh and blood; and (as with her description of Lady Grimston[40]) she can make them live before our eyes.

Sensibility exercised in a sequence of misfortunes and generally doomed to final misery is also the theme of Mrs. Brooke, Mrs. Griffith, Helen Maria Williams and Mary Robinson. But, as they had neither the power nor the individuality of Mrs. Sheridan, there is little escape in their novels from an excess of that fatality which governs lovers in the works of Prévost and Mme Riccoboni.

Mrs. Brooke (1724-1789), daughter of a clergyman named Moore, and wife of the chaplain to the forces at Quebec, was much influenced by Mme Riccoboni. In fact, she englished, in 1764, Mme Riccoboni's *Milady Juliette Catesby*. Prior to that time (in 1763), appeared anonymously *The History of Lady Julia Mandeville*.

Henry Mandeville is reared to expect only £700 a year. He loves his relative, Lady Julia, and considers his chances hopeless. Actually there is an amiable conspiracy between the fathers that the young couple shall marry and so compensate for a flaw in the succession of the family title. But Henry and Julia are kept in ignorance of this design, so that the idea of carrying out a family plan may not destroy the possibility of their falling in love. They keep their love a secret while Henry seeks to improve his fortunes. There is a rumour that the rich Lord Melvin is intended to be Julia's husband. The

39 *Ibid.*, p. 360.
40 *Ibid.*, p. 33.

parents prepare lavishly for the marriage of Julia and Henry, whose secret attachment has become known to them, but these unexplained preparations seem to confirm Henry's suspicions of a rival. He becomes distracted and insists on engaging Lord Melvin in a duel. He is slain and Lady Julia survives him only by a few hours. Prévost is echoed in the descriptions of their deaths, in the awful spectacle of the lovers lying side by side in their coffins, in the despair of their parents and friends. There is a rather interesting suggestion of Gothic terrors in the passage which describes Lady Anne Wilmot's walk in the shrubbery, while the lovers lie dead:

> Pleased with the tender sorrow which possessed all my soul, I determined to indulge it to the utmost; and revolving in my imagination the happy hours of cheerful friendship to which that smiling scene had been a witness, prolonged my walk till evening had, almost unperceived, spread its gloomy horrors round; till the varied tints of the flowers were lost in the deepening shades of night.
>
> Awaking at once from the reverie in which I had been plunged, I found myself at a distance from the house, just entering the little wood so loved by my charming friend; the very moment increasing darkness gave an awful gloom to the trees. I stopped, I looked around, not a human form was in sight. I listened, and heard not a sound but the trembling of some poplars in the wood. I called, but the echo of my own voice was the only answer I received; a dreary silence reigned around; a terror I never felt before seized me; my heart panted with timid apprehension; I breathed short; I started at every leaf that moved; my limbs were covered with a cold dew; I fancied I saw a thousand airy forms flit around me; I seemed to hear the shrieks of the dead and dying: there is no describing my horrors.[41]

This is a very disappointing novel. The story is clear and closely linked, but there is no characterisation, except possibly for the witty and vivacious Anne Wilmot who is a fascinating widow with a kind heart and an ironic turn of mind. Her flirtations, capricious moods and railleries are amusing, but too often overdone ('O mon Dieu! what do I see coming down the avenue? Is it in women to resist an equipage? Papier maché—highly gilded—loves and doves—six long-tailed grey

41 *The History of Lady Julia Mandeville* (British Novelists ed., 1820, xxvii), p. 201.

Arabians. By all the gentle powers of love and gallantry, Fondville himself!').[42]

In *Lady Julia Mandeville* the descriptions of nature and of country life were so idealised as to be pastoral. In *The History of Emily Montague* (1769) Mrs. Brooke, drawing on her knowledge of Canada, achieves some very good effects. This is one of the better aspects of a desultory novel which extends over four volumes a tale which might have been compressed into two. The events are slight. The obstacles to the true love of heroine and hero are all due to their own sensibility or that of others. The macabre element, however, is happily absent. The story is prolonged not only by the complications of sensibility, but by disquisitions on love, marriage, education, colonial politics and scenery. This latter subject is of value since descriptions of nature were all too rare and too unreal in English fiction up to that period. Mrs. Brooke's descriptions in *Emily Montague* are very little idealised, sometimes not at all, and are easily visualised. The best known scene is the breaking-up in spring of the bridge of ice over the St. Lawrence.[43] Very fine also is the description of the Falls of Montmorenci in winter, and there are innumerable other shorter descriptions which show in Mrs. Brooke the ability to observe closely and to reproduce faithfully. For example:

> The rock on the east side, which is first in view as you approach, is a smooth and almost perpendicular precipice, of the same height as the fall; the top, which a little overhangs, is beautifully covered with pines, firs, and ever-greens of various kinds, whose verdant lustre is rendered at this season more shining and lovely by the surrounding snow, as well as by that which is sprinkled irregularly on their branches, and glitters half melted in the sunbeams: a thousand smaller shrubs are scattered on the side of the ascent, and, having their roots in almost imperceptible clefts of the rock, seem to those below to grow in air . . . The torrent, which before rushed with such impetuosity down the deep descent in one vast sheet of water, now descends in some parts with a slow and majestic pace; in others it seems almost suspended in mid air; and in others, bursting through

42 *Ibid.*, p. 35.
43 *The History of Emily Montague* (ed. 1784), iii, p. 22 f.

> the obstacles which interrupt its course, pours down with redoubled fury into the foaming bason below, from whence a spray arises, which, freezing in its ascent, becomes on each side a wide and irregular frozen breast-work; and in front, the spray being there much greater, a lofty and magnificent pyramid of solid ice.[44]

And there are such delightful spring touches as: ''Tis amazingly pleasing to see the strawberries and wild pansies peeping their foolish heads from beneath the snow.'[45]

In this novel sensibility is the ideal. ''Tis the magnet which attracts all to itself: virtue may command esteem, understanding and talents admiration, beauty a transient desire; but 'tis sensibility alone which can inspire love.'[46] Emily Montague is the typical heroine of sensibility, whom we shall meet again in the pages of Mrs. Radcliffe:

> Without being regularly beautiful, she charms every sensible heart: all other women, however lovely, appear marble statues near her: fair; pale (a paleness which gives the idea of delicacy without destroying that of health), with dark hair and eyes, the latter large and languishing, she seems made to feel to a trembling excess the passion she cannot fail of inspiring: her elegant form has an air of softness and languor, which seizes the whole soul in a moment: her eyes, the most intelligent eyes I ever saw, hold you enchain'd by their bewitching sensibility.[47]

The rôle of Belle Fermor resembles that of Anne Wilmot in *Lady Julia Mandeville*. She is a foil for the extreme sensibility of the principal characters. These minor personages, though not well drawn, are at least refreshing and lend a sense of reality. *Emily Montague*, despite its looseness of plot, is preferable to *Lady Julia Mandeville* because the story is more natural and the background much more interesting.[48]

44 *Ibid.*, ii, p. 74 f.
45 *Ibid.*, iii, p. 42.
46 *Ibid.*, i, p. 83.
47 *Ibid.*, i, p. 41.
48 Mrs. Brooke's other novels are:
(a) *The Excursion* (1777). It describes the adventures of Maria Villiers, an impulsive young poetess whose 'wild and Pindaric virtues,' warm heart and social inexperience lead her into difficulties which are worked out in a conventional way. Dr. J. M. S. Tompkins says that she 'is the nearest approach to a female Tom Jones (*mutatis mutandis*) that could

Like Mrs. Sheridan, Elizabeth Griffith[49] was Irish. She first won the attention of the reading public by *A Series of Genuine Letters between Henry and Frances* (1757)—the actual letters which passed between her and Richard Griffith prior to their marriage. In 1769 she and her husband published two companion novels in letters: *The Gordian Knot* by Richard Griffith, and *The Delicate Distress* by Elizabeth.

The Delicate Distress consists of graceful letters in which a number of stories are loosely strung together. The main narrative describes the complications which arise when the Marchioness d'Aumont, once loved by Lord Woodville, tries to regain her hold over him during the first year of his marriage. He really loves his wife, and yet is extremely fascinated by the Marchioness. He alternates between resistance and weakness, and finally determines to join the *femme fatale* in France. A fall from his horse hinders his plans, and in the serious illness that follows, his wife, who has long suspected and now knows all, heaps coals of fire upon his head. They are united more fully than ever, and the wicked Marchioness, intent on other victims, passes out of their lives. Slightly linked with this central theme are various peripheral stories. The chief of these are the story of Lord Seymour and Charlotte; the story of Lady Harriet Hanbury; the story of Lucy Straffon; the story of Lady Somerville; and the story of the Ransfords.

Sensibility and delicacy are the keynotes of this novel. We do not find, however, the exaggeration and artificiality which these terms too often connote in eighteenth century fiction. Sincerity is apparent in Mrs. Griffith's style, and her outlook is thoughtful and generous. Speaking of Miss Fanning who has alienated the

have been offered.' (*The Popular Novel in England*, 1770-1800, p. 169). On page 118 of this work the date of *The Excursion* is given as 1771, obviously a misprint.

(b) *The History of Charles Mandeville* (1790); a sequel to her first novel. Of this there is no extant copy.

Dr. E. A. Baker points out that *Memoirs of the Marquis de St. Forlaix* was not an original work, but merely translated from the French by Mrs. Brooke (1770). See *H.E.N.*, v, p. 146.

49 Lived 1720?-1793.

affections of Sir William Lawson, the husband of her benefactress, Lady Straffon says:

> Had she been led astray, by an agreeable young man, I could have pitied, nay, perhaps, have loved, and even esteemed her ; for I am not such an Amazon in ethics, as to consider a breach of chastity, as the highest crime, that a woman can be guilty of ; though it is, certainly, the most unpardonable folly ; and I believe there are many women, who have erred, in that point, who may have more real virtue, aye, and delicacy too, than half the sainted dames, who value themselves on the preservation of chastity ; which, in all probability, has never been assailed. She alone, who has withstood the solicitations of a man she fondly loves, may boast her virtue; and I will venture to say, that such an heroine will be more inclined to pity, than to despise, the unhappy victims of their own weakness.

She goes on to speak of acidulated and complacent virtue:

> There is no character, I so heartily abominate, as that of the *outrageously virtuous*. I have seen a lady render herself hateful, to a large company, by repeating, perhaps a forged tale, of some unhappy frail one, with such a degree of rancour, and malevolence, as is totally inconsistent, with the calm dignity of real virtue.[50]

Gentleness and magnanimity Mrs. Griffith holds to be the best equipment for life, enabling one to bear all trials and vexations with self-respecting dignity. It is by gentleness that erring husbands are to be reclaimed. It is by magnanimity that treachery is to be repaid. When Sir James Miller jilts Lucy Straffon (because she insists on being inoculated against small-pox!), he marries Miss Nelson, and is soon as deep in debt as his wife is in infidelity. Lucy considers his vices justly punished, but is so grateful to him for leaving her free to marry Lord Mount Willis, that she insists on giving him an allowance anonymously. 'I formerly looked upon him, with horror and aversion; I now consider him as my benefactor; and the saving him from the miseries of extreme poverty will relieve my mind, from a sort of mental debt.'[51]

50 *The Delicate Distress* (1769), ii, p. 112 f.
51 *Ibid.*, ii, p. 101.

To Mrs. Griffith sensibility chiefly means refinement of feeling:

> There is everything to be expected from *sensibility, and delicacy*, joined; but, indeed, I have scarce ever known them separated, in a female heart. Refined manners are the natural consequences of fine feelings, which will, even in an untutored mind, form a species both of virtue, and good breeding, higher than anything that is to be acquired, either in courts, or schools.[52]

Still, the emotional tempests and all the external phenomena of sensibility are strongly evidenced in this novel. When Lord Seymour's adored Charlotte takes her vows as a nun, he says:

> How I got out of the convent, I know not: my senses vanished, with her.—I was fifteen days delirious, and but for the officious kindness of Wilson, should not now feel those poignant agonies, that rend my heart.[53]

When Charlotte failed to win the recognition of her unnatural parents 'she threw herself on the ground, and washed it with her tears.'[54] When Lady Harriet Hanbury learns from her supposed fiancé, Captain Barnard, that he has married another, she treats him with frigid contempt, but later pays for this resolute self-control:

> The heroism of my conduct towards Captain Barnard, had flattered my pride, and kept up my spirits, while he was present, but I was no sooner alone, than I felt all the weight of my misfortunes; and the agitation and distraction of my mind, threw me into convulsions. My maid had immediate help for me, but all the art of the best physician in Paris, could not restore my senses for fifteen days.[55]

The History of Lady Barton (1771) is a very poor novel indeed. It begins in so vague and unconnected a way that several letters pass before we understand the general setting. The plot is straggling and shows no planning. It is interrupted by inset stories of a length out of all

52 *Ibid.*, ii, p. 105.
53 *Ibid.*, i, p. 29.
54 *Ibid.*, i, p. 181.
55 *Ibid.*, i, p. 92.

proportion to the main narrative. Not only are the minor tales inset in the principal story, but they are also inset in each other like Chinese boxes. For example, the story of Mrs. N— is inset in the story of Maria, which is inset in the story of Lady Barton. The use of letters is evidently a mere adherence to a literary fashion, since the peculiar advantages of the epistolary medium are not applied. Nothing could be more mechanical than the manner in which, for instance, the long inset story of Mrs. Walter is continued from letter to letter, the correspondent quoting it verbatim in the first person. The main narrative shows a sorely tempted lady being true to a husband whom she does not love, and rejecting a man whom she adores. In all awkward situations Lady Barton, a victim of extreme sensibility, becomes unconscious and remains so for hours. There is an accouchement of which the contingent circumstances are completely incredible. There is no characterisation. The hero and heroine are exquisitely sensitive paragons; Hume is meant to be a gay gallant worth reclamation; Colonel Walters is a villain of the deepest dye. There is not one convincing touch of human nature, incident or surroundings from beginning to end. The style is prosy and sententious. Tears gush in torrents. The moral is that one must not marry without love: 'It must be the joining of hearts, not hands, that can insure the marriage *rights*—I don't misspell the word—and the woman who stretches out an *empty hand*, at the altar, but mocks the institution; and, if I may hazard the boldness of the expression, becomes *guilty*, before her *crime;* receives an antepast of misery, and puts her trust in miracles, for safety.'[56] All the scenes which are supposed to be vital are absurdly melodramatic: 'Hear me, Sir, while I call Heaven to witness, that Lord Lucan never solicited a criminal indulgence from me! and that my heart has never yet admitted a thought which could reflect dishonour on my husband.'[57] Parents lament that they must, because of undutiful children, 'sink with sorrow

56 *The History of Lady Barton* (1771), ii, p. 116 f.
57 *Ibid.*, ii, p. 149.

to the grave'. A daughter, pressed to marry in obedience to her mother's wishes, on threat of that mother's decease, bathes the bosom of this exigent parent with her flowing tears, and cries out: 'O take me, sacrifice me, do what you will with me. I will not be a parricide! But give me time to conquer this poor heart, and tear my L——'s much loved image from my breast.'[58] No wonder that this victim's sufferings have serious results. 'For five days I continued in a state of mental annihilation, the return of my reason, was like the appearance of an ignis fatuus, it glimmered, and vanished, several times, as if unwilling to return to the wretched habitation which it had forsaken.'[59]

But although Mrs. Griffith adhered to the masculine notion of womanhood, there are occasional glimpses of the feminine point of view. In speaking of the educational advantages denied to women she deplores that the most mediocre man is given, as a matter of course, opportunities beyond the reach of the most gifted woman, but she finds consolation in the reflection that academic learning and character-training are two distinct things: 'The greatest blockheads I have ever known, have been bred in college—Neither absurdity nor meanness prevent a man from becoming a master of language, nor of arriving at a competent knowledge in any particular branch of science.'[60]

The male attitude towards female frailty does not meet with serious opposition in fiction until Mary Wollstonecraft and Mary Hays hit back. The established view was that even the seducer has the right to condemn on moral grounds the woman he has seduced. This inconsistency finds its apotheosis in Hugh Kelly's *Memoirs of a Magdalen; or, the History of Louisa Mildmay* (1767). The Magdalen, who was the affianced of the hero, Sir Robert Harold, yields to him before the marriage ceremony. He writes: 'I have succeeded, fatally succeeded, with this amiable wretch, and both of us

58 *Ibid.*, iii, p. 79.
59 *Ibid.*, ii, p. 162.
60 *Ibid.*, ii, p. 202.

must bid adieu to happiness forever.' Only after she has undergone severe and prolonged penance does he take the risk of marrying this woman he has ruined. Mrs. Griffith puts the mild reply into a man's mouth: 'We first take pains to destroy the foundation of every female virtue, modesty; and are then surprised to find the superstructure totter.'[61]

The sensibility in Mrs. Griffith's novels seems to reflect French influence. Incidentally it is interesting to note in the association of Margarita and Hume[62] an echo of *Manon Lescaut*. Margarita, who has betrayed Hume, and who is now living with a supposed brother, has only to smile at him with ineffable sweetness to win him into the toils again.

Mrs. Griffith's last novel,[63] *The Story of Juliana Harley* (1776), also dealt with domestic cross-currents. It is the story of a forced and loveless marriage between a sensitive woman and a clod. It bears out Mrs. Griffith's view that marriage without love is legal prostitution.

It remains to mention Helen Maria Williams and Mary Robinson, who are alike in several respects. Both wrote highly emotional novels, both were poetesses, both were supposed to have some connection with the Della Cruscans,[64] and (though it is a matter of no literary import) both had strayed from the path of morality. Helen Maria Williams was a fervent believer in the doctrines of the French Revolution. In fact she was imprisoned in the Luxembourg by Robespierre and narrowly escaped being guillotined for her connection with the Girondists. Her political writings involved her in controversies, and drew upon her condemnation as 'a woman whose lips and pen distil venom'; 'whose

61 *Ibid.*, ii, p. 195.

62 In *The History of Lady Barton*.

63 She edited *A Collection of Novels selected and revised* (1777) from the works of Mrs. Behn, Mrs. Aubin and Eliza Haywood.

64 Dr. E. A. Baker says that Helen Maria Williams actually preceded the Della Cruscans, but that Mary Robinson did probably belong to the *coterie* (*H.E.N*, v, p. 150).

wretched pen has long been accumulating on itself disgrace after disgrace.' As the words of a political opponent, these judgments need not be taken too seriously. While in Paris, Miss Williams lived with John Hurford, and some say with Imlay, circumstances which would have caused Fanny Burney to refuse her acquaintance, had she known them when they met at an evening party. Just before that meeting, Miss Williams had published, in 1782, *Edwin and Eltruda*, a legend in verse, and Fanny objected strongly to her air of self-opinionation. She lives for us in Fanny's words: 'A pretty girl rather, but so superfinely affected that, tho' I had the honour of being introduced to her, I couldn't think of conversing with her.'[65] In 1771 Miss Williams published *Anecdotes of a Convent*, a series of letters which tell a straggling story. In 1790 appeared *Julia, a novel interspersed with some poetical pieces*. This story (which has for its background eighteenth century England) has nothing to recommend it.[66] According to the author, it is intended 'to trace the danger arising from the uncontrouled indulgence of strong affections . . . When disapproved by reason, and uncircumscribed by prudence, they involve even the virtuous in calamity.' This prepares one for strong meat, whereas nothing could be more etiolated than the love-story which follows. After tacking backwards and forwards repeatedly among the first chapters, we finally gather that Julia, a paragon of virtue and beauty, is beloved by Frederick Seymour, who is engaged to marry her cousin Charlotte. He marries Charlotte, but continues to love Julia with increasing passion and despair. These emotions he expresses by following her with his eyes and sitting near her. When he is in a very unbridled frame of mind,

65 *The Early Diary of Frances Burney*, 1768-1778 (ed. Bohn), ii, p. 302.

66 Dr. E. A. Baker says: 'But it is in *Julia* . . . that the poetess lets herself go, not only in the verses. The tragic story of Julia's love for the man whom she did not meet till too late, of his death through his impassioned response to her more sober affection, followed by that of his wife, is told with a certain power; and, if the sentiments are excessive, they are at any rate sincere, and, further, Helen Maria could bring out character. The scene is laid in fifteenth-century Spain and so a quasi-historical colour is imparted.' (*H.E.N.*, v. p. 151) Dr. Baker's statements as to the background of the novel and the death of Seymour's wife are probably misprints. Miss William's poems are as washy as her novel. They

he plots to be alone with her so that he may hint his hopeless love, as thus: 'Oh, may every felicity attend you!—may you be happy, when the grave shall have covered my despair, and my heart may retain no longer these sensations, which are interwoven with my existence.' From such speeches Julia shrinks with terrified propriety. She invariably hastens from the room saying that she will conceal herself henceforth in some unknown asylum. These lawless dallyings continue for two volumes.

Julia is purer than the driven snow and of the most delicate sensibility. She is always reading the Bible to her old grandmother; making camelot gowns for the poor; rescuing worms from heedless feet, birds from cats, and flies from bowls of water. She is undoubtedly a noble character. She is very intellectual too, and constantly composes elegant verses which we are never spared. She is tremblingly alive to scenery, particularly at sunset, and she knows the charm of a Gothic ruin, especially if it should have a Gothic gate.[67] Indeed it is when her party is looking at a *snail's nest* in a Gothic abbey that a huge stone almost falls on her, and precipitates her into the arms of Frederick. He keeps his head, however, contenting himself with saying: 'The reflection that I have been the instrument of your preservation, I shall ever cherish as the most delightful that can occupy my mind.'[68] Having struggled gamely to strangle his fatal partiality, he dies of fever. His ravings would melt the heart of a stone. Julia soothes his last moments; Julia breaks the news to Charlotte, whose son has just been born. Thereafter Julia, who refuses to marry, lives with Charlotte and devotes her time to the improvement of Seymour's son; but the memory of her repressed love for Seymour still embitters

are eight in number; chiefly on such subjects as birds, famous poets, the Bastille, and Hope. Only three have any bearing on love: no. 3, a formal idyll; no. 7, in which peace is said to be found only in the grave; and no. 6, in which the faithful woman sadly addresses the man who loves another. Even these poems are all most discreet and mild.

67 *Julia* (1790), i, p. 192.

68 *Ibid.*, i, p. 199.

her life, which otherwise might have been fortunate and happy.

The only parts of this novel which have any link with reality are the descriptions of other women, particularly of venomous gossips. There is a card-party at Mrs. Chartres', which is certainly drawn from Miss Williams's experience. The description of Mrs. Melbourne is also acute. This lady is generally morose and ill-humoured to her family.

> The only seasons memorable for Mrs. Melbourne's tenderness were, when any of her connections or family were ill. She was then the most courteous creature existing, and began to love them with all her might, as if she thought there was no time to lose, and that she must endeavour to crowd such an extraordinary degree of fondness into the short space which was left, as might counterbalance her neglect or unkindness through the whole course of their lives. The way to make her regard permanent was to die.[69]

Miss Williams translated a number of works from the French among them *Paul and Virginia* (1796); and Xavier de Maistre's *The Leper of the City of Aosta* (1817). *The History of Perourou, or the Bellows-maker* (1801), on which Lytton based his *Lady of Lyons*, was said to be original. Dr. Baker believes that she must have adapted it from the French.[70]

Mary Robinson, actress, author, and royal mistress, was of Irish descent. She received her earliest education in the school kept in Bristol by the sisters of Hannah More. Her father, the captain of a whaler (whose family name of McDermott had been changed by a forebear into Darby) appears to have taken only an intermittent interest in his family. He deserted them for long periods, and Mary's upbringing was very haphazard. Her story is too well-known to need repetition. When she, 'the exquisite Perdita', became paralysed, she could no longer rely on love, and she returned to those notions of

69 *Ibid.*, ii, p. 11.
70 E. A. Baker: *H.E.N.*, v, p. 151.

terary fame which had occasionally attracted her since ırlhood. She published a quantity of poetry and several ovels,[71] all highly coloured with sensibility, one an pistolary novel on the Fanny Burney pattern. Space ıakes it necessary to confine ourselves to examining nly one of Mary Robinson's novels—*Vancenza, or the* *angers of credulity* (1792).

This is a very romanticised tale couched for the most art in effusive euphemisms. There is a mingling of the lements of titled romance, Gothicism, and incest. .mid the wild and glowing beauty of Vancenza in Spain :ands the castle of Vancenza, dating back to the twelfth entury. This Gothic pile is the seat of Count Vancenza 'ho lives there in the most perfect happiness with his ster, the Marchioness de Vallorie, her daughter Carline, nd Elvira, 'an illustrious orphan'. Elvira has every ualification for being a heroine—beauty, goodness, xquisite sensibility and mysterious parentage. It needs nly the advent of men into this Eden to set in train all ıe raptures, misunderstandings, villainies and tortures 'hich beset any heroine worthy of the name. It happens ıat the Prince of Almanza is injured while hunting nd conveyed to Vancenza. Elvira loves him at first sight nd so transparently that her secret is an open book to the uke del Vero, who is powerfully attracted by her. The rince departs in ignorance of the conquest he has made, ut del Vero, secretly lingering in the neighbourhood of 'ancenza, determines to pursue his own designs, which o not include marriage to a nameless orphan of no ›rtune. Pretending to be Almanza, he serenades Elvira nd asks her to meet him at daybreak at the cottage of an d woman who is a retainer of the Vancenza family. /ith trembling reluctance she keeps the appointment,

Mary Robinson's fictional works are:
(a) *Celadon and Lydia* (printed in 1777, together with a poem called *Captivity*).
(b) *Angelina* (1796).
(c) *The False Friend*, a domestic story (1799).
(d) *Lyrical Tales* (1800).
(e) *Effusions of Love*, n.d. (purporting to be her correspondence with the Prince of Wales).
(f) *Vancenza, or the dangers of credulity* (1792).

and is so overcome by the sight of the Prince's cloa thrown carelessly on a bench that 'her tottering limb just supported her to the door, she sunk upon the gree sod at the threshold and fainted.' When she recover she finds kneeling before her the Duke del Vero. Sh is filled with rage, shame, self-reproach, pride, and th spirit of insulted virtue. She prepares to wither hin but he insolently tells her that Almanza loves anothe and makes it clear that he, del Vero, will hold over he her indiscretion in coming secretly to meet him. Elvir soon sees the mistake of exposing herself 'to the artific of an abandoned libertine' when del Vero prepares t carry her off there and then. But virtuous indignatio triumphs. Pushing him from her with a look of scor she says resolutely: 'I am above reproach.' She the walks firmly to the castle, but is delirious within a fe hours. She recovers, but 'the icy hand of torpic melancholy chilled the vital source that fed her bein while her fine eyes darted their paly lustre, like th expiring lamps that glimmer in the arches of a sepulchre She keeps her secret, and nobody knows why she ha changed. To divert her the family decides to go on a vis to Madrid. There Almanza falls in love with her, an del Vero troubles her with his minatory attention Carline is privately wooed by the Marquis Petrozi, wh is an impostor, a gamester and a rake. When Cour Vancenza hears Petrozi's real character, he withdraw his family coldly from the acquaintanceship. Petroz in revenge, tries to abduct Carline, but is foiled b Vancenza, whom he slays. His sister, Carline and Elvir return home, and there, having discovered (in Gothi circumstances) a manuscript which reveals that Almanz is her half-brother, Elvira dies.

There is really no characterisation in this nove Almanza is a woman's hero. His eyes beam with sensi bility; his chestnut hair curls beautifully. He wears scarlet hunting dress, bordered with sable, a cloak wit

(g) *Walsingham, or the Pupil of Nature,* a domestic story (2nd ed. 1805). Twice translated into French.

(h) *The Natural Daughter* ?

a brilliant star, and a hat of black velvet with a white plume. Nowadays we should call him a musical-comedy Prince.

Unreality is but too evident also in Mary Robinson's language. Elvira 'enveloped her fair form in a robe of muslin'; the trees are 'the venerable vistas'; the grave is 'the narrow pallet of eternal repose'. 'The villages were crowded with rustics engaged in a variety of gambols.'

But however smothered by high-falutin' nonsense, there is sincere feeling for scenery, and it is evident also that Mary Robinson had taken the Gothic hint from Mrs. Radcliffe. When Elvira leaned out of her window at night:

> All was cold and turbid; not a glimmering star shot forth its feeble rays through the thick clouds that hovered over the forest. The screech-owl, hid within her solitary dwelling, pierced with her horrid shrieks the ear of night; the winds moaned along the battlements, and the long windows rattled round the castle. She stood aghast . . .[72]

When Almanza returned to Vancenza after the Count's death, he found the outer gate unbarred:

> The great court yard was covered with long grass, and the Gothic hall unoccupied by its usual train of domestics. He proceeded through the long gallery; the setting sun cast a gloomy light through the painted windows; the portraits of the family, for many generations, still decorated the damp walls, covered with faded tapestry. His footsteps echoed as he passed along; Elvira heard them as she entered from the terrace; her heart palpitated with apprehension, that some supernatural being occasioned the unusual sound.[73]

Mrs. Robinson's novels are a curious mixture of vulgarity, ignorance, and poetic feeling. She can sum up Gothic splendour in one excellent phrase: 'moth-eaten magnificence', and yet she constantly uses words without understanding their meaning. Her conception of intense emotion may be gleaned from her description of Elvira's

72 *Vancenza, or the dangers of credulity* (1792), i, p. 61.
73 *Ibid.*, ii, p. 70 f.

death (mostly in capitals and with double marks of exclamation as finger-posts to tragedy), and yet with the lyrical spirit of Romantic poetry she tells us that, when the Prince heard the dread news, he shrank 'like a blasted flower that meets the fervid lightning'.[74]

We have been careful to show the faults of that group of women writers who followed the trends of sentiment and of sensibility, but we have endeavoured also to make clear the peculiar value of their contribution. It lay in these women's growing consciousness that female novelists should use a female pen, that with their increasing hold over the reading public they need no longer subscribe to a masculine attitude in fiction. We have already seen a growing individuality in the women's novels—a tendency to write as women. This was the aspect which came fully into view in the novels of Fanny Burney.

[74] *Ibid.*, ii, p. 125.

CHAPTER III

THE DOMESTIC NOVEL AND THE NOVEL OF MANNERS

'*For a young woman's work* I look upon it to be really Wonderful.'
(Dr. Burney)

AT THE end of January, 1778, the London reading public was thrown into high excitement by three small volumes published anonymously. Walpole read them in his Gothic retreat; Dr. Johnson and Mrs. Thrale read them at Streatham; Sir Joshua Reynolds refused to lay them down for sleep or food; Burke forgot to go to bed and was still reading at daybreak. Sheridan, Gibbon, Windham, and even the envious Cumberland, read and wondered. The Blues read and talked profoundly. The circulating libraries circulated at a feverish rate. Lowndes was besieged by eager queries as to the authorship of this new novel. And the first murmurs grew into a shout of triumph for *Evelina*.

Meanwhile at Chesington Hall, near Epsom, the anonymous author was just recovering from pneumonia and heard the first clarions of fame only by letter. Could the literary pundits, the great artists, the politicians, the learned ladies, the fops, the beauties, the society hostesses all clamouring for an opportunity to lionise and monopolise the author of *Evelina*—could they but glance now into the old Samuel Crisp's parlour, they would (like Mrs. Cholmondeley a few months later) start back, exclaiming in consternation: 'It can't be—I don't believe it! no, you are an impostor!' But it is true. This young girl pouring short-sightedly over her sister's exuberant letters—this sallow, sharp-nosed, mouseyhaired, round-shouldered, insignificant young girl is the author of *Evelina*. This is Fanny Burney—about to burst from her chrysalis and to become a butterfly.

But one cannot spend one's life as an obscure caterpillar and suddenly adapt oneself to the glory of the wings. Fanny Burney's overwhelming shyness made public adulation somewhat of an ordeal, but that her family should realise her capabilities was an unmixed joy. Fanny Burney's diaries naïvely record many of her first intimations of success, but none with greater happiness than those which concern her recognition by her own family. Scott loved to think of Fanny Burney dancing round the mulberry tree in Samuel Crisp's garden when she heard that Dr. Johnson had praised *Evelina*, but better still is the picture of Susan Burney listening outside her father's door at seven o'clock in the morning while Dr. Burney reads *Evelina* aloud to his unsuspecting wife—every detail of their laughter and their emotion being written post-haste by the faithful Susan to Fanny at Chesington. Best of all is the scene when Fanny's cousin, the flippant, witty, happy-go-lucky Dick Burney, discovers that she is the author of *Evelina*. He suspects that she knows the author and presses her to tell—never dreaming, of course, of the actual truth. She says finally that she will write the name on a piece of paper, but first exacts a vow of secrecy. He places his hand upon his heart and promises by his honour that he will be faithful; nay, he will even kneel down and swear never to tell a living soul. But at that moment, finding himself observed by Miss Humphries who is also in the room, he holds himself absolved from this mock-heroic detail. Fanny's courage fails, and she writes, not her name, but the cryptic words 'no man'. She hands the scrap of paper to her cousin. 'He read it with the utmost eagerness—but still did not seem to comprehend how the affair stood, till he came to the window—and then, I believe, my countenance cleared up his doubts.' He gazes at her speechlessly, colours violently, and then, having somewhat recovered himself, 'he came again to me, and taking my hand, said: "I believe I must now kneel indeed!" and drawing me to the fire, he actually knelt to me.'

Dick Burney kneeling to Fanny; Dr. Burney's amazed discovery of Fanny's secret five months after *Evelina* had appeared; even Samuel Crisp, who should have guessed, dumbfounded at this extraordinary achievement of his Fannikins—such reactions have a double significance. They prove that Fanny's intimates, like the rest of the world, had rated her too poorly in the past and now rated her too highly.

To estimate the influence of Fanny Burney's environment on her artistic development, it is necessary to refer briefly to the Burney family. On her father's side she came of a family called Macburney, probably of Irish origin but long settled in Shropshire. The Macburneys had possessed a considerable estate, but by perversity and extravagance had reduced themselves to poverty. When Fanny Burney's grandfather, James Macburney, made a run-away marriage with an actress from Goodman's Fields, his father had retaliated by marrying his cook, willing all his property to Joseph, the cook's son, and cutting off James with a shilling. Joseph, however, was in the end no better off than James, for he squandered his patrimony and was forced to earn his living as a dancing-master. James dropped the Mac from his name, and became a portrait painter at Chester. Here was born, by a second marriage, his son Charles Burney, the father of Fanny Burney.

Charles Burney had a considerable talent for music, but a far greater talent for friendship. He early secured the powerful patronage of Fulke Greville, but relinquished it that he might be free to marry. He became an organist and a teacher of music, and worked so hard that he was compelled, after a few years, to seek a less exacting post and healthier air. These he found in King's Lynn, where he remained for ten years and where Fanny was born.

There was nothing in the least brilliant about Fanny Burney's earlier years. In fact, an observer would have considered her a dull child. She was extremely shy and silent, and had such difficulty in learning the alphabet that at eight years old she was still unable to read. Her brothers and sisters called her a dunce, but her mother had no fears for Fanny who showed herself quick-witted in observing people and in inventing games of make-believe. In 1760 the Burney family returned to London and the following year Mrs. Burney died. From that time onward, that is from the age of nine, Fanny Burney's education rested entirely with herself. Of formal education she never had more than some casual instruction in reading and writing, given by a brother or a sister. It is impossible to say why Fanny Burney was denied the educational advantages enjoyed by her sisters. The reasons suggested are not at all convincing. When Hetty and Susan were sent to France, Fanny was kept at home lest she might be tempted to become a Catholic, her affection for her Catholic grandmother being supposed to render her more vulnerable to Catholicism than were her sisters. When Charlotte was later sent to school in Norfolk, Fanny was still kept at home, and this time no other reasons can be suggested than that she was sensitive, and that she was devoted to her father. Devoted indeed she was in the true sense of the word, and as Macaulay has said: 'Her father appears to have been as bad a father as a very honest, affectionate and sweet-tempered man can well be. He loved his daughter dearly; but it never seems to have occurred to him that a parent has other duties to perform to children than that of fondling them.' There is a kind of fantastic humour in the reflection that if Fanny Burney had not so warmly loved her father and her grandmother she might have become a much better novelist. She might perhaps, through education, have developed her mental powers, and acquired a standard of literary judgment. And later, she might have resisted her father's mistaken advice, refusing to abandon her pen for the privilege of becoming a court drudge. Such hypotheses, however, do not lend themselves to proof and must be balanced by what we know of Fanny Burney's character and abilities. Fanny Burney was not more neglected than were the children of Haworth Parsonage. The education of the Brontës had little or nothing to do with their fugitive periods at Cowan Bridge and elsewhere; and they were in their twenties before they went to Belgium—fully developed and self-sufficient. But Charlotte and Emily Brontë were born with powers which 'little Burney' never possessed, and which she would have feared even to imagine. The Brontës were born mature; Fanny Burney died a precocious child. In the visible, tangible possibilities of learning, what was there in Haworth which was not in Poland Street? In each house there was a neglectful father and an extensive library. In Poland Street there was a very happy family and constant intercourse with the most interesting and brilliant people of the age. In Haworth there was a consumptive family, an atmosphere of melancholy and terror, a violent father, a sinister brother, and a sodden graveyard giving on to the storm-swept moors. The children of Haworth found their reality in books. Fanny Burney found hers in her father's drawing room. The children of Haworth read with intuitive genius. When Fanny Burney read, she read like a numbskull. Witness her criticisms of works which she read in her teens. In spite of the erasures and emendations which she made towards the end of her life (when she had learned the opinions of others) one can decipher in the early diary that *The Vicar of Wakefield* did not interest her in the least. Indeed, she was tempted to throw the book aside. 'I began it with distaste and disrelish, having just read the elegant letters of Henry—the beginning of it, even disgusted me—he mentions his wife with such indifference.'[1] There is, nevertheless, a change for the better half way through the first volume. Then 'I was, as I may truly express myself, *surprised into tears*—and in the second volume I really sobb'd.'[2] This method of determining literary value by the tearfall[3] was a characteristic of the period, and was particularly

1 *The Early Diary of Frances Burney*, 1768-1778, (ed. Bohn), i, p. 12.
2 *Ibid.*
3 Mrs. A. R. Ellis coins this witty and useful word.

to be expected of one whose favourite book was Sterne's *Sentimental Journey*. She says: 'Insensibility, of all kinds, and on all occasions, most moves my imperial displeasure.'[4] In keeping with this extreme delicacy of emotion is her criticism of Caius Marius in Plutarch's *Lives*. 'There is a something, a *je ne sçais quoi*, in Plutarch's *Lives* that draws one's attention, and absolutely prevents me leaving off.' But she does not really enjoy herself until she comes to Caius Marius: 'Brutal! inhuman! savage! execrable wretch! *Man* I cannot write—Good God! how shocked, how unaffectedly shocked I am to find that such a *human* brute could ever really exist . . . When he entered Rome—I really trembled—shuddered at the recital of his actions.' And she adds ingenuously 'you may have perceived that I am very earnest and warm in whatever interests me—not of a philosophick or phlegmatick turn.'[5] When Fanny Burney wrote these criticisms she was about sixteen years. She was twenty-one when her brother-in-law Rishton, read Spenser's *Faerie Queen* aloud to Maria and herself. She recorded the fact, and gave her judgment as follows: 'He is reading Spenser's *Faerie Queen* to us, in which he is extremely delicate, omitting whatever, to the poet's great disgrace, has crept in that is improper for a woman's ear. I receive very great pleasure from this poem in which there is an endless fund of ingenuity and poetry.'[6]

It is not in the least unjust to refer to these youthful essays in criticism, because Fanny Burney never reached a higher level of judgment. She must, however, have realised later her lack of critical insight, because in the *Diary and Letters* one cannot but observe how she eluded every effort to draw her into a discussion on books. When Johnson sought to delve into her mind she hedged constantly, and steadfastly refused to utter a single syllable which might reveal her ignorance, playing 'dear little Burney' with all her might, until Johnson gave her

4 *Op. cit.*, i, p. 22.
5 *Ibid.*, i, p. 24.
6 *Ibid.*, p. 252. When Mme d' Arblay revised this diary with a view to publication, she changed the words 'ingenuity and poetry' to 'invention and fancy'.

a fatherly hug and called her his 'little toadling'. But sometimes he returned to the attack. One day he says (though very kindly) that he believes she does not care for reading, because he has never seen her with a book in her hand. She meets the accusation by taking a book from behind a cushion in her chair where she says she has hidden it lest anyone might think her affected. Johnson dropped the subject. Good honest man! he could not be supposed to divine that Fanny's affectation really lay in pretending to hide under an appearance of womanly ignorance, knowledge which she certainly did not possess. If indeed she wished to clear herself of the suspicion of pedantry, she had only to voice the vacuous judgments which she wisely confided to—Nobody. Then would Johnson in stentorian tones have silenced her forever with a tremendous 'Madam — !'

Much has been said as to the value of Fanny Burney's diaries and correspondence. Their importance as a vivid and detailed picture of her time is indisputable, but they are still more interesting as a record of her mind. They provide an explanation of all her literary works, because they fully show her evolution. To her diaries, to her sister Susan and to Samuel Crisp, Fanny Burney confided her inmost thoughts. In Samuel Crisp's friendship she was particularly fortunate, because he was exactly the sort of mentor to aid the development of her mental powers. Crisp was a man of wide literary interests, an excellent critic, and so completely a recluse that he had time and to spare for Fanny Burney. His retirement from social intercourse was generally ascribed to the failure of his tragedy *Virginia*, and there is no doubt that this misfortune never ceased to rankle, but poor health would, in any case, have confined him to his retreat at Chesington. He was, perhaps, the most intimate friend of the Burney family, and Fanny was his especial favourite. From the age of nine she claimed him as her other 'Daddy', and she poured out to him by letter everything that was of importance in her life. Had she been of an inquiring or thoughtful disposition, she might, through Crisp's guidance, have found depth and cultivation. He would have been an excellent confidant for ideas and reflections which she might have been too self-conscious to communicate to her family. But she seems to have been completely free from the long thoughts and obstinate questionings of youth. It does not appear that Crisp had any influence on her development. Fanny's letters to Crisp were merely a transcript of her diary, and her diary was simply a minute record of all the objective life that eddied around her.

Since Fanny Burney had the mind of a newspaper reporter with a keen sense of the ridiculous, it was fortunate for her that she lived in such a maelstrom of events, albeit merely social events. The Burney ménage was the perfect environment for such talents, because a ceaseless tide of life flowed swiftly in at the front door, swirled through the drawing room and music room, and so out again. Not such a tide as moving seems asleep, but the most charming, shallow, babbling, frothy stream in the world. The Burneys' social position was peculiar. It was, so to speak, negative or neutral. Dr. Burney's talents, his versatility and his spontaneous charm attracted to his musical evenings people who belonged to the most various backgrounds. Many belonged to a social stratum much higher than his own. Many, drawn by his mild Bohemianism, were artists. Many had in other ways achieved fame, popularity or notoriety. They came to listen to the music, to meet each other, to be able to say that they had been there. Dr. Burney's 'evenings' became a fashion. These assemblies in Poland Street were heterogeneous and even cosmopolitan. There were people of title, people of the *ton*, visiting Grand Dukes, singers with temporary husbands, painters, actors, composers, explorers, bishops, generals, admirals, ambassadors, human curiosities such as Omiah, the South Sea Islander. Indeed, to 'the silent, observant Miss Fanny' they were all human curiosities. Her shyness in company left her the freer to look on, and caused the people and incidents before her to imprint themselves vividly upon that sensitive photographic film which served her as a brain. She never tried to imagine what went on in the minds of those by whom she was surrounded. Like a child, her interest was caught and held by what the senses could perceive. She never looked beyond externals. Grief, love, beauty, remorse, evil, idealism, despair—unless they had their obvious outward signs they were all one to Fanny Burney. And, because she had no key to human character, she saw life always as a pageant or a masquerade. In her earlier life she could enjoy nothing without feeling impelled to relate it, and so she set down all she saw or heard either in her diaries or letters. These show to a very marked extent her ability to record scenes vividly and to report long conversations verbatim. They show also most of the weaknesses which were later to become so apparent in her novels. In one of the prefaces in *Tom Jones* Fielding had said that the true discerner is he who can distinguish the fine shades of human personality. Such distinctions were always quite beyond Fanny Burney. In the masquerade of life she could recognise the villain by his moustache, the ingénue by her downcast eyes, the fop by his affectation, the miser by his clutching fingers, the vulgarian by his bad manners. Because she could not understand the growth or the diversity of human characteristics, the subtleties which give a great range of variety even to one single trait, she was unconsciously driven to find diversity in peculiarity. She had no taste for ordinary scenes, or for ordinary people. She preferred everything to be strongly marked, strongly contrasted, verging on the grotesque. She was most in her element in describing some gathering of unusual people—Omiah with his quaint broken English, the giant Orloff (reputed to be the murderer of the Czar, and the lover of the Czarina) with his portrait of the Czarina hanging about his neck; Bruce of Abyssinia with his periodic abdominal convulsions; Miss W—, the moron. Even Garrick is shown to us only when he is being temperamental, when he is acting a dozen parts in a moment and sweeping through the house like a whirlwind. We never hear a lively description of Daddy Crisp, or of Susan or of any other normal individual. She never recounts any of Johnson's conversations except those which were eccentric or which eulogised herself. She must have heard some excellent talk in her intercourse with some of the finest intellects of the age. She never records it. The letters and diaries only present life to us photographically, with the emphasis on the ludicrous or on the unusual, and with a selectivity that is merely prudish or egotistic. There is no depth of feeling anywhere to be observed. Fanny Burney professed an absorbing love for music. Did she feel it, or was she simply mimicking the interests of a musical household? She devotes many pages to the divine singing of the Agujari, and if she was sincere we must assume that in the following words she strained every nerve to describe it:

> Such a powerful voice!—so astonishing a compass—reaching from C in the middle of the harpsichord to *two* notes *above* the harpsichord!—Every tone is so clear, so full, so charming!—Then her *shake*—so *plump*—so true, so open! It is as strong and distinct as Mr. Burney's upon the harpsichord. Besides its great power, her voice is all sweetness, and when she pleases, all softness and delicacy. She sings in the highest style of taste and with an *expression* so pathetic, that it is impossible to hear it unmoved. She does the greatest difficulties to be given to her with all the ease and facility that I could say: 'my dear Daddy!'[7]

Such is the shallow jargon with which Fanny Burney records an experience which (we are to believe) stirred her very soul. But she can give an excellent description of the Agujari's first visit, her appearance, her mannerisms and her conversations. At once she pounces on the Agujari's most obvious characteristic: 'Her excessive *vanity* was perpetually betrayed';[8] and she imprints the Agujari on our minds by stressing her foreign tricks: her reputed husband, Signor Colla; her nickname of La Bastardini ('from some misfortune that preceded her birth'[9]); and the story that she was

[7] *Ibid.*, vol. ii, p. 79.
[8] *Ibid.*, vol. ii, p. 2.
[9] *Ibid.*, vol. ii, p. 1.

'mauled when an infant by a pig, in consequence of which she is reported to have a silver side.'[10]

But if Fanny entirely fails to convey the beauty of the Agujari's voice, she can make us see Omiah, the South Sea Islander, singing a native song. He and his song are so bizarre that she is at her best describing them:

> Nothing can be more *curious* or less *pleasing* than his singing voice; he seems to have none; and *tune* or *air* hardly seem to be aimed at; so queer, wild, strange a *rumbling of sounds* never did I before hear; and very contentedly can I go to the grave, if I never do again. His *song* is the only thing that is *savage* belonging to him. The story that the words told, was laughable enough, for he took great pains to explain to us *the English* of the song. It appeared to be a sort of trio between an old woman, a young woman, and a young man. The latter two are entertaining each other with praises of their merits and protestations of their passions, when the old woman enters, and endeavours to *faire l'aimable* to the youth; but as she cannot boast of her *charms*, she is very earnest in displaying her *dress* and making him observe and admire her taste and fancy. Omiah, who stood up to *act* the scene, was extremely droll and diverting by the grimaces, *minauderies*, and affectation he assumed for this character, examining and regarding himself and his dress with the most conceited self-complacency. The youth then avows his passion for the nymph; the old woman sends her away, and, to use Omiah's own words, coming to offer *herself*, says: 'Come! *Marry me*.' The young man starts as if he has seen a viper, then makes her a bow, begs to be excused and runs off. Though the singing of Omy is so barbarous, his actions, the expression he gives to each character, are so original and so diverting, that they did not fail to afford us very great entertainment of the risible kind.[11]

If the Burney 'evenings' were the training ground for Fanny Burney's observations, the diary and letters were an admirable preparation for her fictional works. They contain many rough drafts of situations and characters later employed in the novels. In fact, the first two novels were the natural culmination of those powers which found outlet and development in her journals. *Evelina*, however, was not merely the outcome of the diary. It was a story which had been long maturing in Fanny Burney's mind. Indeed it even had a literary ancestor

10 *Ibid.*, vol. ii, p. 2.
11 *Ibid.*, vol, ii, p. 133.

in the cremated *Caroline Evelyn*. This was a novel which Fanny wrote in her early youth and which she burned with all her other manuscripts when she was about sixteen, in obedience to her step-mother, who strongly disapproved of scribbling young ladies.

Caroline Evelyn was the daughter of a French barmaid and a young gentleman who, when making the grand tour with his tutor, insisted on contracting this very unsuitable marriage. He died shortly afterwards, confiding his child to the care of his tutor, a clergyman named Villars. When Caroline had grown up, Mr. Villars allowed her to visit her mother in Paris, who through a second marriage had become Madame Duval. Caroline secretly married a rake, Sir John Belmont. He returned with her to England, deserted her, and repudiated the marriage. She died at the birth of her daughter, who, disowned and therefore considered illegitimate, was brought up by the good Mr. Villars at Berry Hill, Dorset.

It is clear that such a story had great possibilities of continuation, and long after Fanny Burney had burned the manuscript of *Caroline Evelyn*, her mind continued to dwell on the fate of Caroline Evelyn's daughter. This child, who took the name of Evelina Anville, was most curiously situated. As the obscure ward of a country parson, she was safe and happy enough, although her life was shadowed by the slur of illegitimacy. But, if she were ever to make her entrance into the outer world, it seemed inevitable that she should suffer for the social inequality of her ancestors. She stood between two worlds—the exclusive society in which, as her father's daughter, she had a right to move; and the lower world of petty tradesmen, in which she had relations through her vulgar grandmother, Madame Duval. But she could advance no claim on society, unsupported by her father; and her indeterminate background and her isolation caused her to be ignored and slighted, or else pursued by rakes who considered her fair game. Even against these odds, her innate refinement, beauty, and innocent charm might have triumphed, were it not for the impertinent intrusion of her vulgar relations and the domineering claims of Madame Duval. This was the situation which exercised the mind of Fanny Burney and which developed into the novel *Evelina*.

It is easy to see that such subject-matter was admirably suited to Fanny Burney's powers. It offered to her keen dramatic sense a great variety, indeed a succession of conflicting circumstances and personalities, greatly heightened throughout by continual contrasts. It offered to her sense of the ridiculous all the incongruities of behaviour and of mannerisms which are the proper field of comic writers. Again, the vogue for the epistolary form exactly suited Fanny Burney, who already for so many years had conveyed by letters, to Crisp and others, the most vivid and circumstantial account of life around her. Crisp had called her his little 'anecdotemonger', but she had been far more than that. She had not been content with describing isolated incidents, preferring always to weave together all the events of some particular occasion, and, when ten or twelve quarto pages did not suffice for the narration, continuing it spontaneously from letter to letter. Nothing could have been more natural to Fanny than the epistolary form. For *Evelina* she needed only to make a more prolonged effort and, instead of recounting actual happenings, to invent them. Perhaps, indeed, it would be truer to say that instead of recounting actual happenings, she wrote down imaginary events which she had thought out a long time previously and which had become so familiar to her that the characters lived in her mind, talked, acted and fulfilled their appointed ends without conscious prompting. This maturing, one might also say this autonomy of the characters, left Fanny the letter-writer, almost as free to describe as when she wrote to Crisp. She could still obey the advice he had once given her, when she had feared lest her epistolary style might be too careless and trifling:

You cannot but know that *trifling, that negligence, that even incorrectness*, now and then in familiar epistolary writing, is the very soul of

> genius and ease; and that if your letters were to be fine-labour'd compositions that smelt of *the lamp*, I had as lieve they [travelled elsewhere]. So no more of that, Fanny, and thou lov'st me. Dash away, whatever comes uppermost, and believe me you'll succeed better, than by leaning on your elbow, and studying what to say.[12]

And again: 'There is no fault in an epistolary correspondence like stiffness and study . . . The sudden sallies of the imagination, clap'd down on paper, just as they arise, are worth folios.'[13] The truth of these remarks is seen by comparing the letters of Mr. Villars with the other letters in *Evelina*. In Mr. Villars's letters Fanny leant very heavily on her elbow and the result is grandiloquent sermonising which, although it reduced eighteenth century readers tc floods of tears, is most wearisome to the modern mind.

But the rest of the novel is by no means wearisome. Even by present-day standards it is still worth reading by virtue of a certain quality. In its own day it was like champagne. It came out with a sudden explosive energy. It went to the heads of the reading public, blinding them to its faults. Let it blind us too, for the moment. Later we shall discover its defects in sober sadness, but we must not begin by doing so, or we shall never understand why England went mad over *Evelina*. To judge *Evelina* justly and to understand the furore it caused it is necessary to limit our minds to what had previously been written. *Evelina* appeared at an opportune moment when the public was weary of the school of feeling and extreme sentimentality, and before the Gothic novel had come into power. The four great novelists had left a volume of work which had been imitated, but never equalled. Fanny Burney triumphed because she did not try to imitate them. She may have imagined that she was imitating Richardson since she used the epistolary form and presented the story of a young girl, as told by herself, but we shall see that, in outlook and method, *Evelina* was quite individual. Naturally one does not attempt to compare Fanny Burney to 'the four great

12 *Ibid.*, vol. ii, p. 41.
13 *Ibid.*, vol. i, p. 268.

wheels' of the novel, but it is useful to consider that, within its own limits, *Evelina* showed aspects not hitherto apparent in fiction, and excellences peculiar to itself. Fielding's novels depicted life with a deep, ironic, benevolent insight, but their emphasis was on the picaresque, and they were (though rather unjustly) considered coarse. Richardson, by the exercise of his imagination, created a sort of reality within his own mind, but he did not write from direct observation, and, although he analysed the emotions in great detail, he viewed the human heart through the distorting lens of sensibility. The moral code in his novels was prudential, and they were clouded by a covert eroticism by comparison with which Fielding's novels were robustly clean. Smollett was simply a more sophisticated Defoe. In powers of external portraiture and absence of the subjective Fanny Burney rather resembled him, but most of Smollett's characters were brutal and lewd, and his estimate of human nature was low. Sterne was a slyly sensual sentimentalist. Salacious innuendo was inextricably woven into the fabric of his writings. Like Smollett, he was unable to construct a plot, although indeed, Smollett's roughly-strung succession of episodes seems a master-stroke in architectonics in comparison with the indolent confusion of *Tristram Shandy*. Goldsmith's domestic novel came nearest to the view of life which now interested the female novelists, and its idealism set it apart from the maculate writings of the great men; but the *Vicar of Wakefield* was too consciously didactic. When *Evelina* came out, it must have been apparent to reflective readers that in depth and scope it fell short of the classic novels, but they did not seriously attempt a comparison. It was enough for them that *Evelina* differed in several important respects from all that had gone before—and this so markedly that it must be hailed as something new.

It was new, not because all its constituents were hitherto unknown, but because they were combined in an unusual way. It was new also because its aim had not previously been attempted. By some stroke of genius

Fanny Burney limited the aim of *Evelina* so exactly to her own powers that her success appeared to argue a concentration and not (as it was) a straining of ability to its fullest extent. This aim Fanny Burney states as follows:

> To draw characters from nature, though not from life, and to mark the manners of the times, it is the attempted plan of the following letters. For this purpose, a young female, educated in the most secluded retirement, makes at the age of seventeen, her first appearance upon the great and busy stage of life; with a virtuous mind, a cultivated understanding, and a feeling heart, her ignorance of the forms, and inexperience in the manners of the world, occasion all the little incidents which these volumes record, and which form the natural progression of the life of a young woman of obscure birth, but conspicuous beauty, for the first six months after her *Entrance into the World*.[14]

This aim perhaps, does not seem ambitious, and yet it had never before been achieved. Male novelists had shown themselves able to create minor women-characters convincingly, e.g. acidulated spinsters, redoutable matrons, adventuresses and serving-maids, but they had always failed to create a convincing heroine. For obvious reasons, their heroines were generally high-souled and sentimental creatures.[15] The female novelists mentioned in the preceding chapter did not free themselves from this man-made convention, and though Eliza Haywood makes Betsy Thoughtless anti-sentimental, she goes to the other extreme and creates merely a pert minx. But Evelina is real, and it is important to note that she is not only a real woman, but she is really young.

It has often been said that Evelina was Fanny Burney herself at seventeen. The shy Fanny could well remember the timidities and the self-consciousness occasioned by her first ball, her first admirer, her first feelings of attraction; perhaps, for all we know, her first love. How easy it was for her to enter into the predicaments of Evelina! She had not experienced a tenth of them, but

14 Original preface to *Evelina*.
15 Fielding's Sophia Western is sensible, but she does not count as she is not really a heroine—merely an anchor for Tom Jones.

she had a feeling of oneness with her heroine which helped her to imagine how she herself would have behaved under such circumstances. This feeling of personal reinforcement is strongly evident in the book, and we cannot even say that Evelina's delicacy of sentiment and acute sense of propriety are peculiar to herself, since we know that they were very evident traits in Fanny also ('Poor Fan is such a prude!' her father used to say).

That shyness which was a continuing characteristic of Fanny Burney is represented in Evelina as being due to her rusticity and inexperience. When Evelina is permitted to go with Mrs. Mirvan and her daughter, Maria, on a short visit to London, she is involved in countless new experiences, some pleasurable, some not, but all very interesting because they are so vividly described that to us, also, they seem to be happening for the first time. Not only is Fanny Burney the first to create a convincing heroine, but she is the first writer to show us real life through a woman's eyes. She even catches for us that state of mind (between sharp-cut clarity and delicate illusion) in which a young girl first views the world. It is this spirit of youth which constitutes the greatest charm in *Evelina.* In no preceding novel is it to be observed. Fielding had exuberant energy; Smollett had 'raw-boned high spirits'; Richardson had, at times, a kittenish playfulness; but neither they nor any other writer, prior to Fanny Burney, infused the breath of spring into a novel. Evelina reminds one of a young lamb or a young puppy-dog—all awkwardness, enthusiasm, friendliness, all mistakes, but very much alive and rather pathetic. No doubt it was this ingenuous *élan* which took the great men of the age by storm and closed their eyes to the serious defects.

Another revolution which Fanny Burney effected can best be recognised by a comparison of Pamela and Evelina. Richardson had professed to show a young girl's reactions to a certain set of circumstances. But this young girl is not real and she is not pure-minded. Her sense of values has nothing to do with morality.

Indeed she is so unnaturally overwhelmed by social distinctions that she thinks the vicious Mr. B. far better than she is herself simply because he is richer. Her character is summed up in the incident when Mr. B., all else failing, brings himself to marry her, and at the ceremony says: 'I take thee, Pamela, for my wedded wife'; the self-seeking little toady curtsies and says: 'Thank you, sir!' Women readers did not revolt against that scene because it was in accordance with a male convention in fiction to which they were accustomed, but it is certain that no woman could have invented an episode so degrading to the self-respect of her sex. The complications with which Richardson besets Pamela are the complications a certain type of man would envisage. They all centre in ideas of pursuit and possession. *Evelina* represents a different point of view. There are plots against Evelina's virtue, but these are a minor question. Her main difficulties have to do with the conflicting social circumstances in which she is entangled. She is ignorant of how to behave. She is shy, confused, makes innumerable mistakes. For all her beauty she lacks self-confidence. This is an aspect never presented before *Evelina*—a young girl as she is *to herself*, not merely as she appears to men. Up to then, in fiction, a beautiful woman was supposed to be invulnerable to uncertainties of social procedure. She would not have wondered whether a dress suited her, or have lost her glow merely because she was conscious of dowdy clothes. She would never have needed to find courage and poise in a new style of hairdressing or a new cap. She was never gauche. She had no doubts as to etiquette. But Fanny Burney knew that beauty and self-possession, beauty and tact are not necessarily the same thing. Evelina's mingled delight and fear in her preparations for her first ball reveal perfectly the mind of an inexperienced girl:

> We are to go this evening to a private ball, given by Mrs. Stanley, a very fashionable lady of Mrs. Mirvan's acquaintance. We have been *a-shopping* as Mrs. Mirvan calls it, all this morning, to buy silks, caps, gauzes and so forth.

The shops are really very entertaining, especially the mercers; there seem to be six or seven men belonging to each shop; and every one took care by bowing and smirking, to be noticed. We were conducted from one to another, and carried from room to room with so much ceremony, that at first I was almost afraid to go on. I thought I should never have chosen a silk: for they produced so many, I knew not which to fix upon; and they recommended them all so strongly, that I fancy they thought I only wanted persuasion to buy everything they showed me. And indeed, they took such trouble, that I was almost ashamed I could not.

At the milliners, the ladies we met were so much dressed, that I should rather have imagined they were making visits than purchases. But what most diverted me was, that we were more frequently served by men than by women; and such men! so finical, so affected! they seemed to understand every part of a woman's dress better than we do ourselves; and they recommended caps and ribbands with an air of so much importance, that I wished to ask them how long they had left off wearing them.

The despatch with which they work in these great shops is amazing, for they have promised me a complete suit of linen against the evening.

I have just had my hair dressed. You can't think how oddly my head feels; full of powder and black pins, and a great cushion on the top of it. I believe you would hardly know me for my face looks quite different to what it did before my hair was dressed. When I shall be able to make use of a comb for myself I cannot tell; for my hair is so much entangled, *frizzled* they call it, that I fear it will be very difficult.

I am half afraid of this ball to-night; for, you know, I have never danced but at school: however Mrs. Mirvan says there is nothing in it. Yet I wish it were over.[16]

Better still is Evelina's description of the ball. There is excellent comedy in the contrast between her outward seeming and her inmost thoughts. She appears a heart-subduing beauty, while inwardly she is little more than an awkward child. The confusion and misunderstandings which result from her ignorance of social forms are highly amusing, all the more so since, even when her partners finally consider her 'ignorant or mischievous', or 'a poor weak girl', they are still very far from understanding what is going on in her mind. She has summed them all up to a nicety, and her vivacious descriptions of her adventures would be hard

16 *Evelina* (ed. Bohn), p. 19.

to better. These are her reflections while waiting for the first dance to begin:

> The gentlemen, as they passed and repassed, looked as if they thought we were quite at their disposal, and only waiting for the honour of their commands; and they sauntered about in a careless indolent manner, as if with a view to keep us in suspense . . . and I thought it so provoking, that I determined in my own mind that far from humouring such airs, I would rather not dance at all, than with any one who should seem to think me ready to accept the first partner who would condescend to take me.
>
> Not long after, a young man, who had for some time looked at us with a kind of negligent impertinence, advanced on tiptoe towards me; he had a set smile on his face, and his dress was so foppish that I really believe he even wished to be stared at; and yet he was very ugly.
>
> Bowing almost to the ground with a sort of swing, and waving his hand with the greatest conceit, after a short and silly pause, he said: 'Madam—may I presume—and stopt, offering to take my hand. I drew it back, but could not forbear laughing. 'Allow me, Madam,' continued he, affectedly breaking off every half moment, 'the honour and happiness—if I am not so unhappy as to address you too late—to have the happiness and honour.'[17]

Evelina refuses, saying she believes she will not dance at all, but changes her mind when Lord Orville offers himself as her partner.

Lord Orville, the hero of the novel, is merely a 'condescending suit of clothes',[18] but for some inscrutable reason he attracts Evelina, possibly because he is handsome and because his manners and morals are impeccable. She slips unconsciously into loving him, but it is long before he discloses his intentions. Her peculiar lack of family and background, her vulgar relatives, rival suitors, and a variety of accidents which cause her to appear indiscreet despite her innocence—all conspire to delay his proposal of marriage. They are happy in the end, but only after many weary months, during which Evelina vainly tries to understand the fluctuations in his attitude towards her. We have seen

17 *Ibid.*, p. 20. f.

18 So Hazlitt once called him. See Christopher Lloyd, *Fanny Burney*. (1936), p. 127.

that the women writers of the school of sentiment and sensibility sometimes touched on the aspect of women's passivity before the puzzle of men's minds and intentions. With Fanny Burney this aspect is made the pivotal point of a novel. It was Jane Austen who brought this *motif* of passivity to its full perfection, but even in Fanny Burney's novels we have that tragi-comedy of woman observing a man's attitude to her, her secretly responsive hopes, his inexplicable withdrawal, and the impossibility of showing that she cares, or of asking for the explanation to which she is entitled. When in *Camilla*, for example, that finicking prig, Mandlebert, blows hot and cold for five volumes, Fanny Burney puts into the mouth of Mrs. Arlbery this very trenchant protest against such a quibbling code of honour:

> Mandlebert is a creature whose whole composition is a pile of accumulated punctilios. He will spend his life in refining away his own happiness; but do not let him refine away yours. He is just a man to bewitch an innocent and unguarded young woman from forming any other connection, and yet, when her youth and expectations have been sacrificed to his hesitation . . . to conceive he does not use her ill in thinking of her no more, because he has entered into no verbal engagement. If his honour cannot be arraigned of breaking any bond . . . what matters merely breaking her heart?[19]

Jane Austen shows one woman revolting against the feminine convention of dignified acquiescence, and asking her erstwhile lover why he has suddenly changed. Jane did this to indicate that the convention was a necessary one; and she proves it by showing the young man feigning consternation that Marianne could so have 'misunderstood' him. Marianne has no weapon against that blank disclaimer, although she knows quite well that there is an unstated reason for the change. That is the attitude of Fanny Burney, fully developed in Jane Austen. Another aspect for the first time presented by Fanny Burney and driven home with all Jane Austen's power, is that money and social position often load the dice against beauty and love. It had never been

19 *Camilla* (ed. 1796), iii, p. 380 f.

admitted before, although Smollett shows his heroes as eager fortune-hunters. Smollett's heroes, however, return in the end to the beautiful and pure heroine, whose love outweighs the heaviest money-bags.

One notes, also, another important point on which eighteenth century women-novelists firmly differed from men. Beauty and virtue are the philosopher's stone in the men's novels. Tom Jones may go a-roving from Sophia, but he will return when he is weary of folly; she cannot really lose him if she is beautiful and good. Women knew that beauty and virtue were no talisman, and that one might retain both, without winning happiness. Nor did they account it happiness to await the magnanimous return of the prodigal. Fielding, Smollett, and Richardson take it for granted that the woman is ready to take back the young hero after a thousand amorous adventures. Not so Mrs. Brooke and Mrs. Sheridan, and not so Fanny and Jane. Fanny and Jane never marry vice to virtue. If the young man sows wild oats, then he must eat bitter bread. That is the woman's attitude.

'To draw characters from nature . . . and to mark the manners of the times' was a part of Fanny Burney's aim, but those abilities which made her so pre-eminently a recorder of manners were most calculated to defeat her purpose of characterisation. Her powers of observation were, as we have seen, very acute, but she had no insight. Hazlitt says:

> Madame d'Arblay is . . . a mere common observer of manners . . . There is little in her works of passion or character, or even manners in the most extended sense of the word, as implying the sum-total of all our habits and pursuits; her forte is in describing the absurdities and affectations of external behaviour, or the manners of people in company. There is little other power in Madame d'Arblay's novels than that of immediate observation.[20]

Evelina is Fanny Burney's best novel not only because, as Hazlitt has said, it was her shortest, but also because its subject-matter was least likely to expose her super-

[20] See Hazlitt, *Lectures on the English Comic Writers*, 'Madame d'Arblay'.

ficiality. Life through the eyes of a girl of seventeen is vivid, refreshing and amusing, but it is not deep, and therefore the lack of depth in *Evelina* might be considered in keeping with the writer of the letters. Some of Fanny Burney's studies in manners are, however, extremely clever. She was most successful with vulgar characters, and her best portraits are those of Evelina's shopkeeper cousins, the Brangtons, and Mr. Smith, their lodger.

Evelina's grandmother, the ex-barmaid, Madame Duval, introduces her to the Brangtons, who are at once summed up with withering shrewdness, as follows:

> The relations to whom she was pleased to introduce me, consisted of a Mr. Brangton, who is her nephew, and three of his children, the eldest of which is a son, and the two younger are daughters. Mr. Brangton appears about forty years of age. He does not seem to want a common understanding, though he is very contracted and prejudiced: he has spent his whole time in the city, and I believe feels a great contempt for all who reside elsewhere.
>
> His son seems weaker in his understanding, and more gay in his temper; but his gaiety is that of a foolish, overgrown schoolboy, whose mirth consists in noise and disturbance. He disdains his father for his close attention to business, and love of money; though he seems himself to have no talents, spirit or generosity, to make him superior to either. His chief delight appears to be tormenting and ridiculing his sisters; who, in return, most heartily despise him.
>
> Miss Brangton, the eldest daughter, is by no means ugly; but looks proud, ill-tempered, and conceited. She hates the city, though without knowing why; for it is easy to discover that she has lived no where else.
>
> Miss Polly Brangton is rather pretty, very foolish, very ignorant, very giddy, and, I believe, very good-natured.[21]

The Brangtons are deplorably bumptious and impertinent, and quite look down on Evelina because she is country bred, though they themselves know little more of London that the environs of their shop at Snow Hill. Madame Duval's introduction is so brutally phrased as to make it appear that Evelina's mother 'went astray'. Evelina is so shocked at this suggestion that young Brangton becomes dimly aware that something is wrong! 'If aunt pleases,' said young Mr. Brangton,

21 *Evelina* (ed. Bohn), p. 64.

'we'll talk o' somewhat else, for Miss looks very uneasy-like.' His sisters, however, have no misgivings in returning to a subject which absorbs their crude wonder 'In a few minutes, Miss Brangton, coming suddenly up to her sister, exclaimed, "Lord, Polly, only think Miss never saw her papa!" "Lord, how odd!" cried the other, "Why, then, Miss, I suppose you wouldn't know him?" ' And when Evelina finally runs from the room they insist on following, to comfort her and bring her back! They question her acutely as to what she has already seen in London, and when it appears that she has not been to the Tower their contempt is great When she is forced to confess that she has, nevertheless 'seen such a thing as an opera', it occurs to them that i might be worth their while to see one also, 'for once for the curiosity of the thing'. They arrange to take Evelina to the opera, riding rough-shod over her objections. The Brangtons at the opera is really an inimitable piece of writing. Their squabbles over money the cheese-paring of Mr. Brangton who takes them to the gallery, pausing to beat down the price of every box office on their upward way: the confusion of Evelina who is dressed for the pit, and the added misery of knowing she is observed by her friends in that part of th house: the crass comments of her companions who talk and titter through every act—all are presented to the life, and Mr. Brangton's final comment sums up perfectly the family point of view: 'As for me,' said Mr Brangton, 'they've caught me once, but if ever they do again, I'll give 'em leave to sing me to Bedlam for my pains: for such a heap of stuff never did I hear: ther isn't one ounce of sense in the whole opera, nothing but one continued squeaking and squalling from beginning to end.' No wonder that Dr. Johnson revelled in these characters and used the word *Brangton* to connote a vulgarian ('One would take you for a Brangton sir' he roars at Boswell, when that unfortunate is being more heavy-handed than usual. 'A Brangton, sir? Wha is a Brangton?' 'Where have you lived, sir, and wha company have you kept not to know that?').

Even better than the Brangtons is Mr. Smith, whom Hazlitt calls 'an exquisite city portrait', and whose 'vulgar gentility' delighted Johnson. When Mr. Smith enters, the Misses Brangton fall into ecstasies and beg Evelina to remark his 'smart air'. They consider that he has 'very much a *quality look*'.

'Come,' cried he, advancing to us, 'you ladies must not sit together; wherever I go I always make it a rule to part the ladies.' And then, handing Miss Brangton to the next chair, he seated himself between us.

'Well, now, ladies, I think we sit very well. What say you? for my part I think it is a very good notion.'

'If my cousin likes it,' said Miss Brangton, 'I'm sure I've no objection.'

'O,' cried he, 'I always study what the ladies like—that's my first thought. And indeed, it is but natural that you should like best to sit by the gentlemen, for what can you find to say to one another?' 'Say!' cried young Brangton: 'O, never you think of that, they'll find enough to say, I'll be sworn. You know the women are never tired of talking.' 'Come, come, Tom,' said Mr. Smith, 'don't be severe upon the ladies: when I'm by, you know I always take their part . . .[22]

'Well, Mr. Smith is always in such spirits!' said Miss Brangton.

'Why, yes, Ma'am, yes, thank God, pretty good spirits; I have not yet the cares of the world upon me: I am not *married*,—ha, ha, ha!—you'll excuse me, ladies—but I can't help laughing!'[23]

Such portraits support the truth of Mr. Christopher Lloyd's sound criticism:

Miss Burney was the first novelist to make the ordinary incidents of everyday life significant and interesting. She realised, perhaps unconsciously, a truth which critics have always seen—that one of the chief, if not the true, pleasures of art is the pleasure of recognition. In this way she founded the realistic but polite novel of manners and led the way for that much greater artist, Jane Austen.[24]

But Fanny Burney's portraits are not always so recognisable. Too many of her characters are caricatures. One cannot but remark that Fanny Burney had no fineness of conception, and that her lack of judgment

22 *Ibid.*, p. 191.
23 *Ibid.*, p. 193.
24 Christopher Lloyd, *Fanny Burney* (1936), p. 75 f.

betrayed her into many vulgarities. This lack of good taste is the plague spot in Fanny Burney, and to it we may trace all the worst faults in her writings. It shows itself always in a want of restraint, in the deplorable way in which she always tended to exaggerate, whether it was a character, an emotion, or a style. As to character, it is seldom that she can invest an individual with a mannerism, and then let him behave like a human being. No, he must become an idiosyncrasy masquerading as a human being. This preference for caricature verging on the grotesque is certainly vulgar. It is the same impulse that drives a crowd to pay its penny for a sight of the pig-faced lady. Not only are Fanny Burney's exaggerated characters always displaying the same mannerism—they are always expressing it in the very same words. Captain Mirvan and Madame Duval, for example, are forever quarrelling. The Captain is always damning Frenchies and lauding Britons. Madame Duval is always saying 'Ma foi' and using an unchanging farrago of bad grammar for broken English. Indeed the scenes between this pair are so brutal that they were not approved even by the age for which they were written. They were not necessary to the plot and are in the worst possible taste. We are shown a lout shaking and beating a grandmother, making her the subject of the most savage jeers and horseplay, throwing her in the mud and tying her by her feet to the bough of a tree so that she is unrecognisable for filth. Her face plastered with a mixture of mud and tears; her wig is gone; her voice, from screaming, has become like an animal's howl; she tears the ground with her hands. In this state she is laughed at by the servants, who are in the conspiracy. Fanny Burney does not present this as a disgusting business. She implies that the Captain is a great, rough schoolboy—no more. Then there is the occasion when Madame Duval spits in the Captain's face, and when he tells her that, if she were not so old and ugly, he would spit back; and again the scene where the Captain, to insult a fop, brings in a monkey dressed as a beau and is so overwhelmed with merriment when the monkey bites off a piece of the fop's ear, that he rolls on the floor, shouting with laughter. No wonder that Mrs. Montagu expressed her amazement that 'so delicate a girl could write so boisterous a book,' Even allowing for the liberty with which the century indulged in practical joking, the horseplay in *Evelina* is quite shocking. Captain Mirvan (who, incidentally, is not at all like a sea-captain, but rather resembles a brutal country squire) did not find favour with the reading public, but Fanny Burney was unrepentant. She says: 'The more I see of sea-captains, the less reason I have to be ashamed of Captain Mirvan, for they have all so irresistible a propensity to wanton mischief, to roasting beaus, and detesting old women that I quite rejoice I showed the book to no one 'ere printed, lest I should have been prevailed upon to soften his character.'[25] This aspect of the demure, sensitive and prudish Miss Burney would be surprising did we not remember that she helped to bait the poor moron, Miss W—, and was openly convulsed with laughter at her efforts to sing. Even when Miss W—'s host and bear-leader takes a tablespoon and thrusts it down the front of her dress, while she is singing, Fanny Burney is only the more amused. Indeed she seizes the opportunity later to make Miss W— sing again, for the pleasure of laughing herself sick. This was the paragon whose lady-like decorum at Windsor impressed even 'the sweet Queen'!

But it is when Fanny Burney tries to plumb the depths of passions and of pathos that her lack of restraint most betrays her. Characters which, until then, seemed flesh and blood suddenly seem to be transmuted into card-board. They rant and rave, beat their breasts and liquidate themselves into a pool of tears. All fustian—and there is rarely even a credible cause for these mock-heroic typhoons. For example, one cannot accept as natural Evelina's attitude towards her father. Sir John Belmont had treated her mother abominably. But for Mr. Villars's kindness, Caroline might have died in a ditch, and Evelina might have begged her bread in the

25 *Diary and Letters of Madame d'Arblay* (ed. Dobson), i, p. 375

gutter; nevertheless, this dutiful young woman quivers with eagerness at the possibility that her father may relent. She says: 'My imagination changes the scene perpetually: one moment I am embraced by a kind and relenting parent, who takes me to that heart from which I have hitherto been banished, and supplicates, through me, peace and forgiveness from the ashes of my mother!—at another, he regards me with detestation, considers me as the living image of an injured saint, and repulses me with horror!'[26] When at last they meet the scene out-herods Herod. Sir John cries inarticulately: 'My God! does Caroline Evelyn still live!' And in a few minutes he adds: 'Lift up thy head—if my sight has not blasted thee! Lift up thy head, thou image of my long lost Caroline.' Far from suggesting that the loss was self-imposed, Evelina embraces his knees.' "Yes, yes," cried he, looking earnestly in my face, "I see, I see thou art her child! she lives—she breathes—she is present to my view!—Oh, God, that she indeed lived!—Go, child, go," added he wildly starting, and pushing me from him: "take her away, Madam—I cannot bear to look at her."' With which, and having offered to plunge a dagger in his heart to serve her, he rushes from the room, crying that his brain is on fire. Evelina's intervention when Macartney is about to commit suicide is in the same tone. She bursts into the room, exclaiming: 'O, Sir! have mercy on yourself!'

> The guilty pistols fell from his hands, which disengaging from me he fervently clasped, and cried: 'Sweet Heaven! is this thy angel?' Encouraged by such gentleness, I again attempted to take the pistols; but with a look half frantic, he again prevented me, saying 'What would you do?'
>
> 'Awaken you,' I cried, with a courage I now wonder at, 'to worthier thoughts, and rescue you from perdition.'[27]

Although, in general, the style of *Evelina* is simple and vivacious, there are glimpses of that pretentious pedantry which was later to prove Miss Burney's undoing.

26 *Evelina* (ed. Bohn), p. 132 f.
27 *Ibid*., p. 187.

'During the childhood of Evelina, I suggested a thousand plans for the securing of her birthright; but I as many times rejected them. I was in a perpetual conflict, between the desire that she should have justice done her, and the apprehension that, while I improved her fortune, I should endanger her mind. However, as her character began to be formed, and her disposition to be displayed, my perplexity abated . . . Then did I flatter myself, that to follow my inclination, and to secure her welfare, was the same thing, since, to expose her to the snares and dangers inevitably encircling a house of which the master is dissipated and unprincipled, without the guidance of a mother, or any prudent and sensible female, seemed to me no less than suffering her to stumble into some dreadful pit, when the sun is in its meridian.'[28] She cannot say in plain English: 'To stumble into some dreadful pit in broad daylight.' It must be 'when the sun is in its meridian.' The euphuistic pomposity which was to weigh her later writings to the ground was already beginning to grow. Her aspirations towards Johnsonese, too, are even now to be observed. With careful balancing of thought against thought, of word against word, Fanny Burney writes that it had been Villars's intention to bestow Evelina 'upon some worthy man, with whom she might spend her days in tranquillity, cheerfulness, and good humour, untainted by vice, folly, or ambition.'[29] And Madame Duval is 'too ignorant for instruction, too obstinate for entreaty, and too weak for reason.'[30]

In 1782, four years after *Evelina*, appeared *Cecilia*. It was written after a certain amount of hesitation, and against the advice of Samuel Crisp. He appears to have felt that his young protégée could never equal what she had already achieved, and that an inferior work would only lower her prestige. Above all, he warned her not to force herself to further composition: 'It was not "hard fagging" that produced such a work as *Evelina*. It was the ebullition of true, sterling genius. *You wrote it*

28 *Ibid*., p. 128.
29 *Ibid*., p. 128.
30 *Ibid*., p. 129.

because you could not help it—it came, and you put it down on paper.' Fanny herself felt that 'but for pecuniary advantages, it would be better to write no more.' She seems to have been overwhelmed by the apparent impossibility of repeating her triumph. Indeed, she says: 'I have already, I fear, reached the pinnacle of my abilities, and therefore to stand still will be my best policy.' The wonder with which she was regarded gave her perhaps a sense of unreality. She had no feeling of continuous life with the prodigy who wrote *Evelina* and she must have believed that, if she were to equal that achievement, it would need a herculean effort. She made a herculean effort, which, since she lacked judgment meant that she exaggerated everything. She used too large a canvas; she introduced too many eccentrics she heightened the melodrama; she revelled in the vulgar scenes. Instead of adhering to the epistolary form and to her lighthearted style, she used the ordinary novel form and expressed herself in Johnsonese. The unsuitability of Dr. Johnson's language for a domestic novel of manners does not appear to have struck her.

Cecilia has an elaborate plot, the pivot of which was so unconvincing that Crisp implored Fanny to give it up. She refused. His objection was obviously well founded because the novel appears to depend on an improbable and unreasonable situation. Cecilia Beverley inherits a large fortune on condition that, if she should marry her husband should take her name. She falls in love with Mortimer Delvile, the heir of an ancient family, and he with her. Delvile's parents oppose the marriage, the very mention of which particularly enrages his father Mortimer is torn between love and filial devotion Cecilia suffers intensely and the action moves in a crescendo of drama. Mrs. Delvile grows to love Cecilia and wishes to yield, but feels that it is impossible. Mr Delvile remains uniformly implacable. Finally Cecilia consents to a secret marriage, but the ceremony is interrupted by a mysterious voice, and she refuses to be married on that day or any other. Mortimer now falls into a state of extreme anguish. There is a tremendous scene between the mother, the son and Cecilia, and Mrs. Delvile is so overwhelmed that she cries: 'My brain is on fire', rushes from the room and bursts a blood vessel. This is the scene around which Fanny Burney avowedly wrote the novel, and which nothing would induce her to abandon. It made contemporary readers ill with emotion. Now it merely makes one yawn. With Mrs. Delvile's consent the lovers marry. Mortimer keeps his treasured surname, and all might have been well, had not Miss Burney insisted on introducing further complications. Mortimer fights a duel and finds it necessary to flee the country. Cecilia's marriage is discovered and her fortune is claimed by the next heir. She seeks refuge with Mortimer, but jealousy causes him to misinterpret a situation in which she is innocently involved. He spurns her, and she goes mad and runs about the streets. It is all very distressing, but happiness awaits them in the end.

Ingeniously woven into this main theme is the subsidiary plot dealing with the Harrels. These are friends of Cecilia's with whom she lives for some time in London and who involve her in many difficulties and misunderstandings. Mr. Harrel is a weak scoundrel who gambles away all his money, and then, by threats of suicide, repeatedly blackmails Cecilia into 'lending' him money. She is even driven to borrowing money from Jews. Mrs. Harrel is a brainless and heartless woman, and there is a great deal of amusement in the manner in which this irresponsible couple fluctuate between despair and frivolity. As often as not Mr. Harrel spends the morning sharpening his razor for self-slaughter, only to sally forth at night with Mrs. Harrel to a ball or a rout, leaving the impoverished Cecilia aghast at their volatile insensibility. Harrel really does commit suicide at last, blowing his brains out at Vauxhall, almost in the presence of some of his creditors whom he first entertains to supper, with liberal quantities of champagne. This Vauxhall scene has been much praised by some, notably by Mrs. A. R. Ellis whose critical prefaces to *Evelina* and *Cecilia* are, in general, so interesting that one cannot in this instance quite pass over her remarks, although they are undoubtedly too eulogistic. She says:

> Surely all that leads up to [Harrel's] end, and the chapter which completes it, are the finest parts of the book. In the self-importance of Mr. Hobson and the servility of Mr. Simkins, amid the awful merriment in the box at Vauxhall, there is something not unlike the great dramatists of the sixteenth century.[31]

The characterisation in *Cecilia* shows in excess that tendency toward caricature which was observable in *Evelina*. Macaulay[32] has shown the distinction between writers who can discriminate the fine shades of human character and those who concentrate on exhibiting what Ben Johnson called humours. Such humours exist and are therefore within the province of art, but as they are infrequent in human life, so they should be infrequent in any work which professes to be a representation of human life. The writer who shows genius in representing humours can claim a place among the classics, but it must be a lower place than that of writers who give a balanced view of human character. He goes on to say

> If we have expounded the law soundly, we can have no difficulty in applying it to the particular case before us. Madame d'Arblay has left us scarcely anything but humours. Almost every one of her men and women has some propensity developed to a morbid degree. In *Cecilia*, for example, Mr. Delvile never opens his lips without some allusion to his own birth and station; or Mr. Briggs without some allusion to the hoarding of money; or Mr. Hobson without betraying the self-indulgence and self-importance of a purse-proud upstart; or Mr. Simkins, without uttering some sneaking remark for the purpose of currying favour with his customers; or Mr. Meadows, without expressing apathy and weariness of life; or Mr. Albany, without declaiming about the vices of the rich and the misery of the poor; or Mrs. Belfield, without some indelicate eulogy on her son; or Lady Margaret, without indicating jealousy of her husband. Morrice is all skipping, officious impertinence, Mr Gosport all sarcasm, Lady Honoria all lively prattle, Miss Larolles all silly prattle. If ever Madame d'Arblay aimed at more, we do not think she succeeded well.

31 A. R. Ellis, Preface to *Cecilia* (ed. 1882), p. 13.

32 Macaulay, *Critical and Historical Essays*, 'Diary and Letters of Madame d'Arblay', pp. 601-604.

> We are, therefore, forced to refuse Madame d'Arblay a place in the highest rank of art; but we cannot deny that, in the rank to which she belonged, she had few equals, and scarcely any superior. The variety of humours which is to be found in her novels is immense; and though the talk of each person separately is monotonous, the general effect is not monotony, but a lively and agreeable diversity. Her plots are rudely constructed and improbable, if we consider them in themselves. But they are admirably framed for the purpose of exhibiting striking groups of eccentric characters, each governed by his own peculiar whim, each talking his own peculiar jargon, and each bringing out by opposition the oddities of all the rest. All probability is violated in order to bring Mr. Delvile, Mr. Briggs, Mr. Hobson, and Mr. Albany into a room together. But when we have them there, we soon forgot probability in the exquisitely ludicrous effect which is produced by the conflict of four old fools, each raging with a monomania of his own, each talking a dialect of his own, and each inflaming all the others anew every time he opens his mouth.

But a plot subordinated to the purpose of exhibiting humours cannot really be defended, and the inevitability of each humour and its particular jargon is wearisome in the extreme. The final impression is that stated by Walpole: 'Her great fault [is] that her characters are never allowed to utter a syllable out of character, which is unnatural.' The same point arises when one considers Fanny Burney's classification of the *ton*. She very cleverly groups the society of the day according to the affectations displayed. There are the Insensibilists, the Jargonists, the Voluble, the Supercilious, and later the Ennuyés. Each group has its particular idiom, and when we first hear them speak we are most amused. But boredom very quickly supervenes when we find that we can always anticipate what each type is going to say.

Before we pass on to Fanny Burney's other novels, it may be as well to mention a criticism of Macaulay's with which we find it impossible to agree. He says:

> Madame d'Arblay was most successful in comedy, and indeed in comedy which bordered on farce. But we are inclined to infer from some passages, both in *Cecilia* and *Camilla*, that she might have attained equal distinction in the pathetic. We have formed this judgment, less from those ambitious scenes of distress which lie

near the catastrophe of each of those novels, than from some exquisite strokes of natural tenderness which take us here and there by surprise. We would mention as examples, Mrs. Hill's account of her little boy's death in *Cecilia*, and the parting of Sir Hugh Tyrold and Camilla, when the honest baronet thinks himself dying.[33]

Mrs. Hill's 'little boy' (who was really seventeen) would have been affecting if his mother had not interlarded all her conversation with references to him, but he haunts every sentence with such persistency that we are tempted to hail him with 'Art there, old mole?' As for Sir Hugh Tyrold, his utterances are usually so imbecile that when, for a single paragraph, he deviates into sense, the effect is out of all proportion to the actual value of the incident. As an example of Fanny Burney's more ambitious efforts at pathos, one cannot forget Albany's visit to Cecilia when she is believed to be dying. He makes his entrance (as the author terms it) 'accompanied by three children, two girls and one boy, from the ages of four to six, neatly dressed, clean and healthy.' He apostrophises Cecilia, and begs her to look at the objects of her bounty. Cecilia continues to die, but Albany cannot be deterred from making an oration. He bids the children kneel ('Come, little babies, come! . . . lift up your innocent hands . . .') and thus addresses the unconscious figure:

Sweet flower! untimely cropt in years, yet in excellence mature; early decayed in misery, yet fragrant in innocence! Gentle be thy exit . . . Look at her, sweet babes, and bear her in your remembrance . . . She departs the envy of the world while yet no guilt had seized her soul, and no remorse had marred her peace. She was the handmaid of charity, and pity dwelt in her bosom! her mouth was never opened but to give comfort; her footsteps were followed by blessings! Oh, happy in purity, be thine the song of triumph!—softly shalt thou sink to temporary sleep—sublimely shalt thou rise to life that wakes for ever!'

He then got up, took the children by their little hands, and went away.[34]

33 *Ibid.*, p. 605.
34 *Cecilia* (ed. Bohn, 1882), ii, p. 449.

It is with reluctance that one comes to speak of Fanny Burney's later novels,[35] *Camilla* (1796) and *The Wanderer* (1814). In themselves they are not worth mentioning because they are in no sense a contribution towards the English novel. Nevertheless, because they present a curious problem in the literary career of Fanny Burney, they may be briefly considered. One may begin by saying outright that these two novels are as futile as they could well be. *The Wanderer* is generally held to be the worse, but it is a point not worth determining.[36] What really matters is that these novels reveal an incredible deterioration in the author's powers. *Cecilia*, despite its ambitious scope, had not reached the level of *Evelina*, but in aim and in general characteristics the two novels are alike. On the contrary, *Camilla* and *The Wanderer* might almost be the work of a changeling. There is an occasional echo of the old love of humours, in such characters as Sir Sedley Clarendel and Mrs. Arlbery, but for the most part there is an immense gap between the work of the earlier and the later periods. Where, in the later period, is the keen observation, the striking caricature, the rapid, even abrupt sequence of events, the really excellent dialogue, the vivacity and the sense

35 During this later period Fanny Burney's play *Edwy and Elgiva* was produced (21 March, 1795). This was one of the three historical tragedies which she roughly sketched at Windsor. On leaving the court she arranged her notes, but thought no further about them until the impending birth of her child made it necessary for her to raise money. Kemble and Sheridan, when approached, at once decided to produce the play, giving her no time for revision. The play had a very strong cast, Kemble and Mrs. Siddons taking the leading parts. It was a miserable failure. Mrs. Siddons wrote to Mrs. Piozzi: 'There never was so wretched a thing as Mrs. d'Arblay's Tragedy . . . The Audience was quite angelic and only laughed where it was impossible to avoid it.' When one reflects that *Edwy and Elgiva* was written in very bad blank verse, and that Elgiva, murdered at the beginning of the last act, had to lie prostrate on the stage for twenty minutes, it is clear that its chances of success were poor. This was Fanny Burney's second attempt at the drama, her play *The Witlings* (1779) being, adjudged so like Molière's *Femmes Savantes* that it was not produced, lest it should appear a mere imitation. Actually Fanny Burney had never read Molière's play.

36 In an article in *E.L.H. A Journal of English Literary History*, Dec. 1938, entitled 'An Unpublished Burney Letter', Mr. W. B. Gates finds *The Wanderer* 'considerably more interesting than *Camilla* and not nearly so worthless as Macaulay and Mrs. Ellis would have us believe.' (footnote 8, art. cited.) But a very useful point in this article is that Mr. Gates has listed together all the contemporary reviews on all Fanny Burney's novels. This appears not to have been previously done.

of the ridiculous? If Fanny Burney had retained even this last characteristic she would never have published her last two novels. For what do they contain except the trifling misunderstandings of maudlin nonentities, couched in depraved Johnsonese? Horace Walpole, until then an enthusiastic admirer of Fanny Burney, threw up his hands at *Camilla*, which he said was 'a deplorable book'.

It was well that Dr. Johnson was not alive to see what his style became in the hands of Madame d'Arblay. Inflated with sensibility, deadened by the weight of magniloquent euphuisms and liberally peppered with vulgarisms and grammatical errors, it was a travesty enough to make the good man turn in his grave.[37] But Madame d'Arblay had no hesitation in twisting language to her ill-conceived uses. Indeed she took herself so seriously that she most frequently coined words. 'Surely,' she wrote (somewhat earlier), 'I may make words at a loss, if Dr. Johnson does'—and this despite her incomplete grasp of English and total ignorance of Latin. She had, after a few Latin lessons from Johnson, refused further tuition on the grounds that 'to devote so much time to acquire something [Latin] I shall always dread to have known is really unpleasant.' Trusting thus in her own intuition, she evolves a style of which this extract is a fair example: 'The tide of youthful glee flowed jocund from her heart, and the transparency of her fine blue veins almost showed the velocity of its current.'[38] And again: 'The bird . . . made whatever evolutions were within the circumference of his limited habitation, with wonderful precision.'[39] In the midst of such pretentiousness she does not scruple (as Mrs. A. R. Ellis points out) to use 'me' in the nominative case, adjectives as adverbs, and such expressions as 'to stroam' ('to *roam*'), 'he made up to' ('he approached'), and 'he made off' ('he went away').

37 Speaking of Madame d'Arblay's later style, Macaulay says: 'Nothing in the language of those jargonists at whom Mr. Gosport laughed, nothing in the language of Sir Sedley Clarendel, approaches this new Euphuism.'

38 *Camilla* (ed. 1796), vol. i, p. 16.

39 *Ibid.*, vol. iii, p. 401.

Writing, no doubt, with one eye on 'the sweet Queen' to whom *Camilla* was dedicated, Madame d'Arblay no longer aimed to amuse. Her brain was paralysed by the necessity for extreme refinement and decorum, and in her efforts to sift her material, she was left only with the veriest trifles for her subject. The *motif* is the love and misunderstandings of Camilla and Edgar Mandlebert. These misunderstandings hinge on the most negligible points. Again and again Camilla promises Edgar to avoid some trifling amusement. Again and again her resolution is overthrown not so much by the strength of the temptation as by a concatenation of circumstances. Unfortunately Edgar always discovers these lapses. For example, he finds that she has taken part in a raffle, and that she has been so unwomanly as to attend an exhibition of performing monkeys. Still, he never despairs of helping her to acquire 'the modesty of retired elegance, and the security of established respectability'. Sometimes he withdraws in disapproval, but it is always possible to win him back by asking his advice. Once, for example, a delicate situation is created when Sir Sedley Clarendel, observing her pity for a bullfinch which is ill-treated by its trainer, buys the bird and sends it to her. For the moment, she keeps the bullfinch 'sooner than render [Sir Sedley's] humanity abortive', but she is so overwhelmed by the impropriety that she feels it necessary to ask Edgar's advice, even though he is in a mood of pained aloofness. She looks forward to 'the approaching conference with almost trembling delight'. She loves him with the most quivering sensibility and with the most delicate decorum, but Edgar is evidently determined that she shall, by long trial, fit herself for the true duty of wifehood, which Madame d'Arblay thus defines (in the case of Mrs. Tyrold): 'Had this lady been united to a man whom she despised, she would yet have obeyed him, and as scrupulously, though not as happily, as she obeyed her honoured partner. She considered the vow taken at the altar to her husband, as a voluntary vestal would have held one taken to her Maker; and no dissent in opinion exculpated, in her mind, the least deviation from his will.'[40] But indeed the standard of feminine behaviour and propriety makes *Camilla* incomprehensible to a later age. Who could pretend to understand a period when to kiss the hand of a lady was a vile liberty? Bellamy, a fortune-hunter, feigns a passion for the mis-shapen but kind-hearted heiress, Eugenia, who is intended, by her uncle, to marry Clermont. Clermont remains travelling on the Continent, and has no notion of the honour which awaits him. Madame d'Arblay thus describes the shocking affair :

> Bellamy suddenly took the opportunity of [Eugenia's] being out of sight of all others, to drop on one knee, and passionately seized her hand, exclaiming: 'O, Madam! . . .' When hearing an approaching step, he hastily arose; but parted not with her hand till he had pressed it to his lips.
>
> The astonished Eugenia, though at first all emotion, was completely recovered by this action. His kneeling and his 'O Madam!' had every chance to affect her; but his kissing her hand she thought a liberty the most unpardonable. She resented it as an injury to Clermont, that would risk his life should he ever know it, and a blot to her own delicacy, as irreparable as it was irremediable.[41]

It is curious to recall that Jane Austen praised *Camilla*, and to contrast with that judgment her uncompromising statement that, for heroines, 'pictures of perfection make me sick and wicked'.[42] Jane, like the rest of Madame d'Arblay's public, could not forget the joy she had found in the early novels of Fanny Burney, and no doubt forgave much because she had loved much. *Camilla* had a huge sale; so had *The Wanderer*, but one cannot think of either work without repeating the words of Sir Sedley Clarendel: 'O, a very crush! a cannon ball would be a butterfly in the comparison.' Though *The Wanderer* was her last novel, *The Memoirs of Dr. Burney* show the depths to which her style of writing finally sank. Thus she describes how her father met his second wife:

40 *Ibid.*, vol. i, p. 18.
41 *Ibid.*, vol. i, p. 304.
42 *Letters of Jane Austen* (ed. Brabourne, 1816), ii, lxxxiv.

> Six heartless, nearly desolate, years of lonely conjugal chasm, had succeeded to double their number of nearly unparalleled conjugal enjoyment—and the void was still fallow and hopeless!—when the yet-very-handsome-though-no-longer-in-her-bloom Mrs. Stephen Allen, of Lynn, now become a widow, decided, for promoting the education of her eldest daughter, to make London her winter residence.

What happened to the genius which, despite its limitations and faults, was yet apparent in *Evelina*? How can one explain not merely the decline of Fanny Burney's powers, but her apparent metamorphosis from a genius into an idiot? Her years at Court, however miserable, could not surely have changed her into an entirely different person. Her lack of education could not be directly responsible for her later style, since her first style, when she had not more education, was her best. Speaking to Hannah More of *Camilla* Walpole said: 'Alas! [Madame d'Arblay] has reversed experience . . . this author knew the world and penetrated characters before she stepped over the threshold: and now she has seen so much of it, she has little or no insight at all.'[43] Johnson, who died before the rot set in, speaks in almost identical terms of *Evelina*: '*Evelina* seems a work that should result from long experience, and deep and intimate knowledge of the world. Miss Burney is a real wonder. What she is, she is intuitively.'[44] There appear to be only two possible solutions to the problem of Fanny Burney's later writings. It may be that her first impetus of inspiration died, or that by deliberately changing her aim and methods of composition she destroyed her literary powers. Hazlitt held this latter view. He says, in reference to *The Wanderer*:

> We are sorry to be compelled to speak so disadvantageously of the work of an excellent and favourite writer; and the more so, as *we perceive no decay of talent, but a perversion of it*. There is the same

43 *Works of Horace Walpole* (5 vols., folio, 1798) i, p. 623. Letter to Hannah More dated August 29, 1796.

44 *Diary and Letters of Madame d'Arblay* (ed. Dobson) i, p. 247. It is worth noting that Johnson must have thought Fanny Burney younger than she was, when she wrote *Evelina*. His words were part of a conversation with Mrs.

> admirable spirit in the dialogues . . . as in her former novels, but they do not fill a hundred pages of the work; and there is nothing else good in it. In the story, which here occupies the attention of the reader almost exclusively, Mme d'Arblay never excelled.[45]

It is true that Hazlitt's opinion would seem to be supported by the fact that, though Fanny Burney's diary becomes rather dull during the Court period, it still contains lively and vivid descriptions (e.g. her meeting with the king during his madness, and Goldsworthy's amusing talk). It is also true that from the moment she went to Court, Fanny Burney seems to have become ashamed of being a novelist—so much so, indeed, that she racks her brains for some other way of describing *Camilla*: 'I own I do not like calling it a novel; it gives so simply to the notion of a mere love story that I recoil a little from it. I mean this work to be sketches of character and morals put into action—not a romance.'[46] Novels were still in low repute, and she who had been privileged to mix the royal snuff could no longer allow herself the freedom of a private person. In *Camilla*, at any rate, she wrote to please her patron, and she did not write in vain. Her Majesty allowed the three elder princesses, aged respectively thirty, twenty-eight, and twenty-six to read *Camilla*, without first censoring it. If Madame d'Arblay sold her genius for a mess of patronage, verily she had received her reward.

But however great her snobbishness, her desire for dignified decorum, had Fanny Burney retained her first impetuous inspiration, she could not, one believes, so stem and check it that, from a sparkling spring, it became a stagnant pool. It seems more likely that, by the time she wrote *Camilla*, her youthful powers had waned and there was nothing to take their place—not even the judgment by which she could truly have compared her later and her earlier productions. We have

Thrale, in which they were comparing Pope's *Windsor Forest* with *Evelina*. Pope was sixteen when he began *Windsor Forest* (1704) and twenty-five when he finished it (1713).

[45] *Edinburgh Review*, 24 (Feb. 1815), 320-338.
[46] Letter to Susan Burney.

already said that Fanny Burney died a precocious child. We should have said rather that, when she died, she had already experienced that strange eclipse which precocity so often suffers. Youthful prodigies very frequently become stodgy adults. So it was with Fanny Burney. When life weighed her down, when she could no longer remain a carefree onlooker, when it became necessary to struggle and to endure, then it seemed that what had lent her wings had been little more than youthful spirits. A light heart may go all the way in life, but it rarely goes far in literature. There comes the time when exuberance and excess of energy no longer imperiously seek expression, when the shallow nature can no longer feed on external impressions because they are no longer pleasurable. Such minds must either flit over the surface of life or go under. Fanny Burney went under at Windsor, and when she came to the surface again she had become—the prosy Madame d'Arblay.

Still, she had fulfilled her literary destiny. She had written one novel which, although it was superficial, was great. It was great because, in some respects, it excelled the technique of previous novels, and because it projected new and important aims in fiction; because it marks the point at which the feminine movement in fiction comes fully into view, and because it aided the development of Jane Austen and Maria Edgeworth. Fanny Burney's mental development is not unlike the evolution of the silk-moth. The silk-moth begins as an insignificant caterpillar of unpromising appearance. At this stage of its life it occupies itself entirely with preparations for its future activities. Then comes the inevitable moment; it begins to spin out of itself a thin fibre of silk, and it continues to spin thus out of its being until it has enveloped itself completely in this cocoon. Then, spent and exhausted, it remains hidden within its own creation which has cost it such vital energy. So did Fanny Burney lie hidden while *Evelina*, which she spun out of the substance of her life, engaged the public attention. But the silk worm never spins again; it changes entirely; grows wings; emerges from its hiding place a beautiful white moth. It flutters about a little, mates and dies. So did Fanny Burney. *Evelina* is her only lasting achievement, and it would have been better for her fame if she had never attempted any other.

CHAPTER IV

THE GOTHIC NOVEL

"Sonitus terroris semper in auribus."

THE GOTHIC novel was at once a part of the Romantic Revival and a prolongation of the cult of sensibility. One characteristic of the Romantic movement was that writers turned to bygone ages for imaginative scope. Early in the eighteenth century this new interest had shown itself in poetry and in essays. Antiquarian research in mediæval poetry and romances increasingly attracted attention, and even led to such impositions as MacPherson's *Ossian* and Chatterton's luckless forgery. But although this interest in literary antiquities was a notable aspect of the new orientation, it was not strong enough in itself to kindle the Romantic spirit, and it soon became evident that the architectural approach to mediævalism was to prove the main channel by which olden times were to influence modern literature. A Gothic cathedral or more particularly a Gothic castle was the nucleus of great imaginative activity. Such a building could not be considered without reference to the people whose lives centred therein, and nothing was more natural than to weave about it ideas of human life and thought, and to make it the background for events which might be supposed to have occurred within its walls.

Although the impetus to this kind of story-telling was first evidenced in poetry, novelists did not long delay in seizing upon inspiration so suited to their craft. It was an escape from the gamut of domestic themes, and offered an almost unlimited freedom of invention. It was necessary only that the events described should be such as might be expected to happen in a Gothic castle—the interpretation of verisimilitude depending merely on the author's fancy.

Nowadays when such writers as Sigrid Undset bring to the writing of historical fiction not only artistic conception, but the perfect accuracy of an archaeologist, it is somewhat difficult to realise the insouciance with which the Gothic writers set themselves to depict the life of ancient days. It was not that they ignored, but that they did not conceive the essentials of an historical novel. Prior to Scott, nothing had been written which could with any justice be called an historical novel. *The Castle of Otranto* contained historical elements, but it cannot be claimed as an historical novel. Still less can this claim be advanced for Sophia Lee's *Recess*, unless one is satisfied to accept as an historical novel a tale without the slightest historical verisimilitude woven around certain historical personages. It does not even seem possible to credit Sophia Lee with the originality of introducing historical characters, as there is little room to doubt that she got the idea from Prévost, and modelled *The Recess* on *Cleveland*.

But even if writers of the English Gothic school had known enough to reproduce the real life of ancient times, they would not have done so, because they would have been profoundly shocked at its lack of refinement. Julia Kavenagh treats this point very well. She remarks that Walpole, the English Gothic school, and even Scott followed the only feasible plan in presenting to the finical reading public only a romantic and polite picture of bygone days, but she stresses the fact that theirs was a very bad method, because in giving a romanticised version of the past they omitted 'the rudeness, and with it the breadth and geniality of those wonderful times.' She continues:

> Our ancestors have been shown to us with singular capacities for bloodshed, because we could bear this, our humanity not having progressed in proportion to our delicacy; but of their joyousness, of that mad mirth which went hand in hand with deeds heroic or terrible, of that roughness which pervaded every rank of society,

> we have not been told. The knight has been clothed in modern gentleness, politeness, and refinement, and in that smoothing down of features offensive to the modern taste, the largeness, that great characteristic of the Middle Ages, and perhaps the greatest, the manly and noble frankness, have been irremediably lost.[1]

The Gothic novel stressed terror—a twofold terror compounded of physical dangers and the more paralysing fear of the supernatural. The proportion and degree of these two elements constituted the main difference between the English, German and French schools. Prévost's power of creating an atmosphere of sinister gloom, his mysterious and bloody incidents, foreshadowed the main elements of the Gothic novel, and Baculard d'Arnaud's charnel-house conceptions strongly influenced one group of novelists. In Germany the tale of terror developed by contact with the folklore of gnomes, spirits and diabolism. Schiller's *Die Rauber* (1781) and his *Der Geisterseher* (1789) represent the aspects of brutality and supernaturalism which became the most outstanding characteristics of the *Schauerroman*. The German conception of the novel of terror became the chief influence during the later English period, of which 'Monk' Lewis and Maturin are the most outstanding writers. Lewis's violence and obscenity show one side of the German influence carried to excess. Maturin's *Melmoth* shows what genius can make of a supernatural legend. But Maturin's psychological technique sets him apart from other Gothic novelists who, as a rule, did not trouble themselves with the intricacies of character. Of the women writers only Mary Shelley was influenced by the German school, and then only by its ghostly elements. The other women novelists with whom we are concerned belong to the earlier period of English Gothicism which found its best expression and, in a sense, its origin in Mrs. Radcliffe.

The popularity of terror as a literary theme during the second half of the eighteenth century led to enquiry as to the cause of such enjoyment and as to the technique

Julia Kavenagh, *English Women of Letters* (1863), i, p. 242.

by which terror should be presented so as to produce pleasurable effects. Edmund Burke considered that 'whatever is qualified to cause terror, is a foundation capable of the sublime'[2] and this because terror rouses the mind to exercise its strongest faculties. Such expense of energy is pleasurable in itself. Miss Aikin explained 'the strange luxury of artificial fear'[3] as being due to the reader's feeling of curiosity. She held that stimulation of curiosity not only made a terrible story pleasurable, but brought imagination and feeling into full play. Suspense maintains the mind in full activity and 'the pain of terror is lost in amazement.'[4] Dr. Nathan Drake[5] did not enquire why fear is 'welcome' and why it is 'salutary' for the reader. He was interested in determining how best to manipulate the terrible so as to produce the most pleasurable results, without dependence on the supernatural. He believed that Mrs. Radcliffe's balancing of beauty and suspense was the most effective way of making pleasure overcome the painful sensations induced by the narrative. Such views approached from different angles the fundamental interest in the Gothic novel.

However much the Gothic novel may have aided the evolution of the historical novel, it seems clear that the Gothic novelists merely played at reproducing the past. That they did not burthen themselves with the task of historical accuracy greatly simplified their labours. They had only to expand their minds in the direction of antiquity, to unleash their imaginations. The term 'Gothic' was abstracted from its architectural connotation. It was loosely used to designate some bygone period, not necessarily the Middle Ages, and was even protracted by Mrs. Radcliffe to include the year 1758. A Gothic novelist kept well in mind such general notions of antiquity as were common property. These were his historical boundaries, and within them loomed the Gothic castle, rich with hints for the development of

2 *Inquiry into the Sublime and Beautiful* (1756).
3 See *Monthly*, Nov., 1794, on 'The Mysteries of Udolpho'.
4 J. and A. L. Aikin, *Miscellaneous Pieces in Prose* (1773).
5 Dr. Nathan Drake, *Literary Hours* (1798).

the story. In itself this mighty stronghold was a visible commentary on contemporary social conditions. It had been built to withstand the sieges of men and time, and by its very construction it implied the determination to defy and to exert force. Dizzying battlements, dark and winding stairways, dark dungeons, instruments of torture, groans and gouts of blood, secret passages with many a suggestion of spectral life, ghostly music, tapestries which sway with the wind and which betray the secret watcher or the assassin—this was the stuff of the Gothic novel. This was the stuff of romance. No wonder that minds long shackled to sensible themes cast reason to the winds, and played the Gothic game of make-believe—a game in which anything might happen so long as one began with 'Once upon a time'. This flight from the present into the past was really a romantic quest—an effort to discover strange aspects of beauty, to give a loose to the restlessness, the curiosity, and the sense of wonder which excessive normality had stifled. At best the Gothic novel was a blending of beauty and terror. It was an attempt to convey by story-telling 'the tempestuous loveliness of terror'.[6] This is why in such novels as Mrs. Radcliffe's we find not merely patches of beauty which relieve the tension, but very often an intermingling of beauty and fear. Fear is the element which transmutes this loveliness, or loveliness is the element which makes this terror bearable. And both viewed in the perspective of antiquity take on a variety of quickly-changing shapes. Antiquity is the Gothic moonlight which shadows or illumines everything. It creates beauty and it is beautiful in itself. It is to stress antiquity that we are always shown a Gothic building in decay. This emphasis on dilapidation marks not only the contrast between then and now. It gives also a sense of tradition outbraving the ravages of time. In the Gothic castle ancestors gaze down from their portraits in the gallery—nay, they even step down out of their frames, as in Otranto. Tattered banners rustle on the walls of the banqueting hall. And this castle, these portraits and these

6 Shelley's poem *On the Medusa of Leonardo da Vinci.*

banners are usually first shown to us at sunset—a symbolism which at once suggests a dying glory and a romantic splendour.

That the Gothic novel was a part of the Romantic Revival is not more apparent than that it was a development of the cult of sensibility. Indeed one might consider it as the last resource of authors seeking some new irritant for emotion. The gamut of domestic distresses was exhausted, and, as we have already seen, English novelists, like their French brethren, turned to that wider field of sensibility which dealt in dangerous adventures and tragic strokes of fate. Here were already the elements of suspense and peril which were so prominent a feature of the Gothic tale. The key to the relationship of the Gothic novel and the novel of sensibility is the heroine. This trembling girl who now endures every variety of horror is the very same who formerly suffered more normal vicissitudes. The events described in a Gothic story are enough to harrow up the spirit of a brave man, but it is always a trembling girl who has to endure them. Thus the fullest effects of terror and anxiety are achieved. We gain our knowledge of these dread adventures through the perception of the heroine. As we read, we become identified with her, and since her sensitiveness is extreme and her reactions intense, we are caught up in a mounting wave of sensibility. This heroine is always friendless, often ignorant even of her parentage, and her isolation makes her sufferings all the more exquisite:

> Un coeur isolé, forcé de se replier sur lui-même, de se parler, de se répondre, de se nourrir, si l'on peut s' exprimer ainsi, de sa propre substance, en acquiert plus de ressort et d'énérgie dans ses mouvements. Il n'est point de faibles oscillations pour une âme solitaire: tout y porte de violentes secousses.[7]

But though the persecuted heroine is extremely sensitive, she is not weak. She may weep and swoon but she does not succumb. Indeed she cannot succumb if the

7 So Baculard d'Arnaud describes an isolated soul. His words apply very well to the Gothic heroine. See Baculard d'Arnaud, Preface to *Euphémie, ou Le Triomphe de la Religion* (Paris, 1768).

story is to continue. Neither can she yield to tyrannous demands, because it is essential that the state of tension be maintained. This necessity of reconciling strength and weakness forced the novelist to trim his sails. He compromised by making the heroine not defiant, but firm. She will not yield to oppression so as to end it, but she feels the oppression in every lacerated nerve. This, of course, is quite possible, but the reader is afflicted with a sense of improbability when he observes this shrinking girl not merely enduring unescapable terrors, but deliberately incurring them. Well might Jane Austen burlesque the well-worn sequence of the heroine who, despite extreme nervousness, insists on adventuring into a deserted wing, listens behind the arras to the foul plots of bloody men, and sits up all night to read, by the light of an expiring lamp, a manuscript found under the most sinister circumstances. Whether or not the author realised this inconsistency, he could scarcely avoid it, if he was to maintain a ceaseless onslaught of terror. The fitness of such a purpose does not appear to have given these novelists pause, and no doubt even the sensitive Mrs. Radcliffe would have been overwhelmed with surprise had she been confronted with such arguments as Swinburne later advanced against the tale of terror. Speaking of Wilkie Collins's novels, Swinburne said: 'The suggested or implied suffering of such poor innocent wretches, the martyrdom of perpetual terror and agony inflicted on the shattered nerves or the shaken brain of a woman or a girl, is surely a cruel or a painful mainspring for a story or a plot.'[8]

We have been speaking of Gothic fiction at its peak, so as to examine its main characteristics. It would be well to refer very briefly to some of the main evidences of its evolution. Prior to *The Castle of Otranto* (1764), which was avowedly the manifesto of a new genre of fiction, Gothic touches had shown themselves from time to time in English fiction, notably in Smollett's *Ferdinand, Count Fathom* (1753) and to a lesser extent in Leland's *Longsword, Earl of Salisbury* (1762). In *Ferdinand, Count*

8 See A. C. Swinburne, *Studies in Prose and Poetry* (1894).

Fathom there is definite proof that Smollett had chanced upon the Gothic idea, and upon the very technique which Mrs. Radcliffe later employed. Smollett aimed at nothing more than to enliven his picaresque tale with some new kind of adventures—horrible and mysterious events which he depicts with great vividness. He creates an atmosphere of terror and employs all those properties which were to become so dear to the school of Gothic novelists. Like them, he appeals directly to the innate superstition in his readers, plays on their nerves by hinted horrors and keeps them in taut suspense. Darkness and solitude are the constituents of his atmosphere. In the description of the Count's journey through the dark forest there is a suggestion of the Gothic treatment of nature. Having aroused fear and anticipation, Smollett makes our flesh creep by means of unburied corpses, robbers, owls screeching in ruined battlements, a midnight visit to a chapel lighted only by a glimmering taper, a spectre, a heroine who sleeps at the end of a long gallery and who hears in the still watches the ghostly music of an aeolian harp. Smollett later explains away all his mysteries, as did Mrs. Radcliffe.[9]

The Castle of Otranto was a contribution to the Gothic and also to the historical novel. Which was really Walpole's aim? In his preface he states that it is his intention to unite the imagination and invention in old romances with the probability of modern fiction, and he justifies his introduction of the supernatural by claiming that it was necessary for verisimilitude: 'Belief in every kind of prodigy was so established in those dark ages, that an author would not be faithful to the manners of the times who should omit all mention of them.'[10] But the superstitious element in his tale was so ill-conceived that it contradicts instead of establishing the appearance of veracity. Walpole's supernatural phenomena appeal only to the risible faculty. The plumed

[9] The fragment *Sir Bertrand*, included in J. and A. L. Aikin's *Miscellaneous Pieces of Prose* (1773), shows the appositeness of Godwin's remark that tales of terror have a sort of resemblance to nursery tales. *Sir Bertrand* is *The Sleeping Beauty* as one might imagine it in a nightmare.

[10] Preface to 2nd. ed. of *The Castle of Otranto*.

helmet is really too large even for the most voracious reader to swallow, and the three drops of blood would have done better to issue from any part of Alfonso's statue than the nose. Such a sanguinary effusion calls merely for a doorkey, and the terror it inspires in the onlookers merely adds to the ludicrous effect. Nor is the supernatural giant a more fortunate invention. This double appeal to our fear seems to cancel itself out. Enormous ghosts do not terrify. The more a ghost retains the proportions of humanity, the more it is driven home to us that here is one who has been what we are, and who has gone where we must surely follow. That is the terror on which the skilful narrator of ghost-stories relies. And it is amusing to consider that whereas Walpole's supernatural fails in its effect, Mrs. Radcliffe's mysterious suggestions impress and terrify so much that we are indignant when she explains them away. Who would not prefer to dwell in Otranto rather than in Udolpho? The blood on the turret-stairs in Udolpho is much more frightful than Alphonso's nasal effusion, even though the one had a harmless explanation and the other denoted ghostly vengeance. The sword which at Otranto weighed down one hundred men was slight by comparison with the strange light which flickered on the sentry's spear on Udolpho's battlements. The ghostly portrait of Manfred's grandfather is far less appalling than the veiled picture which Emily St. Aubert dared to view. Did Walpole introduce the historical merely as a background for his tale of terror? Or did he use the supernatural merely as a stimulus to his readers—to key them up to the imaginative state which would enable them to live vicariously in his mediæval tale? Whatever was his purpose, *Otranto* fails as a Gothic novel, and is not much more successful from an historical point of view. Its best contribution to Gothicism is the character of Manfred, whose dark passions drive him onward to his doom.

Clara Reeve (1729-1807), the daughter of a clergyman

resident at Ipswich, came under the influence of *The Castle of Otranto*, but she quarrelled seriously with Walpole's method of introducing the marvellous. She says:

> The opening excites the attention strongly: the conduct of the story is artful and judicious; the characters are admirably drawn and supported; the diction polished and elegant; yet with all these brilliant advantages, it palls upon the mind . . . and the reason is obvious; the machinery is so violent that it destroys the effect it is intended to excite. Had the story been kept within the utmost *verge* of probability, the effect had been preserved, without losing the least circumstance that excites or detains the attention.
>
> For instance; we can conceive, and allow of, the appearance of a ghost; we can dispense with an enchanted sword and helmet; but then they must keep within the limits of credibility.[11] A sword so large as to require a hundred men to lift it; a helmet that by its own weight forces a passage through a courtyard, into an arched vault big enough for a man to go through; a picture that walks out of its frame; a skeleton ghost in a hermit's cowl:—when your expectation is wound up to the highest pitch, these circumstances take it down with a witness, destroy the work of imagination, and instead of attention excite laughter.[12]

This is excellent criticism; worthy, in fact, of the author of the *Progress of Romance* (1785). What follows is an excellent prognostication which, although she voiced it, she herself did not take seriously. She says that she decided to attempt a work upon the same plan, in which she would avoid Walpole's defects: 'But then I began to fear it might happen to me as to certain translators and imitators of Shakespeare: the unities may be preserved while the spirit is evaporated.'[13] These words exactly describe *The Old English Baron*.

Published, in 1777, under the title of *The Champion of Virtue, a Gothic tale*, this novel reached a second edition the following year, and was named *The Old English Baron*. Neither title is apt. There are so many

[11] Scott, in his Life of Clara Reeve, disagrees with her objections to the *Castle of Otranto*. He says: 'If we are to try ghosts by the ordinary rules of humanity, we bar them of their privileges entirely. For instance, why admit the existence of an aerial phantom and deny it the terrible attribute of magnifying its stature? Why admit an enchanted helmet and not a gigantic one?' The reasons suggested on page 137 seem a possible answer to Scott's argument.

[12] Preface to *The Old English Baron* (ed. 1883).

[13] *Ibid.*

champions of virtue in this story that one cannot well distinguish the one Miss Reeve had in mind. As for the second title, it does not refer to the principal character, and is useful only to indicate contrariwise the chief faults of this novel. In a word, the setting is not sufficiently old, the characters are too aristocratic and the hero is too excessively of the type which Miss Reeve mistakenly considered English. Edmund (for this is the paragon's name) is like the bespectacled and earnest young curate so dear to the comedian's heart. He is too good, too long-suffering and too humble. Our difficulty is not the belief that he has blue blood in his veins, but the belief that he has any blood at all. He has all the virtues, but no vigour. He wins through all his difficulties simply by being harmless—an affecting but rather improbable circumstance. We see him first as the lowly Edmund Twyford, a peasant lad of unknown parentage, a servant in the house of Baron Fitz-Owen. But we at once recognise in him the young heir, whose parents have been foully murdered. He is loved by the Baron and the Baron's son William, the Baron's daughter Emma, the chaplain, Father Oswald, and an old retainer, Joseph, as well as by all the servants and country folk. He is hated by the Baron's son Robert, and by two villains who do all they can to disgrace him in war and malign him in time of peace. He is finally challenged to sleep in the haunted room. Phantoms haunt his slumbers, and emit groans from underground, like Hamlet's father; but Edmund's strength is as the strength of ten because his heart is pure.

He solves the riddle of his birth, bids Emma an enigmatic farewell and seeks the help of Sir Philip Harclay, a knight so benevolent that his castle is something between Chelsea Royal Hospital and a home for decayed gentlemen. On hearing that Lord Lovel, Edmund's wicked uncle, murdered Edmund's parents, Sir Philip Harclay decides to engage this caitiff in single combat. Haughty challenges ensue and finally they take the field, Sir Philip determined to wring a confession from his opponent.

> The lists were cleared, and the combatants began to fight. They contended a long time with equal skill and courage; at length Sir Philip unhorsed his antagonist. The judges ordered that either he should alight or suffer his enemy to remount; he chose the former, and a short combat on foot ensued. The sweat ran off their bodies with the violence of the exercise. Sir Philip watched every motion of the enemy, and strove to weary him out, intending to wound, but not to kill him unless obliged for his own safety.
>
> He thrust his sword through his left arm, and demanded whether he would confess the fact. Lord Lovel, enraged, answered he would die sooner. Sir Philip then passed the sword through his body twice, and Lord Lovel fell, crying out that he was slain.
>
> 'I hope not,' said Sir Philip, 'for I have a great deal of business to do with you before you die.'[14]

This business-like method of inquisition succeeds. Lord Lovel is banished to the Holy Land. Edmund is reinstated, Emma becomes his wife, and the moral is 'the over-ruling hand of Providence, and the certainty of RETRIBUTION.'

Clara Reeve's story is cursed with all the faults of its qualities. The plot is clear, but it is only too clear; there is not much sentimentality, but there is far too much commonsense; it is moral, but it is too moralising; it does not exaggerate the marvellous, but it reduces the marvellous to the commonplace. Clara Reeve's horrors arouse no fear.[15] Her ghost groans, and it is no more than if a harmless old gentleman cleared his throat; it appears in blood-stained armour and we perceive nothing amazing; it speaks and, despite its words, we feel that it is only making a polite reference to the weather. Its skeleton is found tied neck and heels in a buried chest. We attend the exhumation and are as unmoved as if we watched a gardener transplanting lettuce. Indeed Edmund himself is most philosophic, not to say absent-minded, as to the remains of his murdered parents. With much difficulty he finds and reassembles their skeletons. Then we observe him enter into his inheritance, and become affianced to the fair Emma. All is happiness and joy:

14 Clara Reeve, *The Old English Baron* (ed. 1883), p. 144.
15 See Julia Kavenagh's sound criticism (*English Women of Letters*, 1862, i, p. 239).

> After they had refreshed themselves and recovered from the emotions they had sustained on this interesting occasion, Edmund thus addressed the Baron: 'On the brink of happiness, I must claim your attention to a melancholy subject. The bones of both my parents lie unburied in this house; permit me, my honoured lord, to perform my last duties to them, and the remainder of my life shall be devoted to you and yours.' 'Certainly,' said the Baron, 'Why have you not interred them?'[16]

He might well ask.

Clara Reeve published, in 1793, an historical novel called *Memoirs of Sir Roger de Clarendon*. This dealt with the most important events in the reigns of Edward III and Richard II. It was her intention to weave a romantic tale around the historical facts. Her facts are correct, but there is no historical atmosphere, and this story, like *The Old English Baron*, is a cold and commonplace production. In 1788 appeared another Gothic attempt: *The Exiles, or Memoirs of the Count of Cronstadt*. This was based on two of Baculard d'Arnaud's novelettes.[17] Cronstadt was the gloomy and self-doomed character who so often figures in Gothic tales, and probably was the inspiration for Harriet Lee's Kruitzner. Indeed Cronstadt takes for a time the name of his servant Albert Kreutzer, a fact which may have influenced Harriet Lee in the choice of her hero's name. In addition to the novels which we have mentioned, Clara Reeve wrote two stories of her own period: *The Two Mentors* (1783) and *The School for Widows* (1791). Like all her fictional compositions, these were deliberately didactic, the latter envisaging a sort of educational Utopia. Clara Reeve's influence on Harriet Lee is really her best claim to remembrance. She had not the temperament for Gothic fiction which required vivid and almost unbridled imagination both in creating atmosphere and in inventing and employing elements of

16 Clara Reeve, *The Old English Baron*, (ed. 1883), p. 203.

17 See E. A. Baker, *H.E.N.*, v., p. 180. Clara Reeve's borrowings were from Baculard d'Arnaud's *The History of Count Gleichen* (so called in the English translation), 1785, and d'Almanzi, *Anecdote françoise* (1776), apparently never translated. Dr. Baker says that Prévost's *Doyen de Killerine* probably gave to Clara Reeve's book 'as much of the tone and atmosphere as Baculard's two stories.'

terror. Clara Reeve writing a Gothic novel calls up a picture of a maiden lady in elastic-sided boots, endeavouring to control a mustang.

Far more important was the contribution made by Harriet Lee (1757-1851) and her elder sister Sophia (1750-1824). These women really caught the Gothic spirit, and are amongst the most notable writers who aided its development in fiction. They were daughters of the irascible John Lee, author and actor. Years before his death in 1781, they had taken to the writing of novels and plays, partly, no doubt, because of an inherited flair, and partly because their father's continual quarrels with theatre managers made it necessary for them to supplement the meagre family finances. On the death of their father, the sisters opened a school in Bath, where they had amongst their pupils one Anne Ward of whom, as Mrs. Radcliffe, we shall hear much more presently.

Many claims have been made for Sophia Lee's first novel, *The Recess* (1785). Her sister Harriet called it 'the first English Romance that blended interesting fiction with historical events and characters, embellishing both by picturesque description. *Cleveland*, written as I believe, by the Abbé Prévôt, had precedence of all.'[18] Various critics since that time have agreed in substance with Harriet's assertion, and it has been suggested that *The Recess* gave hints for *Kenilworth*. Scott may possibly have been attracted by the idea of writing an historical novel on the more personal aspects of Elizabeth's reign. Genius can find an inspiration in the most unexpected and even worthless material. That *The Recess* is worthless there is little doubt. It is historical only in the sense that its background is Elizabeth's reign. Raleigh, Essex, Leicester, Sir Philip Sydney and his sisters, and the two rival queens are integral parts of the story. Sophia Lee represents that Mary Queen of Scots, believing Bothwell dead, secretly married the Duke of Norfolk during her imprisonment in Bolton Castle. There is much plotting

18 Preface to *The Canterbury Tales*.

to release Mary and finally, through the agency of the Regent Murray, Elizabeth discovers the truth. Norfolk is arrested. Meanwhile twin daughters are born to Mary and, as she wishes to conceal a marriage which would cost her husband his life, she causes them to be secretly conveyed away. Norfolk's sister, Lady Scroope, arranges that the children shall be cared for in some subterranean quarters formerly the refuge of persecuted priests, and known as the Recess. Bothwell reappears; and Norfolk, deprived thus of any legal connection with Mary, is released, but further plotting leads him to the block. Mary's twin daughters, Mathilda and Ellinor, reach maturity in their gloomy retreat, and though they have never once seen the sun, they are, when the story opens, very lovely young women. With their mother's beauty they inherit her fatality, and it is not long until they are involved as deeply as she in love and political intrigue.

Mathilda, the elder, encounters the Earl of Leicester by a strange accident and wins his heart. He marries her and takes her and her sister Ellinor to Kenilworth. To escape Elizabeth's wrath the marriage is concealed, but she is not deceived, and carries them off to the court so that she may have them under supervision. The story now splits into two strands, narrating Mathilda's adventures as the wife of Leicester and Ellinor's as the beloved of Essex. Elizabeth is the villain of the piece, and by every means in her power she destroys the happiness of the lovers. Mathilda and Leicester eventually flee to France where he is slain. She is decoyed to the West Indies, persecuted by wicked lovers, and imprisoned for long years, but she at last returns to England with Leicester's child.

Meanwhile Ellinor has been parted from Essex. Elizabeth discovers the secret of the sisters' birth and, under threat of executing Essex, forces Ellinor to sign a confession that their royal pretensions are imposture. To make assurance doubly sure, Elizabeth forces Ellinor to marry Lord Arlington who is too stupid for intrigue. Thereafter Ellinor's reason gives way and, after the execution of Essex, she becomes quite demented.

Mathilda, after many trials, the greatest of which is the poisoning of her daughter, dies at last.

Sophia Lee makes no attempt to create the atmosphere of Elizabethan times, or to reproduce the customs or language of the period. She forestalls criticism thus: 'I make no apology for altering the language to that of the present age, since the obselete stile . . . would be frequently unintelligible.' Evidently she also considered her readers incapable of understanding the outlook and the behaviour of the Elizabethan age, and felt it necessary to make her characters conform to eighteenth century fictional standards. Indeed it is probable that she was honestly unaware of any differences in relation to period, and was unconscious of the anomaly of an Elizabethan age peopled with etiolated beings and speaking the jargon of sensibility. An anæmic Raleigh goes on polite tours around the world; so languishing a Sydney could never have fought at Zutphen; Drake, had she presented him, would have played croquet, but never bowls. That Sophia Lee could have thought her Essex consistent with his fate shows how far she was from estimating the quality of her work. Otherwise she would have known that such a nincompoop could never have achieved the dignity of decapitation. Elizabeth alone lives, and she only because Miss Lee outraged her own feelings to create her. No sensible reader would give one such Elizabeth for a wilderness of Ellinors.

From beginning to end this novel is bathed in tears. Though sometimes the self-dissection is accurate, it is devitalised by an extreme lack of restraint. When presenting the emotions, Sophia Lee makes Pelion and Ossa like a wart. One might quote in proof of this by opening any of the three volumes at random. For example, there is the occasion when Leicester and Mathilda are captured and imprisoned by a vengeful villain from whom nothing is to be feared but dishonour and death. This really beggars description.

From a humorous point of view it is a pity that space does not permit us to give some of Ellinor's adventures in Ireland. Miss Lee sees no reason to doubt that in

Elizabeth's reign Scotland was a Hesperides peopled with refined and benevolent men, while Ireland, on the contrary, was inhabited by beings who in 'their language, manners, and lives' resembled the 'inhabitants of the Torrid Zone'. Ellinor falls into the hands of 'Tiroen', a villainous savage with the most dishonourable intentions. Tiroen lays his plans, but Ellinor, several moves ahead of him, thoughtfully provides herself with laudanum which she induces him to quaff as a love-pledge. Ellinor in relating this incident is so reminiscent of a spinster aunt that one cannot resist quoting:

> I was one evening alone in the tent allotted to me . . . when Tiroen approached me unawares—his complexion was flushed with wine, and his eyes and air shewed a determination at which my nature shuddered—no longer regarding decorum or respect, his manners made me in a moment sensible I had deferred taking my laudanum too long. An idea, at which I have never ceased to wonder, suggested itself to my mind; and while fluctuating between the possible and impossible, I a little soothed the boisterous wretch at whose profligate vows I trembled . . . convinced by the tenor of his discourse and conduct, that I could escape his licentious purposes only by feigning an intention of yielding to them, I smoothed my agonised features into a smile which almost stiffened me into a convulsion, and complained of thirst—a glass of water stood by, of which I drank—inclination no less than gallantry, made him insist on pledging me . . . He eagerly swallowed the beverage. Sleep had before hovered over his eyelids; it was now forerun by stupefaction.[19]

Yet, though rarely, this fustian is sometimes relieved by such a passage as describes the escape of Mathilda, Leicester and their friend, Rose Cecil, to France:

> We ascended the deck, and seating ourselves in a little boat lashed to it, every fear, every hope seemed suspended, and the present all our lives for which any had a sense. The gentle breezes only played upon the white sails, and the vessel cut with a safe and pleasant motion, through those green waves whose points the full moon exquisitely silvered, as breaking they gave life to the stillness of the night. I turned my eyes with the sweetest satisfaction from my love to my friend, from my friend to my love; the same mild orb deli-

[19] Sophia Lee, *The Recess* (2nd. ed. 1786), iii, pp. 73-75.

> cately illumin'd either face . . . These sacred pauses in life which lovers only know, invigorate the soul, as sleep does the body and alone can enable us to sustain the past and coming ill.

That Sophia had not Harriet's ability as a novelis was proved by *The Canterbury Tales* which appeared i 1797. This was a collection of stories planned by Harrie who wrote most of them, Sophia contributing *The Tw Emilys* and *Pembroke*. *The Canterbury Tales* are o the *novella* type, most of them suffering from undu condensation. The subject matter is generally domesti and sentimental, and often shows a democratic spiri unusual in days when readers dearly loved a lord. Th stories are very uneven in technique. In many of ther time is badly managed, notably in *Montfort* an *Constance*. ('And what is become of Constance? Nin years are past—nine long years, in about as many line This is going full speed indeed! Patience, courteou reader! The ensuing years will perhaps creep a snail' pace.') But despite the faultiness and improbabilit of some of these stories, there is much evidence o originality, of realism. One observes in such fiction sure instinct to develop a technique equal to its concep tions. For example, there is the spirit of experiment i which Harriet Lee begins *Constance* with conversatior then explains the background and works in th characters. The characterisation is usually convincin sometimes achieved with crisp deftness.

The best of Harriet's domestic stories is *Th Landlady's Tale*. This bears the impress of the suppose narrator. It is told with convincing power and complet naturalness. Mary, a shop-girl, is betrayed by Captai Mandeville, an army officer whom the landlady describ as follows: 'He was one of those rattling sparks, Si who dash on in life without looking to the right or th left, through a long lane of the maimed and the blin whom they have made so; till, being come to the journey's end, they are obliged to cast their eyes bac and see the sad spectacle of human misery.'[20] Whe

20 *The Canterbury Tales* (2nd. ed. 1805), v, p. 45.

Mary is deserted by Mandeville she goes to his native place, discovers he is married, and bears her child, which dies. At the same time Mandeville's wife has a child, and she dies soon afterwards. Mary offers herself as nurse to the baby son, and lives at the Hall. Mandeville returns, persecutes her with his demands, and threatens to have her dismissed without a character. On an impulse she rushes to the nursery, bundles his son into her arms, walks to Newcastle and takes ship for London. There she lives until the boy is twelve years old, and then goes to Weymouth. She and the boy are taken in by Mrs. Dixon, the landlady, who engages Mary as a seamstress. The death of her father calls Mary from home and in her absence Mandeville, now a member of Parliament, comes to stay at Mrs. Dixon's. He little knows that under the same roof is his son, now aged seventeen. This youth, Bob, falls under the bad influence of Mandeville's groom, and agrees to 'borrow' some of Mandeville's valuables, and to pawn them so as to raise money for betting. They are sure they can return the articles in time to avoid detection, but they are wrong. Mandeville exonerates the groom and all the blame falls on Bob, who is shipped to Botany Bay. Mary returns and, distracted at what has happened, tells Mandeville that he has ruined his own son. Mandeville falls into a fit. All efforts to free the boy are vain, but he frees himself by dying on the outward voyage. Mary's reason becomes impaired; Mandeville's health remains enfeebled, and public censure forces him to leave Weymouth.

Of the dignified pathos which characterises this story, one brief example must serve. When Mary was in despair,

> After turning her thoughts a thousand ways in search of comfort, she found no gleam of it but in the idea of going back to her own village. She had been innocent—she had been comparatively happy there. She believed she should find something to love, and Mary could not live without loving something.[1]

1 *Ibid.*, v, p. 120.

The three Gothic stories in *The Canterbury Tale* are all by Harriet Lee. They are *Constance* (the French man's tale), *Lothaire* (the old woman's tale), an *Kruitzner* (the German's tale).

Constance is a good story told with animation. Th heroine is a beautiful and innocent girl who lives wit her godparents in a cottage on the Marquis of Valmont' estate in Languedoc. Her loveliness attracts the attentio of the Marquis and his guests and, to avoid them, i is arranged that she shall be sent to some friends i Dauphiné. But Constance is more in love than she know with one who calls himself Valrive, a servant of th Valmont household, but who is actually the Chevalie de Valmont. She agrees to say farewell to him in little house in the forest, but is kidnapped and taken to château of the Marquis of Valmont. Some three month later the Marquis arrives, but his dishonourabl attentions are in abeyance as he is a fugitive from th Revolutionaries. Constance's effort to escape is describe with Gothic effect. Her fears, her midnight exploration of the grim château are exciting. She accidentally come upon an emaciated prisoner in the castle dungeon— the rightful Marquis of Valmont who has been incarcer ated for almost a century, and this despite the fact tha he is not above forty years of age. The arrival of th *sans-culottes* frees both him and Constance. She discover that he is her father. He dies, and Constance after man vicissitudes marries her lover.

Kruitzner is not only the best of Harriet Lee's Gothi stories, but the best of all her writings. The story begin with the arrival at an obscure town in Silesia of a man his wife and their son. This man is Kruitzner wh from the moment of his appearance, impresses th villagers with a sense of mystery. Kruitzner's illnes detains these strangers in this little backwater, althoug they wish to press forward on their journey. They ar miserably poor, and the Intendant of the Prince d T— (who has his own purposes to serve) allows ther the use of an empty house near the Palace. A junto c village schemers sets itself to spy on Kruitzner and to discover his secret.

The secret they so long to discover would not disappoint them, for the family sheltered in the dilapidated house was destined for strange adventures and had already felt the hand of fate. Kruitzner, whose real name was Siegendorf, was the heir of Count Siegendorf of Bohemia, disowned for the licentiousness of his private life and for his incapacity and indifference in defence of his country. Thus disgraced, he went into Saxony where he continued his profligate course until he saw and loved Josephine Michelli, the daughter of a poor scientist. At first he is ideally happy, but soon memories of his high birth and all that he has lost torture him, and he pours out the whole story to his wife and her father. They are amazed; and Michelli is alarmed lest in Kruitzner's new desire for reconciliation with his father he may be prepared to abandon Josephine. He resents also the way in which Kruitzner has deceived him, and they quarrel. Kruitzner, in his anger, makes another of his fatal decisions and, at once putting it in action, sets out secretly for Bohemia with the object of making a personal appeal to his father. On the way he communicates with the old Count who, in response, arranges to have an allowance paid to Kruitzner, but forbids him to return to Bohemia until he has redeemed the name of Siegendorf. Determined to reform, Kruitzner continues his journey homewards, but at Cassel his good intentions break down before the argument of a full purse and opportunity. He again falls into evil ways and spends all he has, even the money he left in Hamburg for his wife and son. His father hears of his dissipations and renounces him forever.

From that day forth Kruitzner's nature undergoes a change. He believes himself deeply wronged by his father, and he withdraws into himself to feed upon his own bitterness. When the old Count offers to take Kruitzner's little son, Conrad, and to rear him for succession to the title and estates, Kruitzner cannot refuse, although this offer is the final proof that he himself has been disinherited.

Years elapse, and Kruitzner and his wife continue in poverty while their son grows into manhood. But there is a secret pretender to the estates in Bohemia, the cold and avaricious Stralenheim who, on the death of the old Count, reveals his real nature. He contests Conrad's legitimacy, and claims his inheritance. Conrad leaves Bohemia; Kruitzner and his wife try to reach it. Stralenheim seeks Kruitzner to destroy him. All their ways meet at the remote village in Bohemia where Kruitzner's illness has detained him. There are spies, searches, evasions, a secret passage, a theft and finally a murder—the murder of Stralenheim. A Hungarian, who disappears immediately after the murder, is suspected of the crime, but there is no real proof. Kruitzner, freed of Stralenheim's evil pursuit, returns to Bohemia and succeeds to his inheritance, but his son's strange remoteness of manner and his reluctance to live at home afflict Kruitzner with a fear that he himself will know the sufferings of a father who watches, but cannot reclaim, a wayward son.

Finally, it transpires that Conrad was the murderer of Stralenheim. Conrad is killed in a skirmish, and is not long survived by his parents. Kruitzner rests at last, after a weary cycle of error and expiation.

Kruitzner is a story which suffers from compression. Reading it is like entering a house where great things are toward; we are enveloped in an atmosphere of intrigue; we see people hastily passing to and fro, talking together, going out, re-entering. We have been given a hint of what is happening, but so rapidly that it is with difficulty we take in the complicated plot. But the character of Kruitzner is the focal point. That is so finely conceived so minutely dissected, driven home to us with such living force that it gives reality and coherence to the involuted story. Kruitzner is an egoist of turbulent passions, cursed with all the morbidity of introversion. He has a consciousness of fatality which sets him apart invests him with strange and sinister individuality, and gives a gloomy grandeur to his tragic life. Kruitzner should have been born in the fury of a storm when earth and sky were convulsed with demoniac rage. He carries with him his own dark atmosphere, and the deadly lightning of his will brings ruin to himself and to those around him. He has depths easily stirred to good or evil, but moving in obedience to some law of his own nature. He errs, and he is so embittered against himself for his mistakes that he perversely continues in courses that can lead only to destruction:

> It is the wrong we commit against ourselves that corrodes and most bitterly envenoms the heart; that we receive from others sometimes displays its noblest faculties, either by the act of repelling or enduring the evil. [Kruitzner] owed half his faults and almost all his miseries to a secret tearing consciousness of error, which he never permitted to rise into reformation.[22]

After he has forfeited his father's affection and the respect of his country, he is for a while redeemed by the love and goodness of his wife. But not for long. Soon thoughts of what he has thrown away break the tranquillity of his days, and he deceives himself with the idea that it is remorse which disturbs him and which urges him to a reconciliation with his father. It is not remorse.

> The radical fault of his character was yet far from being extirpated: for whether under the influence of virtuous or illicit passions, whether revelling in the courts of princes, or living in the bosom of frugality and temperance, it was self and self only, that had hitherto guided all his actions; and even at a crisis, when he was willing to believe that filial duty and honour gave rise to his returning sensibility, it was strangely compounded of that pride and self-love the avenging angel had not yet wrung out his heart.[23]

Even when he has ruined his life, he is not willing to live in the future of his son Conrad. It rankles within him that Conrad will have what might have been his own. And yet he loves his son, and yields him up to his grandfather with relief at the thought that this child, at

22 *Ibid.*, iv, p. 215.
23 *Ibid.*, iv, p. 198.

least, will come into his own. No wonder that a heart devoured at the same moment by pride, remorse, envy, love and bitterness can never for a moment find peace.

The end of *Kruitzner* is finely conceived. The Count, reinstated in his honours and possessions, is still gnawed by the remembrance of the means he has employed, and by doubts of his son's nature which too much appears to resemble his own. Nor is he spared the final horror of finding that Conrad has put into action the very deed which his own mind had secretly contemplated. He has to endure the misery of having begotten an instrument for the performance of those dreadful promptings from which his own mind recoils in horror. His punishment is not merely remorse for his own sins, but responsibility for that of his son. The suffering he inflicted on his father is as nothing to what he himself has now to endure.

Harriet Lee set herself the task of making us understand the nature of Kruitzner, and how he precipitated and endured the events of his life. At the same time she claims our sympathy for him. That she succeeded in achieving these purposes gives her the right to be considered as a most valuable contributor to English fiction. We have in *Kruitzner* not merely Gothic mysteries, but the mysteries of a soul. Hartley Coleridge says of it: 'The motif—a son predestined to evil by the weakness and sensuality of his father, a father's punishment for his want of rectitude by the passionate criminality of his son, is the very key-note of tragedy.' Byron read this story when he was about fourteen, and it affected him powerfully: 'It made a deep impression on me,' he says, 'and may, indeed, be said to contain the germ of much that I have since written.' In 1821 he dramatised it under the title of *Werner, or the Inheritance*.

In *Kruitzner* there is a very sparing use of Gothic paraphernalia. Indeed of external adjuncts there is little more than a ruined house and a secret passage. The real action is in the mind. There is a steady growth of suspense, fear, and mental torture. Harriet Lee did not need the rack of the Inquisition. She knew that a certain kind of nature tortures itself, and she introduced outside forces merely to tighten the screw. The result is Gothic in the psychological sense. Kruitzner is in excelsis a Gothic hero—a figure of isolated and tormented grandeur.

Another woman who aided the development of the Gothic novel was Mrs. Charlotte Smith (1749-1806). Poverty drove her to commence author, and she brought to her work a great natural talent and no education. Her schooling, such as it was, ended at the age of twelve. At fifteen she was forced by her step-mother into a marriage which was distasteful to her, and which proved a disastrous failure. Her worthless husband involved her in many misfortunes, even in imprisonment, and she was forced to support not only her twelve children, but their irresponsible father. These were the circumstances of a writer who provided Mrs. Radcliffe with some valuable hints, and who made a signal contribution towards the development of the Gothic novel.

Her first works were a volume of poems, and a translation of *Manon Lescaut* (1786). In 1788 appeared her first novel *Emmeline, the orphan of the castle*. This story of domestic sensibility is not worth recounting from a Gothic point of view. Except for the formal background of the castle, and some hints of sentimental landscape, it has no Gothic characteristics. This love of romantic scenery is very important. Rousseau and such writers as Madame de Genlis[24] may have prepared the way by popularising harmonious landscapes, but to Mrs. Smith must go the credit for adding this most prominent trait to the Gothic novel. There is no doubt that it was from Mrs. Smith that Mrs. Radcliffe derived this very interesting aspect of Gothicism. In Charlotte Smith's second novel *Ethelinde, or the Recluse of the lake* (1789) the Cumberland setting is carefully elaborated, but it is in *Celestina* (1791) that we find awe and beauty mingled in the true Gothic proportions. Here also, in

[24] e.g. her *Adèle et Théodore* (1782).

the descriptions of the Pyrenees, we find proof of Mrs. Radcliffe's indebtedness.

Celestina is a curious mixture of tendencies. It unites the elements of domestic sensibility, doctrinal didacticism and Gothicism. The plot is loose and straggling with several inset stories given at a length out of all relation to their importance. These are: the story of Jessy and Cathcart, the story of Mrs. Elphinstone and the story of the Count de Bellegarde. This latter tale has the Pyrenean background which Mrs. Radcliffe used three years later in *The Mysteries of Udolpho*. Both women obviously used the same source: Ramond de Carbonnières' *Observations faites dans les Pyrénées* (1789), but it seems more than probable that Mrs. Radcliffe turned to de Carbonnières after she had read *Celestina*. Charlotte Smith's instinct as a novelist gauged the value of the Frenchman's descriptions. The might and splendour of the mountains, the glaciers, the torrents, the gloomy pine forests, the little valleys like oases in this rugged isolation, the swirling mists, storm, thunder and lightning, the hollow cry of the vulture, awe and fear—in adapting all these to the purposes of fiction Mrs. Smith anticipated Mrs. Radcliffe. Here, too, is the half-ruined castle on an airy summit, the nearby convent and the story of cruel wrongs, imprisonment, plotting Jesuits, and pitiful maidens forced to take the veil. None of it, of course, is presented with Mrs. Radcliffe's artistry of suspense and mystery, but the paraphernalia are there. It is notable that Mrs. Smith here arrives also at a suggestion of that chiaroscuro technique which Mrs. Radcliffe had already employed, and which she was later to bring to a fine art. Mrs. Smith may have taken the hint from Mrs. Radcliffe's previous novels, or may simply have followed closely Ramond de Carbonnières' contrasted use of the storm and peril of the mountains and the peaceful security of the valley. Indeed the Vallée de Luron (to which Willoughby comes after his dangerous wanderings) suggests to Mrs. Smith the words applied by Rousseau to a similar spot among the rocks of Meillerie: 'Il semblait que ce lieu désert dût être l'asyle de deux amants échappés seuls au bouleversement de la nature.' Such exquisite moments of happy security Mrs. Radcliffe always gave her persecuted lovers, before she sent them relentlessly forward on the dark path of their fate.

But it was not only in her use of nature that Mrs. Smith sounded the Gothic note. The Count of Bellegarde's castle, situated on a height with masses of ruined fortifications, is unmistakably Gothic:

> The gate of the castle, and all beyond the moat . . . was yet entire, as were the walls within its circumference, bearing everywhere the marks of great antiquity, but of such ponderous strength, as time alone had not been able to destroy . . . The towers, at each end, rose in frowning grandeur, above the rest of the building; and having only loops, and no windows, impressed ideas of darkness and imprisonment, while the moss and wall-flowers filled the interstices of the broken stones; and an infinite number of birds made their nests among the shattered cornices, and half-fallen battlements, filling the air with their shrill cries.[25]

The interior of the castle is no less romantic:

> An immense hall, barbarously magnificent; it was roofed with beams of oak, and the sides covered with standards, and trophies of armour, the perishable parts of which were dropping to pieces. The narrow Gothic windows were filled, not with glass, that admitted the light, but with glass, painted with the atchievements of the family; mingled with the heads of saints and martyrs.[26]

No wonder that 'Willoughby as he marched gravely along, through the long galleries, and across the gloomy hall, fancied himself a knight of romance, and that some of the stories of enchanted castles, and wandering adventures, of which he had been fond in his early youth, were here realised.'[27]

Desmond, an epistolary novel which appeared in 1792, is again a *mélange* of the same tendencies which were evident in *Celestina*, but in *Desmond* the doctrinal

25 Charlotte Smith, *Celestina* (1791), iv, p. 220 f.
26 *Ibid.*, iv, p. 224.
27 *Ibid.*, iv, p. 231.

didacticism is so shameless that the book is less a novel than a social and political tractate. The domestic framework sets forth the love of an idealistic young man for Geraldine, the patient wife of a wastrel named Verney. Verney's wretched behaviour reaches the limit when he tries to decoy his wife into becoming the mistress of the Duc de Romagnecourt. She manages to evade this situation. Then she hears that her husband has been seriously wounded near Avignon, and hastens to join him. On the way she has a terrible adventure in an inn which is really a house of call for robbers. She is rescued in the nick of time by Desmond who has followed her to France and unobtrusively watched over her. They take refuge in the Count d'Hautville's Gothic castle, which, although the embers are still glowing on the hearth, seems deserted. The gloom, their fears, their discovery of a man's cap pierced by a bullet and covered with blood, the mysterious sounds of low breathing, their final discovery of a hideous man—one of a troop organised by d'Hautville for the defence of the castle against the revolutionaries—all arouse curiosity and fear. It transpires that the Count d'Hautville has gone to Italy and the garrison become outlaws. Eight of the bandits are out marauding when Geraldine and Desmond arrive. On hearing this, Desmond has the drawbridge raised and prepares to defend the castle against the robbers should they return while he and Geraldine are still there. They get safely away to Avignon, however, and do all in their power to nurse Verney back to life. But Verney, with a singular tact, dies repenting all his misdeeds and recommending the sorely-tried lovers to marry—which they do.

Arising from a description of the estate of Montfleuri, there is a reverie of Desmond's which blends the two main elements of Mrs. Radcliffe's Gothic conception. Here Charlotte Smith unites the romantic loveliness of nature and of terror, and creates about them a widening sense of the strangeness of human existence. She says:

I know this betrays a very Gothic and exploded taste, but such is the force of early impressions, that I have still an affection for 'the bowed roof'—the cathedral-like solemnity of long lines of tall trees, whose topmost boughs are interlaced with each other . . . But I account for my predilection, by the kind of pensive and melancholy pleasure I used to feel, when in my childhood and early youth, I walked alone, in a long avenue of arbeal, which led from a very wild and woody part of the weald of Kent, to an old house my father, at that period of my life, inhabited. I remember the cry of the woodpeckers or the yaffils, as we call them in that country, going to roost in a pale autumnal evening, answered by the owls, which in great numbers inhabit the deep forest-like glens that lay behind the avenue. I see the moon slowly rising over the dark mass of wood, and the opposite hills, tinged with purple from the last reflection of the sun, which was sunk behind them.—I recall the sensations I felt, when, as the silver leaves of the aspins trembled in the lowest breeze, or slowly fell to the ground before me, I became half-frightened at the increasing obscurity of the objects around me, and have almost persuaded myself that the grey trunks of these old trees, and the low murmur of the wind among their branches, were the dim forms, and hollow sighs of some supernatural beings; and at length, afraid of looking behind me, I have hurried breathless into the house.[28]

The best of all Mrs. Charlotte Smith's novels is *The Old Manor House* (1793). Once again the elements which most interested her are apparent, but they are more evenly balanced, and they are not, as formerly, merely collateral, but are fused in the greater part of the story. In her previous novels there had really been no characterisation, although there had been the ability to sketch the minor characters with a few touches of realism or malice. These portraits, however, were merely external, but in *The Old Manor House* Mrs. Smith shows herself interested in human reactions and motives. The character of Mrs. Rayland is most effectively and consistently drawn. She dominates the action of the story, not only during her lifetime, but even after her death, since the mystery which surrounds her will causes the involvements in the second part of the novel.

Mrs. Rayland, the owner of Rayland Hall and its

28 Charlotte Smith, *Desmond* (ed. Dublin, 1792), i, p. 104 f.

extensive estates, is a rigid autocrat whose greatest pleasure lies in the power which she derives from her illustrious ancestry and her great wealth. Her only relatives are a family called Somerive who live a few miles away and whom she despises because they are descended from a branch of the family which has repeatedly demeaned itself by misalliances. Mrs. Rayland has it in her power to do as she wishes with all her property and, by her arrogance and grudging condescension, she keeps the Somerives in a state of perpetual suspense as to her intentions. The profligacy of the elder son, Philip, alienates her sympathies from him; and Orlando, the younger son, who is her favourite, seems to have the best chance of succeeding to her property. Mrs. Rayland, however, does not commit herself as to her intentions, and Orlando has to be content with frequenting Rayland Hall and awaiting her pleasure. This he does, not so much for selfish motives as for the benefit of his needy family. But a complication arises from the presence at Rayland Hall of Monimia, the orphan niece of Mrs. Lennard, the housekeeper. Orlando falls deeply in love with Monimia. The necessity for keeping their affection a secret from Mrs. Rayland leads to midnight meetings, to which they come through a secret passage and a ghostly chapel. With much power Charlotte Smith shows that, though Mrs. Rayland is an inflexible autocrat, she is being watched silently and rapaciously by Mrs. Lennard and Pattenson, the butler, both of whom are interested in feathering their nests, and who would oust Orlando from favour if they could. Mrs. Lennard's motives are very well dissected. We are shown that she is fiercely opposed to the love of Orlando and Monimia because, if Orlando does not become heir, the estate will probably be split up, and Mrs. Lennard in that case would get a much smaller legacy. Pattenson hates Orlando because he foolishly suspects him of intriguing with one of the maids whom Pattenson himself hopes to seduce, and because Orlando's mysterious movements around Rayland Hall at night seem to menace Pattenson's secret commerce with smugglers. Pattenson has some unexplained hold over Mrs. Lennard which makes it necessary for her to placate him when their interests clash. All these separate motives of intrigue are most skilfully interwoven, and it is against this background of fear, spying, ruthlessness and self-interest that the guileless Monimia and Orlando pursue the course of true love. Although Mrs. Rayland plays with Orlando as a cat with a mouse, her hard nature softens towards him, and although she dissimulates her affection and her intentions, it becomes clear that he has a very good chance of becoming her heir.

At this juncture an elderly admirer of one of Orlando's sisters, for reasons of his own, wishes him out of the way, and offers him a commission in the army. Mrs. Rayland, who comes of a martial line, encourages Orlando to accept, and he has no choice but to go, thus leaving Monimia to the tyranny and restraint of Mrs. Lennard, who has the strongest suspicions of their secret understanding. After enduring many terrible adventures in the American war, Orlando escapes from the red Indians who are his captors, and with great difficulty gets back to England. He finds his father's house in the possession of strangers, his father dead and his mother and sisters gone without a trace. Rayland Hall is shut up, and he learns that, by Mrs. Rayland's will, it now has passed with all the rest of the property into the possession of an avaricious clergyman called Dr. Hollybourn. Mrs. Lennard has taken her legacy and married a scheming rascal young enough to be her son. Monimia is nowhere to be found. The rest of the novel deals with Orlando's efforts to find her, to help his family and to bring to light Mrs. Rayland's last will, which is in his favour. He succeeds in all these undertakings, and the story ends with a full measure of justice for all the characters.

In setting, in its mysterious or brutal events, and in its use of scenery *The Old Manor House* is Gothic. Rayland Hall provides the architectural background necessary to a Gothic tale. When Orlando first sees Monimia, it is 'by the faint light which the old gothic casements afforded at that hour of the evening.'[29] Their secret interviews involve breathless moments like an eternity when they steal down the winding staircase from the turret, feeling their way in the inky darkness, hearts racing madly at every sound which may denote human spies or ghostly hauntings. Very interesting as an exposition of Mrs. Smith's use of terror is the incident when Orlando and Monimia, in the study at midnight, see a face at the window. We are told at once that it is a human face, but we are kept in suspense as to the origin of the voice which, when they are returning to the turret through the chapel, pronounces in the deathly silence the words 'Now, now!' This supernatural effect is later explained away—a fact which shows that, in the use of terror, Mrs. Smith and Mrs. Radcliffe were in agreement. The difference in their Gothic technique lay only in the degree and frequency of the appeal to the reader's fears. Mrs. Smith possessed to a very marked extent the power of creating a ghostly and terrible atmosphere, and her use of nature resembled Mrs. Radcliffe's not only because it was romantic, but also because Mrs. Smith, like her more famous contemporary, brought to her descriptions a lyrical gift. Not only does she, like Mrs. Radcliffe, continually interpolate poems throughout the narrative, but she gives us sometimes prose lyrics, in which the poetic intention is all the more clearly marked by the repetition of a *motif*. Mrs. Radcliffe had done this in *The Romance of the Forest* (1791). In *The Old Manor House* we find a similar kind of composition. When Orlando bade farewell to his native countryside before going to America: 'The night was overcast and gloomy; chill and hollow the wind whistled among the leafless trees, or groaned amid the thick firs in the dark and silent wood; the water-falls murmured hollow in the blast, and only the owl's cry broke those dull and melancholy sounds, which seemed to say—"Orlando, you will revisit these scenes no more!"' These valedictory words run like a refrain through the chapters which lead up to Orlando's actual departure. The misery of his family, his father's

29 Charlotte Smith, *The Old Manor House* (1793), ii, p. 47.

illness, the destitute state of Monimia, his own uncertain fate—'all combined to sink and depress him and again to lend to the well-known paths he was traversing, horrors not their own, while every object repeated: "Orlando will revisit these scenes no more!"'[30] In Rayland Hall 'he traversed the library, yielding to these tormenting thoughts; and, by the light of the solitary candle he had set down in the window seat, every thing appeared gloomy and terrific. Every object and every sound seemed to repeat the sentence that constantly occurred to him— "Orlando will revisit this house no more."'[31] When, many months later, he returned to Rayland Hall:

> The sight of the many well-known objects on his way—every tree, every shrub, recalled to his mind a thousand pleasing ideas; and as he passed hastily through the fir wood, where in a dreary night of December he had last parted from Monimia . . . he compared his present sensations with what he had at that time felt, and laughed at the superstitious impression given him then, and on some former occasions, by the gloom of the winter sky—when he fancied that, in the hollow murmur of the breeze, he heard, 'Orlando will revisit these scenes no more!'[32]

Monimia is just such a heroine as Mrs. Radcliffe's Emilys and Adelines, and her fearful predicament in the main resembles theirs. For example, in the turret room:

> As I lay, listening of a night to the howling of the wind in the great melancholy room at the end of the north gallery, where I was locked up every night, I have frequently started at the visions my fancy raised; and as the dark green damask hangings swelled with the air behind them, I have been so much terrified as to be unable to move or summon to my recollection all the arguments . . . against superstitious fear—Then too I have been glad to hear the rats as they raced around the skirting boards, because it convinced me there were some living creatures near me, and helped me to account for the strange noises I sometimes heard . . . Good God! how weak I was to add imaginary horrors to the real calamities of my situation.[33]

30 *Ibid.*, i, p. 308.
31 *Ibid*,. i, p. 330.
32 *Ibid.*, ii, p. 46.
33 *Ibid.*, ii, p. 270 f.

The domestic element in *The Old Manor House* is worth noting. There is an echo of *Evelina* in the descriptions of Orlando's relations who are in trade. Dr. Hollybourn and his egregious daughter are in the same vein, and we have a further example of this aspect in Isabella's humour at the expense of her foppish old wooer, General Tracy. The practice of tilting at purse-proud cits had long been established in the novel, and it is amusing to reflect that Mrs. Smith's democratic sympathies led her, in this regard, to make common cause with the snobbish tradition in fiction which had ever mocked at bourgeois crudities.

Charlotte Smith is one of the most interesting writers of her time. In her effort to unite the Gothic, domestic and *tendenz* genres she attempted the impossible, yet, as a reflection of the chief trends in the second half of the eighteenth century, her novels repay careful examination. Their chief value lies in their Gothic aspect. That Charlotte Smith and Mrs. Radcliffe had the same conception of Gothicism is quite clear, and Mrs. Smith's best claim to remembrance rests in the fact that she provided Mrs. Radcliffe with some of the raw materials of the Gothic craft.

To see the possibilities of a trend in fiction, and to choose for its development the most effective materials and technique was the peculiar achievement of Mrs. Radcliffe. What had been hinted sporadically by others became her entire theme, and the instruments which they had fingered experimentally she used with the certitude of genius. Thus she gains the credit of initiating the most characteristic type of English Gothic fiction.

Mrs. Radcliffe was more fortunate than many of her sister-novelists. She wrote not under financial compulsion, but simply to while away the hours when her husband's editorial duties took him daily from home. She had had the usual smatterings of polite education and the usual feminine taste for novel-reading. She was of a most sensitive and retiring disposition, and found in the exercise of her imagination the pleasure which more gregarious women find in social intercourse. What began, no doubt, in day-dreams, in a fireside game of make-belief, soon took form as her pen set down the strange adventures which grew within her mind.

Mrs. Radcliffe's first novel *The Castles of Athlin and Dunbayne, an Highland story* (1789) merited the severe criticisms of the *Critical*[34] and *The Monthly*.[35] The *Critical* bluntly stated that she knew nothing about the Highlands, and *The Monthly* found her wonders 'insipid, if not disgustful'. The book contained some of the Gothic paraphernalia of secret passages and supernatural hints, but it is clumsy and unconvincing. Somewhat better, although still quite undistinguished, was *The Sicilian Romance* (1790). The *motif* is pursuit. The story might be summed up in Keats's lines:

> 'Ages long ago
> These lovers fled away into the storm.'

Mrs. Radcliffe's lovers begin their flight at an early stage of the story, and continue to be pursued until the end. The action takes place towards the close of the sixteenth century. The Marquis of Mazzini marries as his second wife Maria de Vellorno, a beautiful and unscrupulous woman. They live mainly at Naples, returning only once a year to their Gothic castle at Mazzini. Here live Emilia and Julia, the Marquis's two daughters by his first wife. Julia is loved by a young man called Hippolitus de Vareza, but this earns her the hatred of her stepmother who hopes to enslave Hippolitus. To avoid a forced marriage with a libertine, Julia determines to elope. She gets safely away, but Hippolitus is struck down at the moment of escape. He is taken by his servants to his ship which lies waiting. Then follow, on the one hand, the pursuit and evasion of Julia; on the other, the terrible experiences of those who try to solve the mystery of the haunted wing of the castle of Mazzini. It appears later that the Marquis's first wife is imprisoned in a subterranean chamber in this wing.

34 See *The Critical Review*, Sept., 1789.
35 See *The Monthly Review*, Dec., 1789.

Julia's flight takes her, amongst other places, to a convent of monks with an annexe of nuns, all under the rule of an Abate. Here she finds Hippolitus's sister, a nun who dies of consumption with great pomp before the high altar at midnight, surrounded by all the nuns and monks. This is a foretaste of the pseudo-Catholic procedure with which Mrs. Radcliffe astounds us in her later novels. Julia escapes from this peculiar ecclesiastical ménage, finds Hippolitus (who is not dead after all), and the pair continue to be pursued through a maze of caverns, forests, subterranean passages, and vaults opening only by a spring lock on the outside, until they arrive back at the castle of Mazzini. Here they rescue Julia's mother. The Marquis dies of poison. Maria de Vellorno stabs herself, and all ends happily.

The plot of this novel is confusing and weak. The general atmosphere is one of extreme sensibility. There is a deliberate striving for exquisite beauty in effects which always seem meretricious. Anachronisms are many, but no seasoned reader of Gothic fiction will cavil at pianofortes and 'sophas' towards the close of the sixteenth century. Mrs. Radcliffe's device of tricking us into false alarms is very evident.

In comparing these first totterings with Mrs. Radcliffe's balanced stride in *The Romance of the Forest* (1791), one observes a great advance in technique. *The Romance of the Forest* shows for the first time Mrs. Radcliffe's power to unite and sustain the elements of beauty and terror. For these elements, as they take form in this novel, Mrs. Radcliffe appears to have been to some extent indebted to Charlotte Smith. As we have already seen, Mrs. Radcliffe found in *Celestina* (which had just appeared) not merely an indication of a valuable source of scenic descriptions, but also very useful hints as to the employment of these sources. A second debt which Mrs. Radcliffe owed to Charlotte Smith has been suggested by Miss. C. F. McIntyre. Mrs. Radcliffe stated that she found La Motte's story in Guyot (or Gayot) de Pitaval's *Causes Célèbres*. Miss McIntyre believes that Mrs.

Radcliffe's source was actually Charlotte Smith's *Romance of Real Life*.[36]

The events of Mrs. Radcliffe's tale take place in France during the seventeenth century. The story opens with the predicament of Pierre de La Motte who, to escape imprisonment, flees from Paris with his wife. They are benighted near a ruined house and, on seeking shelter, are given the alternative of taking away with them an unknown girl called Adeline, or of sharing her doom. Naturally they choose to live, and they take Adeline under their protection. They continue their journey until their carriage breaks down in a lonely part of the forest of Fontanville, and they see before them dark towers rising above the trees. This is the Abbey of St. Claire—the perfect example of a Gothic ruin in which lurks every possible terror. The travellers decide to shelter there for the night, but the morning brings delay, and delay gives time for the conclusion that here more than anywhere should they be safe from discovery. But these fugitives, already involved in the web of their own difficulties, soon find that the Abbey is a perilous refuge. There are secret trapdoors, dungeons, a skeleton, a rusty dagger and a parchment revealing a tale of cruel wrong. There are also the cross-purposes of human behaviour, chiefly instigated by a wicked marquis who, in pursuing Adeline with his vicious attentions, little guesses that she is the niece whom he has ordered to be assassinated. Adeline makes repeated efforts to escape and succeeds at last. She is finally united to her faithful lover, Theodore, and her villainous uncle swallows poison.

In this, as in Mrs. Radcliffe's other novels, there is really no characterisation. In fact, for the most part, Mrs. Radcliffe weaves her story about the same stock types. Adeline in *The Romance of the Forest* becomes Emily in *The Mysteries of Udolpho* and Ellena in *The Italian*. Madame La Motte becomes Madame Cheron in *Udolpho* and the Marchesa di Vivaldi in *The Italian*.

36 See C. F. McIntyre: *Ann Radcliffe in relation to her time* (Yale Univ. Press, 1920), pp. 51-58.

Theodore becomes Valancourt in *Udolpho* and Vivaldi in *The Italian*. There are always precisely the same honest and garrulous maid and man-servant, the direct descendants of Bianca and Jaquez in *Otranto*. Only in the creation of Schedoni did Mrs. Radcliffe penetrate beneath the surface of character and motive.

The method of working on the reader's nerves by mysterious suggestions and by suspense comes fully into view in *The Romance of the Forest*. For example, Adeline's reading of the parchment is protracted for three chapters by such devices as the sudden extinguishing of the light, or an ungovernable access of fear which makes it impossible for her to continue. All the circumstances connected with the reading of this parchment (the howling of the wind, the moving of the arras, the voice whispering Adeline's name) exemplify what Scott calls the 'dressing-up of the very phantom by which we are to be startled.'[37] But Mrs. Radcliffe's conception of terror had nothing in common with the rude shocks of the German school. It was rather an extreme sensibility to impending danger and a sense of isolation by which one reached an ineffable mood. When La Motte approached the Abbey of St. Claire he was conscious of this upsurging of emotion which had its source in a profound apprehension of beauty, of antiquity, and of the mystery of human existence. Thus he felt when he entered

> the chapel of the Abbey, where the hymn of devotion had once been raised, and the tear of penitence had once been shed; sounds, which could now only be recalled by imagination—tears of penitence which had long since been fixed in fate. La Motte paused a moment, for he felt a sensation of sublimity rising into terror—a suspension of mingled astonishment and awe! He surveyed the vastness of the place, and as he contemplated its ruins, fancy bore him back to past ages.[38]

It is *The Romance of the Forest* which first brings home to us the appositeness of Scott's criticism that 'Mrs.

37 *Mrs. Radcliffe's Novels* (Ballantyne ed. 1824), Scott's prefatory memoir, p. xxiv.

38 Ann Radcliffe, *The Romance of the Forest* (Ballantyne ed., 1824), ch.xi, p. 82.

Radcliffe has a title to be considered as the first poetess of romantic fiction.' Her descriptions of the forest of Fontanville have a wild and dewy freshness which puts us in mind of the forest of Arden. In Fontanville the birds are always singing; flowers spring beneath our feet; it is eternal spring—the springtime of a poet's fancy. And Mrs. Radcliffe not merely gives lyrical descriptions of nature but actually, in the account of Clara and her lute,[39] proves that her mind sought the movement and the form of lyric poetry. This passage is far too long for quotation, but with some omissions it could easily be arranged to show the growth of the lyrical thought, and the development of the *motif* which runs through it and gives it unity:

> I have been playing all day on my lute under the acacias by the lake . . .
>
> She at length found herself, she scarcely knew how, beneath her beloved acacias by the side of the lake . . .
>
> I fear I should again have forgotten them while I played on my lute on the banks of the lake . . .
>
> The evening was still, and uncommonly beautiful. Nothing was heard but the faint shivering of the leaves, which returned but at intervals, making silence more solemn, and the distant murmurs of the torrents that rolled among the cliffs. As she stood by the lake, and watched the sun slowly sinking below the Alps, whose summits were tinged with gold and purple; as she saw the last rays of light gleam upon the waters whose surface was not curled by the lightest air, she sighed. 'Oh! how enchanting would be the sound of my lute at this moment, on this spot, and when everything is so still around me!'

She went to fetch her lute and 'returned with the instrument to her dear acacias, and beneath their shade continued to play till the surrounding objects faded in darkness from her sight. But the moon arose, and, shedding a trembling lustre on the lake, made the scene more captivating than ever . . . She was perfectly enchanted "no! nothing was ever so delightful as to play on the lute beneath her acacias, on the margin of the lake, by moonlight."'

39 *Ibid.*, ch. xxi.

This is the imagery and the rhythm of lyric thought, and it is notable that in the last sentence she gathers up and weaves together the elements of her conception.

Mrs. Radcliffe's descriptions of nature would lead one to expect great things of her poetry, but alas! her interpolated poems are worthless in themselves and absurd in their settings. And so we are faced with the riddle of this woman who could in prose write of flowers seen at daybreak 'while the dew yet hung glittering on their leaves': and yet who, desiring a poetic expression of the same idea, perpetrates a luxuriantly futile sonnet which begins:

'Soft silken flower that in the dewy vale . . .'

Mrs. Radcliffe should have been a poet, but she failed as a poet. She finds expression in prose, but her attitude to nature is not that of a prose writer. It is not merely a reflection of the romantic vogue. It is the result of her temperament. Not only, in common with such writers as Mrs. Smith, does she use nature excessively to reflect individual moods, but she elaborates her descriptions of nature out of all proportion to the story. Such a prose poem as that of Clara and her lute is an excrescence in a novel, and yet if she had detached it and given it poetic form it would at once have become a sickly platitude. It was Mrs. Radcliffe's misfortune that, like Hamlet (and how she would have enjoyed such a comparison!), she was poised between two worlds. She had not made M. Jourdain's discovery that what is not verse is prose, and what is not prose is verse. She is the supreme example of genuine literary power misdirected for want of education. Any one of her novels contains a thousand testimonies of this fact. All her novels constitute a depressing avalanche of proof. Her style is the style of a poet gone astray. It is the style of one who had not subjected herself to intellectual discipline. There are no bones and sinews, and far too much soft flesh. Had she been censured for this in the beginning, she might have rectified it, but, unfortunately, to the school of sentiment and sensibility an excessive billowing of the emotions did not appear an error of taste. Thus the period in which she wrote gave the added impetus of approval to the defects of Mrs. Radcliffe's style. Perhaps she was aware of her lack of education for she is continually straining after cultural effects. She is everlastingly enumerating statuary and paintings. In the words of a contemporary writer:

> She affects in the most disgusting manner a knowledge of languages, countries, customs, and objects of art of which she is lamentably ignorant. She suspends *tripods* from the ceiling by chains. . . . She covers the Kingdom of Naples with India figs . . . . and she makes a convent of monks a necessary appendage to a monastery of nuns . . . Whenever she introduces an Italian word it is sure to be a gross violation of the language. Instead of making a nobleman's servant call him *Padrone* or *Illustrissimo*, she makes him address him by the title of *Maestro* which is Italian for teacher.[40]

This critic is prejudiced against novels of terror and particularly against their high-priestess; therefore his condemnation is too pitiless. Yet in Mrs. Radcliffe's novels we are too often afflicted with pretentiousness. For example, we hear that 'in the cool of the evening, the ladies took the *fresco* along the banks of the Brenta';[41] and that 'the *Lagune* soon displays a gay scene of innumerable little barks, passing from *terra-firma* with provisions.'[42] Then again, our acceptance of the following passage depends on whether we believe that cows sip: 'Under the shade of the oak and chestnut, herds of cattle were grazing. Groups of them, too, were often seen reposing on the banks of the rivulet, or laving their sides in the cool stream, and sipping its wave.'[43] And it is not only in such ways that Mrs. Radcliffe reveals her weakness. In *The Sicilian Romance* there is a description of midnight festivities in the woods which is either naïve or vulgar, according to one's point of view. The woodland vistas are hung with variegated lamps;

40 Note appended to a letter on 'Terrorist Novel Writing' in *The Spirit of Public Journals* (1797), i, p. 323.
41 *The Mysteries of Udolpho* (ed. Ballantyne, 1824), ch. xvii.
42 *Ibid.*, ch. xviii.
43 *Ibid.*, p. 236.

collations are spread under the trees; music touched by unseen hands breathes around, the musicians being concealed in the most embowered spots so as to elude the eye and strike the imagination. Nothing meets the gaze but beauty and romantic splendour. All is mirth and melody, and 'Julia seemed the magic queen of the place'. This romantic effusiveness is Mrs. Radcliffe's most evident fault. It is not enough that the heroine finds herself amongst beautiful surroundings. No, it must be at sunset (or sunrise), the perfume of flowers must rise as an odorous exhalation, the birds must warble in the shimmering air, the trees must sigh in unison: the mountains must rise majestically in the background and the music of an aeolian harp must be heard in the distance. If the heroine is near the sea, then a single sail must glide gracefully over the polished surface of the water, and a luminous star glow with effulgence in the serene of heaven. One would suppose that even an author's economy would prevent the discharge of all this ammunition at once, but Mrs. Radcliffe has no hesitation in producing the same effects over and over again. She will vary the background, or the order of her images: the trees may sigh before the birds warble, or the star may glow before the flowers exhale their perfume. One part of this programme, however, remains immutable: the music of the aeolian harp must always be heard at the last. It is the aesthetic apex—the thinnest, highest note of all the tight-strung play on our emotions.

But it is not only in scenic descriptions that Mrs. Radcliffe ignores the aesthetic possibilities of a disciplined imagination. There is in *The Romance of the Forest* an incident which proves that the nature which Mrs. Radcliffe knew was not human nature. When Theodore La Luc is going to be executed he asks his friends to spend the last night with him in his cell, and they do so. Now, apart from any consideration as to the likelihood of this incident, it is highly improbable from a psychological point of view. No man would so lay himself open to a protracted ordeal of farewell. Indeed, even

Mrs. Radcliffe is struck by the difficulty of filling in this painful period. She says: 'The night was passed in embarrassed conversation; sometimes interrupted by long fits of silence, and sometimes by the paroxysms of despair.'[44] The final interview between Theodore and his relatives takes place next morning. La Luc (his father, an aged clergyman), Clara (his sister) and Adeline (his beloved) come to say good-bye. It is impossible to describe the orgy of emotion that ensues. The father preaches a sermon; they all invoke heaven, and talk about their hearts at great length. Swoons are almost uninterrupted by consciousness and the sufferers are nearly drowned in their own tears. Dry-eyed despair, heroism without heroics did not occur to Mrs. Radcliffe, and she arouses in us something like contempt when, having dragged us through these puling farewells, she reprieves the prisoner at the last moment. Nothing but death could decently follow the scene in the prison cell.

It must not be imagined that these criticisms are aimed at lowering Mrs. Radcliffe's literary prestige. On the contrary, it is precisely because she had genius that it has seemed necessary to determine the explanation of those inequalities so apparent in her novels. Genius is natural bent developed to the fullest capacity. Lack of education certainly impedes such development, however much that bent may succeed in expressing itself merely through its own strength. It was really more by the strength of her natural impulse that Mrs. Radcliffe succeeded. In 1863 Julia Kavenagh asked what might have been the literary result 'had Ann Radcliffe been John Radcliffe and received a vigorous and polished education.' And the answer seems to be that then surely Ann Radcliffe would have lived on, not merely through her influence on the minds of great men, but in her own writings; not merely as the half-forgotten initiator of a phase of fiction, but as the creator of some imperishable beauty in verse or prose.

44 *The Romance of the Forest* (ed. Ballantyne, 1824), ch. xxi, p. 203.

Mrs. Radcliffe was unaware that beauty is created chiefly through an impassioned control of inspiration. Nevertheless, she did, with practice, perfect the better aspects of her work, although she was not sufficiently conscious of her faults to eradicate them. The two last novels published during her lifetime are certainly her best.

The Romance of the Forest established Mrs. Radcliffe as a successful novelist. *The Mysteries of Udolpho* (1794) reinforced her fame. The story begins slowly and takes some time to get really under way. Monsieur St. Aubert, a gentleman of Gascony, is left, on the death of his wife, with failing health and fortunes. His one comfort is his daughter Emily. It becomes necessary for him to travel for the sake of his health, and, accompanied by his daughter, he journeys towards Provence, only to die on the way. Emily, poor in everything but the love of a young soldier named Valancourt, goes to live with her aunt, Madam Cheron, who despises her for her poverty and discourages Valancourt's suit. Soon Madam Cheron abandons her widow's weeds to marry the mysterious Italian, Count Montoni, who boasts a palace in Venice and a castle at Udolpho. To Venice they repair. Montoni shows the cloven hoof from the first moment of his married life, and proves a tyrant not only to his wife, but to Emily. Her he endeavours to force into an unsuitable marriage, but before he can complete his design he has made Venice too hot to hold him, and flees to Udolpho, taking with him his wife and Emily. At this point the interest of the story really begins. In the mountain stronghold of Udolpho Montoni is lord of all. Too late his wife discovers that he is really a penniless ruffian who has married her only for her money. She refuses to sign over her possessions to him, and dies tormented but unyielding.

Emily is now alone in what is virtually a robbers' stronghold—driven almost to madness by spectral voices, apparitions, bloody scenes and insulting attentions. Her unwelcome Venetian suitor, Morano, pursues her to Udolpho and makes several efforts to abduct her, but is foiled by Montoni who has now formed the idea of taking for himself Emily's estates. Emily steadfastly refuses to sign a document of surrender, but is made to yield by Montoni's threat to abandon her to the insults of his subordinates. Then, by a wonderful stroke of luck, she escapes from Udolpho.

Here the interest of the story becomes moribund, although it gasps on for twenty chapters or more. Emily reaches France and is given refuge in another castle which soon becomes as haunted as Udolpho. While Emily's sojourn at Château-le-blanc was peaceful, it provided a welcome contrast to the horrors at Udolpho. Mrs. Radcliffe always provides her heroine with such tranquil respites. But the repetition of the ghostly *motif* at Château-le-blanc is inartistic. Udolpho has already exhausted the reader's nerves to such an extent that these fresh mysteries fail to arouse any response. Furthermore, Mrs. Radcliffe's method of bringing Emily to Château-le-blanc is extremely awkward. We see Emily, escaped from Udolpho, safely embark for France, and are then forced to endure two chapters describing the Villefort family, the quarrels of Monsieur with his wife, and the mawkish raptures of his daughter Blanche, fresh from her convent school. We are even condemned to endure a lamentable poem of sixteen stanzas entitled *The Butterfly and his Love*, composed by this soulful young creature, before we see Emily's ship approaching, and witness her arrival at Château-le-blanc. Possibly our thwarted disgust at these irrelevancies is a proof of our interest in Emily, but if Mrs. Radcliffe created this interlude to heighten our suspense, she was sadly mistaken, because these chapters would certainly be 'skipped' by the unconscientious reader.

These are the weaker aspects of the novel. Its perfections are far greater than its faults. The journey to Udolpho is a crescendo of majestic scenery and human premonition so interwoven that they create a single effect of mounting awe. As the travellers climb higher and higher into the Apennines, among the dark pine forests and dizzy precipices, they are awed by sensations of dreadful sublimity. Emily's mind is oppressed by strange foreboding. She is entirely without a friend and she is powerless. Thus Mrs. Radcliffe describes the first view of Udolpho:

> Towards the close of day, the road wound into a deep valley. Mountains whose shaggy steeps appeared to be inaccessible, almost surrounded it. To the east a vista opened, and exhibited the Apennines in their darkest horrors; and the long perspective of retiring summits rising over each other, their ridges clothed with pines, exhibited a stronger image of grandeur than any that Emily had yet seen. The sun had just sunk below the top of the mountains she was descending, whose long shadow stretched athwart the valley, but his sloping rays, shooting through an opening of the cliffs, touched with a yellow gleam the summits of the forest that hung upon the opposite steeps, and streamed in full splendour upon the towers and battlements of a castle that spread its extensive ramparts along the brow of a precipice above. The splendour of these illumined objects was heightened by the contrasted shade which involved the valley below.
>
> 'There,' said Montoni, speaking for the first time in several hours, 'is Udolpho.'
>
> Emily gazed with melancholy awe upon the castle, which she understood to be Montoni's; for, though it was now lighted up by the setting sun, the gothic greatness of its features, and its mouldering walls of dark grey stone, rendered it a gloomy and sublime object. As she gazed the light died away on its walls, leaving a melancholy purple tint, which spread deeper and deeper, as the thin vapour crept up the mountain, while the battlements above were still tipped with splendour. From these, too, the rays soon faded, and the whole edifice was invested with the solemn duskiness of the evening. Silent, lonely and sublime, it seemed to stand the sovereign of the scene, and to frown defiance on all who dared to invade its solitary reign. As the twilight deepened, its features became more awful in obscurity, and Emily continued to gaze, till its clustering towers were alone seen rising over the tops of the woods.[45]

Speaking of this description, Scott says that if six artists endeavoured to embody it on canvas, the result would be six pictures entirely dissimilar to each other, and yet all authorised by Mrs. Radcliffe's printed words. Scott compares the description of Udolpho with Mrs. Radcliffe's description of Hardwicke ruins, which she

45 *The Mysteries of Udolpho* (ed. Ballantyne, 1824), ch. xviii, p. 325.

wrote with her eye on the object. He contrasts the precision of this latter description with the romantic glamour of Udolpho, which he considers 'a beautiful effect-piece', and he emphasises that in accuracy and realism Mrs. Radcliffe's descriptions are inferior to those of Mrs. Smith. Nevertheless, it was the poetic alchemy of Mrs. Radcliffe's mind which intoxicated Byron with the magic of a Venice which she had actually never seen,[46] and which inspired the unforgettable stanzas on Venice in *Childe Harold.*

Lewis himself stated that *The Mysteries of Udolpho* had influenced him in writing *The Monk* (1795). There is a possibility that Mrs. Radcliffe found in this otherwise distasteful book some hints for the chief character in *The Italian* (1797); and it seems possible also that she was influenced by Schiller's *Der Geisterseher.*

Apart from the deliberate incorrectness of the historical background into which Mrs. Radcliffe was betrayed by her animosity towards Catholicism, *The Italian* is the best of all her novels. But Mrs. Radcliffe's attitude towards Catholicism is so typical of the Gothic school that it deserves a few words of literary criticism.

46 At the time when Mrs. Radcliffe wrote *Udolpho* she had not visited the countries with which she was so familiar. Miss C. F. McIntyre and Dr. J. M. S. Tompkins have made most valuable discoveries as to the sources on which Mrs. Radcliffe drew. Acting on a suggestion in the *Diary of a Lover of Literature* Miss McIntyre traces Mrs. Radcliffe's description of Venice and of the voyage up the Brenta to Mrs. Piozzi's *Observations and Reflections made in the course of a journey through France, Italy and Germany*. Dr. Tompkins reinforces Miss McIntyre's opinion, and adds two more sources used by Mrs. Radcliffe in *Udolpho*: Ramond de Carbonnières' *Observations faites dans les Pyrénées* (1789), and P. J. Grosley's *New Observations on Italy and its Inhabitants* (English translation, 1794). The evidence in Grosley's case is conclusive; in de Carbonnières' a strong probability can be established. Dr. Tompkins also suggests the influence of Arthur Young's *Travels in France* and Henry Swinburne's *Journey from Bayonne to Marseilles*, the latter appearing as a supplement to the 2nd. ed. of *Travels through Spain* (1787). Dr. Tompkins believes that it was probably Mrs. Smith's *Celestina* which stimulated Mrs. Radcliffe's interest in the Pyrenees and which turned her attention to de Carbonnières' book. De Carbonnières had just that spirit of lyrical romanticism which would appeal to Mrs. Radcliffe. Miss Tompkins notes that, though Mrs. Radcliffe certainly drew on Grosley, she avoided his less romantic touches and preferred always to give an idealised version of what he described. Dr. Tompkins gives a most detailed account of Mrs. Radcliffe's debt to Grosley, showing how Emily St. Aubert followed Grosley's route into Italy and experienced on the way many incidents which Grosley describes. At Udolpho we come to Mrs. Radcliffe's greatest debt to Grosley: the incident of the veiled picture. Grosley describes (vol. i, p 205) that in Ravenna, at the Benedictine Church of St. Vital, he was shown the waxen

One cannot do better than quote in this connection the remarks of a sound and temperate commentator. She says:[47]

> The dealings of the literary men of Protestant England in the eighteenth century with the institutions of the Roman Catholic Church are a little disingenuous. They are very conscious of the picturesque attractions of convents, vows of celibacy, confession and penance; they are seduced by the emotional possibilities of the situations that can be based on these usages; but they seldom fail to make it quite clear that they regard the usages as superstitious and irrational, and, if they did, there was not wanting a critic to blame this 'attempt to gloss over the follies of popery, or to represent its absurdities as sacred'.[48]

In her earlier novels Mrs. Radcliffe had shown anti-Catholic bias coupled with a complete ignorance of Catholic beliefs. These misrepresentations might have been made unsuspectingly, but such a plea cannot be entered for *The Italian*. In *New Observations on Italy and its Inhabitants*, which was a source book most lavishly used by Mrs. Radcliffe, Grosley makes light of the Roman Inquisition, distinctly stating that when he was in Rome, in 1758, the Inquisition had passed no capital sentence for over one hundred years. He continues: 'Everything there is transacted in private by spiritual and pecuniary penalties.' Did Mrs. Radcliffe, who drew so heavily on Grosley, accept these statements? She did not. On the contrary, she defiantly dates *The Italian* exactly at 1758. She says: 'It was in that very year that Vivaldi in the vaults of the Inquisition heard the thrilling groans of the tortured and was bound by masked familiars on the rack.'[49]

image of a woman, representing the horrors of the grave by such details as a devouring worm, lizard and toad. This was exactly the sort of material to suit Mrs. Radcliffe's purpose. *The Italian* also shows Grosley's influence. See C. F. McIntyre: *Ann Radcliffe in relation to her time* (Yale Univ. Press 1920), and J. M. S. Tompkins: 'Ramond de Carbonnières, Grosley and Mrs. Radcliffe' (*Review of English Studies*, July, 1929).

47 J. M. S. Tompkins, *The Popular Novel in England*, 1770-1800, (1932), p. 274 f.

48 See *Critical*, March, 1792, on Mrs. Robinson's *Vancenza*.

49 See J. M. S. Tompkins, 'Ramond de Carbonnières, Grosley and Mrs. Radcliffe' (*Review of English Studies*, July, 1929).

Scott's remarks as to the authenticity of Mrs. Radcliffe's background would seem to indicate that, when the canons of literary criticism run counter to ingrained prejudice, literary criticism is cast to the winds. He says: 'We have been told, that in this beautiful romance [*The Italian*] the customs and rules of the Inquisition have been violated; a charge more easily made than proved, and which, if true, is of minor importance, because its code is happily unknown to us.' In a word, it was unnecessary for Mrs. Radcliffe to know what she was talking about, and it was unnecessary for Scott to possess enough knowledge of the Inquisition to be able to judge the verisimilitude of her novel.

The plot of *The Italian* opens with the Marchesa di Vivaldi's violent opposition to the proposed marriage of her son and one Ellena, whose birth is obscure. The Marchesa is supported in her opposition by her confessor, the mysterious and terrible Schedoni. The death of Bianchi, Ellena's aunt, leaves the young girl quite unprotected, and makes Vivaldi all the more determined to marry her. Ellena, however, is carried off by masked men, and confined in the Convent of the Black Penitents. Here she is treated with rigorous contempt by the stately abbess, but not more so than the unfortunate nuns, all of whom are racked by secret sufferings and treated like convicts in a particularly inhumane prison. Vivaldi succeeds in finding Ellena at the very moment when she is being forced to take the veil. He helps her to escape. They evade many dangers and throw dust in the eyes of their pursuers. Ellena takes refuge in an Ursuline Convent at Celano.

Meanwhile the Marchesa di Vivaldi is passing through a storm of passionate resentment at the attitude of her son. Schedoni skilfully plays on her feelings, and, at a moment when her mood might have softened, he sedulously aggravates her pride and anger until he has wrought her to his purpose, which is the murder of Ellena. The subtlety with which he works upon her temperament and mood shows that Mrs. Radcliffe at last understands the interplay of character. Schedoni is like a cat playing with a mouse. Detailed arguments at length give place to broken-off phrases which suggest the murder, but avoid plain speech. Schedoni finally manœuvres the Marchesa into imagining that the idea is hers, not his. The next day, at the Church of San Nicoli, she is led deeper into the toils, and she authorises him to do the deed which he offers himself to perform. Her acquiescence, her sudden fear of the course to which she has committed herself, and of Schedoni in whose power she must henceforth be—these are excellently shown. At the last moment she postpones the final decision. Schedoni is disappointed, but does not despair. He sets in motion the machinery of the Inquisition, and Vivaldi and Ellena are both found and taken into custody. There is a tremendous scene in which Vivaldi is examined by the chief Inquisitor. Ellena is taken to a lonely house by the sea, where Schedoni comes to murder her. At the very moment when his arm is raised to strike, he observes that she is wearing a miniature of himself, and recoils in horror at the idea that he has attempted to kill his own daughter.

Ellena is not really the daughter of Schedoni. She is his niece. Schedoni, really the Count Ferando di Bruni, has a past stained with many crimes. Having caused his elder brother to be assassinated, he married that brother's wife, but stabbed her when he feared she would detect his crime. This unfortunate woman survived, however, and lived on in the Convent of the Black Penitents long enough to meet Ellena, the child of her first husband. Schedoni, at the last, poisons himself in prison. The Marchesa di Vivaldi dies repentant, and Ellena and Vivaldi marry.

Of the many magnificent descriptions in this novel we must omit all save that of Schedoni, and that which leads up to the appointed murder at Spalatro's lonely house by the sea. Thus for the first time we see Schedoni, a being who resembles Milton's Satan, a further development of Kruitzner, a fore-runner of Byron's sinister heroes:

His figure was striking, but not so from grace; it was tall, and, though extremely thin, his limbs were large and uncouth, and as he stalked along, wrapt in the black garments of his order, there was something terrible in its air; something almost superhuman. His cowl too, as it threw a shadow over the livid paleness of his face, increased its severe character, and gave an effect to his large melancholy eye, which approached to horror. His was not the melancholy of a sensible and wounded heart, but apparently that of a gloomy and ferocious disposition. There was something in his physiognomy extremely singular, and that cannot easily be defined. It bore the traces of many passions which seemed to have fixed the features they no longer animated. An habitual gloom and severity prevailed over the deep lines of his countenance; and his eyes were so piercing, that they seemed to penetrate, at a single glance, into the hearts of men, and to read their secret thoughts; few persons could support their scrutiny, or even endure to meet them twice. Yet, notwithstanding all this gloom and austerity, some rare occasions of interest had called forth a character upon his countenance entirely different; and he could adapt himself to the tempers and passions of persons whom he wished to conciliate with astonishing facility.[50]

The scene between Ellena and Schedoni on the sea-shore is finely conceived; the scene in which Schedoni comes to murder Ellena and makes his terrible discovery surpasses anything that Mrs. Radcliffe wrote. This entire chapter is perfectly sustained. There is the rising tide of fear and evil, the altercation between Spalatro and Schedoni, with its turgid dialogue hinting at horrors, and culminating in the words: 'Give me the dagger'. Mrs. Radcliffe, that lover of Shakespeare, found this inspiration in *Macbeth*. 'You forget,' says Schedoni, threatening Spalatro, his reluctant minion, 'You forget that I know you; you forget the past.'

'No . . . I remember it too well; I wish I could forget; I remember it too well. I have never been at peace since. The bloody hand is always before me; and often of a night, when the sea roars, and storms shake the house, THEY have come, all gashed up as I left them, and stood before my bed! I have got up, and run out upon the shore for safety.'

'Give me the dagger,' said the confessor after a long pause;

50 *The Italian* (ed. Ballantyne, 1824), ch. ii, p. 546.

'Take up the cloak and follow to the staircase. Let me see whether your valour will carry you so far . . . Give me the dagger.'

'You have it already, Signor.'

'True,' said the monk, 'ascend softly or our steps may awaken her.'

'You said I was to wait at the foot of the stairs, signor, while you—'

'True, true, true!' muttered the confessor, and had begun to ascend, when his attendant desired him to stop. 'You are going in darkness, signor, you have forgotten the lamp' . . . Schedoni took it angrily, without speaking, and was again ascending, when he hesitated, and once more paused. 'The glare will disturb her,' thought he, 'it is better to go in darkness.' Yet—he considered that he could not strike with certainty without a light to direct his hand.[51]

This chapter not only excels in the vivid urgency of the action, but reveals also a psychological insight which ordinarily Mrs. Radcliffe was very far from possessing. She shows Schedoni in the grip of the ruthless determination which has devoured his life—the determination to win power by any means. But this deed which he contemplates is more appalling than any he has already perpetrated, and his meeting with Ellena on the shore has awakened in him the unusual feeling of pity. Pity and ambition struggle within him, and he betrays this inner tumult by his abrupt and contradictory commands, his hesitations, and his assumed stoicism. Mrs. Radcliffe thus gives us the clue to his thoughts:

The emotions of his mind were violent and contradictory. At the very instant, when his heart reproached him with the crime he had meditated, he regretted the ambitious views he must relinquish if he failed to perpetrate it, and regarded himself with some degree of contempt for having hitherto hesitated on the subject. He considered the character of his own mind with astonishment, for circumstances had drawn forth traits, of which, till now, he had no suspicion. He knew not by what doctrine to explain the inconsistencies, the contradictions, he experienced, and, perhaps it was not one of the least that in these moments of direful and conflicting passions, his reason could still look down upon their operations, and lead him to a cool though brief examination of his own nature. But the subtlety of self-love still eluded his inquiries, and he did

51 *Ibid.*, ch. xx, p. 635.

> not detect, that pride was, even at this instant of self examination, and of critical import, the master spring of his mind.[52]

It is not merely for the reasons we have stated that *The Italian* is Mrs. Radcliffe's best work. In structure also it is far superior to her other writings, and most of its terrors have the advantage of being real. Mrs. Radcliffe's method of creating mysteries only to explain them away ended by exasperating the nerve-racked reader. Schedoni and Spalatro could not be explained away, and the reader, sharing vicariously in Ellena's dangers, does not feel that he has been deliberately fooled.

After *The Italian*, Mrs. Radcliffe wrote no more for a considerable time. Her public had grown weary of being tricked by false alarms, and criticism became more audible. Furthermore the market was flooded by an immense crowd of imitators, who fastened only on such sensational parts of Mrs. Radcliffe's technique as were imitable. Terror was divorced from beauty; terror was divorced from virtue; and Mrs. Radcliffe had the misery of observing the degeneration of the novel she had initiated. It was but too easy to confuse the originator with her self-styled disciples and to attribute to Mrs. Radcliffe's influence the egregious works of those who were incapable of understanding her aim. There is proof that Mrs. Radcliffe was hypersensitive to the acid criticisms now launched against the Gothic novel. She withdrew more and more from a publicity which she had never coveted and which now became most painful to her. When she again took up her pen, it was to attempt an historical novel. This had 'all the faults of the historical novel before Scott, and none of her own merits.'[53] She devoted much time to studying in old sources the social background of Henry III's reign. The result of these researches was *Gaston de Blondeville*, written in 1802 and published posthumously. Since Mrs. Radcliffe was so dissatisfied with this novel that she left it

52 *Ibid.*, ch. xx. p. 632.
53 George Saintsbury, in *Camb. Hist. of Engl. Lit.*, xi, p. 301, footnote.

unpublished during the remaining twenty-one years of her life, it would not be just to criticise it seriously. In *Gaston de Blondeville* Mrs. Radcliffe deliberately abandons the elements of her characteristic type of fiction. Her romantic descriptions are no more; sensibility is eliminated; and her peculiar technique of creating terror from trifles is cast aside in favour of a real ghost. This flat-footed apparition alarms far less than the tiniest mouse scurrying in the wainscot of Udolpho. Mrs. Radcliffe's historical data stick out through the skin of her narrative, and on this sorry steed she jerks her weary way through the forest of Arden—a forest not a revelation of primeval beauty as at Fontanville, but simply a large number of trees growing close together.

Mrs. Radcliffe must be judged not merely by her works, but by their influence. Turning one's eyes from the more sensational aspects of the Gothic novel which have produced such a spate of modern 'thrillers', one can find evidence of the more subtle elements, handed down to us through such writers as Maturin, Godwin, Ainsworth, Hawthorne, Poe and Henry James. These owe much to other sources than Mrs. Radcliffe, and no doubt many of them would have repudiated the notion of being indebted to her, however indirectly, but it must be remembered that it was, nevertheless, Mrs. Radcliffe who gave the tale of terror its first real impetus in England. More interesting still was her influence on poets. She helped to turn Scott's attention to the past; she kindled the imagination of such men as Byron. It was her fate that greater minds than her own should fully express her half-articulate inspirations. With all her faults (and they are great) Mrs. Radcliffe deserves to be remembered amongst these who have permanently influenced English literature.

Of the many women who followed the Gothic vogue only one other deserves mention. Mary Shelley, influenced by German ghost stories and by the vague scientific notions current at the time, determined to write a tale which would terrify her readers. This intention was the result of a competition proposed by Byron to while away an evening at Lake Leman. At first Mary Shelley could not hit upon a subject. Then she had a dream which she embodied in *Frankenstein* (1818).[54] The story is so well-known that it is unnecessary to outline its plot. The most glaring fault in its structure is due to the fact that, having begun 'It was on a dreary night in November', Mrs. Shelley later inserted four prefatory chapters. The theme of the mechanical monster too great for his creator to control gave ample scope for frightful adventures. This monster, oppressed by his isolation among human beings who fear and hate him, becomes a satanic character, terrible in his pride and malignancy. There are queer echoes of Godwin and Mary Wollstonecraft in the protracted account of his education, and in the evil effects upon him of humanitarian doctrines. This aspect of *Frankenstein* links it to the *tendenz* fiction of this period, which must be considered briefly in the following chapter.

54 Mary Shelley also wrote:
(a) *Valperga, or the life and adventures of Castruccio, Prince of Lucca* (1823).
(b) *The Last Man* (1826).
(c) *Perkin Warbeck* (1830).
(d) *Lodore* (1835).
(e) *Falkner* (1837).

Chapter V

THE DIDACTIC NOVEL

'Our unsexed female writers now instruct, or confuse, us and themselves in the labyrinth of politicks, or turn us wild with Gallick frensy.'
(Mathias, *Pursuits of Literature*)

'I know that the earth is the great Bridewell of the Universe.'
(William Godwin, *Fleetwood*)

The difference in aim between *tendenz* and other kinds of fiction, during the eighteenth century, was the difference between sensitiveness and sensibility. Sensibility had luxuriated in trumped-up causes of emotion. In the *tendenz* novel there was real sensitiveness. It was in closer contact with the facts of life, and took cognizance of real aspects of human suffering. Such aspects became increasingly evident towards the end of the century, and the output of *tendenz* fiction grew in proportion. Many reasons contributed towards this preoccupation with social and political problems. Social neglect might truthfully be regarded as a characteristic of eighteenth century England. The criminal code, the prison system, the conditions of the working class, the lack of adequate educational and medical facilities for the poor, the neglect of the aged and infirm, the misguided and cruel treatment of the insane—these for a long time had needed reform, but now such miseries were aggravated by the enclosure of common land, and by the beginnings of the industrial revolution. Increasing discontent was fanned by the new spirit of democratic enquiry which made itself felt in England during the American War of Independence and the early phases of the French revolution. Radicals were inflamed by the spectacle of France embattled against class distinctions and invidious privilege. The reflections of philosophers were based on the theories of Voltaire and Rousseau. One might have supposed that only faith and courage were needed to bring the ideal of justice to earth. It followed that, if a political conception of justice could be realised, justice could be established as the foundation of human existence. It seemed (as it still seems) as if all the evils of life might be banished by the application of just principles. Justice was a flaming sword by which the hydra-headed monster of oppression and suffering might be slain, and a new era of freedom might dawn. Nothing is more intoxicating than an ideal. In this divine intoxication it seemed possible to assert that men are born equal and free. Starting from these premises lovers of freedom, that is to say lovers of justice, developed an argument which could be applied to all forms of human bondage. Of these the bondage of civilisation seemed responsible for all the miseries of civilised society, and the life of the natural man alone seemed to offer the conditions of a free and harmonious existence. Social grievances seemed to arise from the assertion of baseless privilege, and so this declaration of the human being's right to justice had many facets. It sought to abolish the prerogative of rank and wealth, the traditional privileges of institutions whether political, social, or ecclesiastical; it abhorred the slave trade; it anathematised the endless bondage of the poor. Certain women extended the argument of justice to their own sex, and showed that the subjection of women was no less flagrant than any other aspect of traditional injustice. On all these fronts the wordy battle raged, and the philosophic champions of justice ingenuously imagined that because their arguments were irrefutable those who profited by power and privilege must be convinced, and therefore must yield. Every literary means was employed to drive home the principles of justice, and the novel, because of its popular appeal, was regarded as an excellent means of propaganda.

But unfortunately propaganda and art neither propose the same aims nor employ the same means. Art may teach, but only obliquely, and, however much it may convey some judgment of life, it seems certain that this result must be incidental to its purpose. The philosophic novelists used fiction as a convenient means of expression and were not primarily concerned with the artistic possibilities of the novel. It was, therefore, to be expected that their contribution to fiction would be meagre. They did a service to the novel by introducing the wider issues of human life, but we cannot estimate the value of their contribution by the value of their philosophic ideas. Fiction may (and, it may be contended, should) suggest the abstract, but it is inherent in the technique of the novel to use life as its symbolic medium. It is only by such means that fiction may teach. To reduce the characters in the novel to mouthpieces for doctrine, or to puppets whose behaviour must prove some philosophic contention is to negate the purpose of fiction. Those who achieved success as didactic novelists did so only when, in obedience to an artistic impulse, they created real people and involved these characters in a plot which, while it bore out the didactic purpose, was yet compatible with human existence. In a word, success in didactic fiction is possible only when the writer succeeds in reconciling the didactic purpose with the technique of art.

John Moore of *Zeluco* fame, although he had seldom lost a chance of exposing the errors of human society, was, nevertheless, chiefly interested in the psychological aspects of his novels. Robert Bage, Thomas Holcroft and William Godwin had a more doctrinal purpose. Their novels reveal at once the individuality and the strength of their inspirations, and the weakness due to their didactic aim. Bage and Holcroft unquestioningly used the epistolary form, which was, in fact, quite unsuited to their kind of story-telling, and yet, by the power of their convictions and by flashes of realism, they compensated in part for their too obvious pedagogy. Godwin's *Caleb Williams* (1794), that peculiar mixture of sociology and Gothicism, is in a sense a masterpiece, but its power is due not to its sociological purpose, but to its use of suspense and terror.

There were opposing tendencies influencing the attitude of women novelists towards *tendenz* fiction. They had thrown themselves wholeheartedly into moral didacticism not only because it was moral, but because its serious purpose pleased their earnestness. Now the novel of doctrine offered further scope for teaching, but unhappily the social and political problems involved were regarded either as beyond women's ability, or as a most unsuitable field for feminine speculation. Thus it was that few women took sides in the vexed questions which now cloaked themselves in fiction. Not many women indeed could have vindicated political interests as did that lady who incurred the disapproval of Robespierre. He asked witheringly: 'Since when have women interested themselves in politics?' And he was answered: 'Since they have become liable to be guillotined.' Mrs. Smith's reply is as convincing, though less deadly:

> Women, it is said, have no business with politics. Why not? Have they no interest in the scenes that are acting around them, in which they have fathers, brothers, husbands, sons, or friends, engaged? Even in the commonest course of female education, they are expected to acquire some knowledge of history; and yet, if they are to have no opinion of what *is* passing, it avails little that they should be informed of what *has passed*, in a world where they are subject to such mental degradation; where they are censured as affecting masculine knowledge if they happen to have any understanding; or despised as insignificant triflers if they have none.[1]

In *Desmond*, as we have already seen, Mrs. Smith used the novel form as a mere frame-work for her political views. Still, she struck some shrewd blows through the mouths of those dramatis personæ whom we must hesitate to designate as characters. She despises the corruption of party politics, the arrogance of ancient titles, the insolence of 'mushroom nobility' and the ignorant pretentions of the new rich. The conversation between General Wallingford and Lord Newminster concerning the French Revolution and its repercussions

1 Charlotte Smith, *Desmond* (Dublin ed., 1792), Preface, p. iii.

in England is most amusing. Mrs. Smith manages very skilfully the constituents of comedy in this scene. We listen to the inveterate prejudice and stupidity of these self-appointed critics, each reinforcing the bellowing of the other, to the accompaniment of Mrs. Fairfax's ladylike lamentations.

> 'Rot the people,' cried the noble Peer: 'I wish they were all hanged out of the way, both in France and here too. What business have a set of blackguards to have an opinion about liberty, and be cursed to them? . . . By Jove, Sir, I'd set fire to their assembly, and mind no more shooting them all, than if they were so many mad dogs.'[2]

But alas! too soon these glorious imbecilities are reduced to the level of actual controversy by Desmond's address on the evils of the feudal system.[3] Later we are given the queasy views of the church dignitary: ' 'Tis an uneasy thing, a very uneasy thing, for a man of probity and principles to look in these days into a newspaper. Greatly must every man be troubled to read . . . wrath of heaven . . . perfidious and irreverent people . . . They have done the most unjust and wicked of all actions in depriving the church of its revenues.'[4] This Doctor of Divinity blusters and browbeats at the slightest effort to take the opposite view ('I won't argue, I won't commit myself, nor endeavour to convince a person whose principles are, I see, fundamentally wrong'); and, when a quiet man who opposes him scores several points, the Doctor swells with rage, crying: 'I don't know who that person is, but he is very ignorant, and very ill-bred.'[5]

At the beginning of *Desmond*, Mrs. Smith makes her characters sufficiently alive to rebut the suggestion that they are merely pegs on which to hang her arguments. They are, of course, merely types, but they are presented *en ronde* and, without being in the least individual, they are human. They look and speak as such types look and

2 *Ibid.*, i, p. 37.
3 *Ibid.*, vol. i, p. 40.
4 *Ibid.*, vol. i, p. 47.
5 *Ibid.*, vol. i, p. 48.

speak in real life. It is for that reason that their statements do not appear a deliberate pattern of didacticism, but are the natural expression of their opinions and prejudices, that is to say of the opinions and prejudices of their caste. This touch of humanity, however, soon vanishes and we are left with a trackless waste of doctrine.

Mrs. Smith went far in her revolutionary doctrines, but she did not really apply the principle of freedom to women. It was reserved for Mary Wollstonecraft to throw down the gauntlet for her sex. She was not the first to see in education the best way of raising the status of women. Mary Astell, a hundred years before, had made a reasoned plea for women's education, but Mary Wollstonecraft had views undreamt of by the gentle Mary Astell. That we are here concerned simply with Mary Wollstonecraft's contribution to fiction restricts us to the barest summary of her life and of her epoch-making book *The Vindication of the Rights of Woman*, and yet it is only through the knowledge of these that we can interpret her attempts at fiction.

Mary Wollstonecraft was the eldest daughter of a most unhappy marriage. Her mother was an Irish woman of good family. Her father, the son of a wealthy manufacturer in Spitalfields, started out in life with £10,000, but soon reduced his children to beggary and his wife to despair by his profligacy and tyranny. Mary's childhood burned into her mind squalid scenes of drunkenness, violence and domestic misery. This helps to explain her distrust of marriage and her corroding consciousness of women's subjection. The poverty in which the family lived made schooling impossible. She picked up what learning she could in the midst of household drudgery and everlasting migration from place to place in obedience to her father's whims. She had always had to contrive some sort of livelihood for herself and her family. After her mother's death, she no longer had a home and turned to governessing as a means of support. Her employer, Lady Kingsborough, is the original of Mary's 'fine lady' in the *Vindication*—her conception of what a woman should not be. No doubt, life as she saw it at Mitchelstown Castle was vapid and heartless, but her pride and her loneliness as a dependent must have added to her feeling of isolation. It was not merely the minor tragedy of a lonely governess: it was the consciousness of mental powers undeveloped and failing to find expression; it was the consciousness of youth, beauty and capacity for emotion withering unused. But Mary was not long to remain in this servitude. Lady Kingsborough, jealous of her daughter's affection for the governess, found an occasion to get rid of her, and Mary went to try her literary fortunes in London. At this point she really began to live as a woman and as a writer, but she brought to this new life the memories of the old. Her struggles, her generosity to her useless and disloyal sisters, her removal to Paris and her life with Imlay are too well known to need elaboration. *The Vindication* coupled with her unsanctified union drew upon her horrified condemnation. Her attempts at suicide and her marriage with Godwin offered the public further sources of criticism. Her death released her from the struggle of trying to solve the problems of woman's emancipation and woman's happiness.

The Vindication of the Rights of Woman caused the chivalrous Walpole to stigmatise the author as a 'hyena in petticoats', a 'philosophic serpent'. To the modern reader it appears a gallant but rather badly written statement of obvious facts. To Mary Wollstonecraft's contemporaries it was a shocking proclamation of revolt not merely against men's authority, but against female propriety. Indeed Mary deliberately attacked the superficiality of feminine conventions. She wished them to abandon the pernicious cult of sensibility, the 'deluge of false sentiments and overstretched feelings', the narrow opportunism of their upbringing. Rousseau had denied women the power of reasoning, and had stated that works of genius were beyond their capacity. He had recommended that 'all the ideas of women . . .

should be directed to the study of men.' 'Educate women like men', said Rousseau, 'and the more they resemble our sex the less power will they have over us.' This training for the seraglio disgusted Mary Wollstonecraft. She replied: 'This is the very point I aim at. I do not wish them to have power over men; but over themselves.'[6] In education she saw the key to this self-government. Through education women might realise their mental powers, and share in the wider possibilities of life. Women's economic dependence on man induced in them a hypocritical attitude and an undue preoccupation with emotions. And what of the women who, for one reason or another, were cast upon their own resources? Education would, at least, give them a means of self-support. Women should purify their hearts. They should develop a sense of dignity. They should remember, said Mary, that until now they had never had a chance to show what they might become: 'Men of genius and talents have started out of a class, in which women have never yet been placed.'[7]

Since Mary Wollstonecraft disliked novels, it is curious that she should have attempted to become a novelist. She may have done so simply because she believed in the didactic power of fiction, or she may have sought in such writing to express, and thus to rid herself of, the memories which preyed upon her. Fiction, however, was not her medium. Hers was a philosophical, though not always a logical, mind. She had not the novelist's gift of creating characters and weaving a pattern of life. All her attempts at fiction are thinly veiled autobiography, and since the circumstances of her life had aroused in her a strong sense of women's grievances, her fragments of fiction are strongly polemical. Indeed, by a curious anomaly, it is in the main this propagandist purpose which galvanises her stories into life. The character who represents herself lives by the impassioned sincerity of her sufferings and her beliefs. Other characters only come to life when they

A Vindication of the Rights of Woman (ed. Pennell), p. 80.

Ibid., p. 102.

are impassioned by their theories or by their wrongs. These crude and confused outpourings are not really novels, and yet there are grim patches of reality, sudden glimpses of power which make it impossible to dismiss Mary Wollstonecraft as a novelist. There is occasionally a passage which shows the style which she might have achieved, had she lived long enough to find a mental outlook which would have permitted her to remember without agony, and to fight against social injustice without sacrificing artistic principles.

Mary Wollstonecraft's first attempt at story-telling was *The Cave of Fancy* which she began in 1787, and never finished. This is a strange mixture of morbid reminiscence and philosophic deliberation. It begins in Johnsonian style, and seems to have an echo of *Rasselas*. A sage, who lives in a hut and has control over spirits, adopts a child whose mother has been drowned in a shipwreck, and decides to educate her. One branch of her education is by means of a variety of stories and characters presented to her in the Cave of Fancy. Then follows a specimen of these stories, which begins 'My mother was a most respectable character, but she was yoked to a man whose follies and vices made her ever feel the weight of the chain. The first sensation I recollect, was pity.' That is Mary's youth. There is a blending of identifiable incidents and inventions, and here appear the chief constituents of her later novels. We hear of an unhappy love affair, of a marriage to a family benefactor, undertaken to please her mother. A consciousness of unusual gifts and dreams of a great love are here expressed for the first time. 'I was afraid of the unmarked vacuity of common life'.[8]

> I grasped a mighty whole and smiled on the king of terrors; the tie which bound me to my friends he could not break; the same mysterious knot united me to the source of all goodness and happiness. I had seen the divinity reflected in a face I loved; I had read immortal characters displayed on a human countenance and forgot myself while I gazed.[9]

8 Mary Wollstonecraft, *The Cave of Fancy* (*Posthumous Works*, 1798), iv, p. 142.
9 *Ibid*., p. 151.

Mary, a Fiction (1788) is a further development of the same theme—the theme of Mary's life. There are scenes from her childhood, presentation of the characters of her father, mother and elder brother. Her friend, Fanny Blood, here appears as Ann, and there is a description of Mary's journey to Portugal and of Fanny's death. The rescue during the storm at sea is autobiographical also. Mary wrote this novel before meeting Imlay. It is evidently the work of one in great mental distress. The heroine reveals a pressing need to be understood and loved, a need which is frustrated by her mother's preference for her elder brother, by Ann's passive acceptance of her affection, and by her lover's death. She ends by dragging out her life with a husband to whom she has been joined in a marriage of convenience. The concluding words show her anticipating death with a sense of relief.

The Wrongs of Woman; or Maria, a Fragment[10] develops Mary Wollstonecraft's subject more fully, and brings into prominence her arguments against women's subjection. At the opening of the story we find Maria in a private asylum where her husband has caused her, though sane, to be confined. One of the attendants, called Jemima ('she had only a claim to a Christian name, which had not secured her any Christian privileges'), impressed Mary as a person who might help her to escape. She convinces Jemima of her sanity. Meanwhile she becomes interested in a fellow prisoner called Henry Darnford, and is soon assured that he, like herself, is the victim of an intrigue. He lends her books in which political theories are expounded. Through Jemima's help, he visits her, and tells her the story of his life, in which Imlay's is partly embodied.

Jemima's story is not an echo of anything in Mary's own life. It is an accumulation of misery designed to show the injustices which a woman might endure. Jemima's father seduced her mother. They were both servants in a rich house. The erring woman was dismissed in disgrace. The man was slightly reproved

10 Published posthumously in 1798.

and allowed to keep his position. Jemima is born at the expense of her mother's life. Her father marries, and Jemima is apprenticed to one of her step-mother's friends who keeps a slop-shop in Wapping. There she endures the harshest treatment. At the age of sixteen, the unwilling victim of her master's brutality, she is thrown into the street by her jealous mistress. Nothing remains but the life of the streets, which she describes with a grim ferocity. She finally becomes the mistress of a literary man. He dies. She is friendless again. Want of a character prevents her from getting domestic employment, and she cannot sew well enough to support herself by needlework.

> At last I got recommended to wash in a few families, who did me the favour to admit me into their houses, without the most strict enquiry, to wash from one in the morning till eight at night for eighteen or twenty pence a day. On the happiness to be enjoyed over a wash-tub I need not comment; yet you will allow me to observe, that this was a wretchedness of situation peculiar to my sex. A man with half my industry, and, I may say, abilities, could have procured a decent livelihood.[11]

She hurts her leg, suffers from the wretchedness of the hospital system, and is dismissed scarcely able to stand and with nowhere to go. She is refused a piece of bread by a householder who bids her go to the workhouse. She does, and this is her comment: 'What are the common run of workhouses, but prisons, in which many respectable old people, worn out by immoderate labour, sink into the grave in sorrow, to which they are carried like dogs.'[12] After she has spent some time in the workhouse, she is offered the position of attendant in an asylum, which she accepts, although she knows the cruelties to which she will become a party. 'What should induce me to be the champion of suffering humanity? Who ever risked anything for me? Who ever acknowledged me to be a fellow-creature?'[13]

11 Mary Wollstonecraft, *The Wrongs of Women* (*Posthumous Works*, 1798), i p. 116.
12 *Ibid.*, p. 124.
13 *Ibid.*, p. 127.

Then follows Maria's narrative, written for the future information of her infant daughter. Maria is Mary Wollstonecraft, and again we have a presentation of her youth, this time fully elaborated. It is a terrible indictment of her father and of her elder brother, 'the deputy-tyrant of the house'. There is a poignant description of her mother's death. She tells of the long months of watching by her mother's bed; of her brother's neglect of this mother who adored him. Mary describes her mother's last moments:

> I shall not dwell on the death-bed scene, lively as is the remembrance of the emotion produced by the last grasp of my mother's cold hand; when blessing me, she added, 'A little more patience, and all will be over!' Ah! my child, how often have these words rung mournfully in my ears—and I have exclaimed—'A little more patience, and I too shall be at rest.'[14]

Maria marries George Venables to escape from a home made unbearable by the authority of her father's servant-mistress. Venables turns out a drunken profligate. (Possibly Mary Wollstonecraft drew him with her eye on Bishop, the husband of her sister Eliza). A benevolent uncle (for whom alas! there was no parallel in Mary's family) supplies Maria with money which her husband invariably seizes. Here Mary Wollstonecraft lashes the law by which a husband owned all his wife's property, and might even (as did Venables) force a lock to get at her money. On the other hand, a mother could not lawfully snatch from her unwilling husband even enough to keep her children alive. 'When such laws were framed, should not impartial lawgivers have first decreed . . . that the husband should always be wiser and more virtuous than his wife, in order to entitle him, with a show of justice, to keep this idiot or perpetual minor, for ever in bondage?'[15]

Venables finally tries to compromise his wife with one of his friends so that he may blackmail him. In a similar situation Charlotte Smith shows the wife evading

14 *Ibid.*, p. 174.
15 *Ibid.*, p. 280.

the danger, but still considering it her duty to care for her husband. Mary Wollstonecraft shows Maria at once leaving her husband forever. At this juncture Maria's rich uncle dies, bequeathing all his money to Maria's little daughter and appointing Maria as guardian. Baulked of his hopes, her husband has her kidnapped and imprisoned in an asylum. He keeps the child, this being within his legal rights. While in the asylum Darnford becomes Maria's lover. They escape. Her husband sues Darnford for seduction. Darnford is obliged to leave England on urgent business, but Maria fights the case alone. In court she vindicates women, and states their grievances. The judge condemns her attitude, and the story breaks off here. A few notes indicate a possible end. Darnford deserts her. She hears that her child is dead and determines on suicide. Jemima enters with her child who has merely been hidden by the vengeful Venables, and Maria decides to live for her daughter's sake.

It is a very badly constructed novel, too obviously intended as a fictional supplement to the *Vindication*, but apart from its bearing on doctrinal fiction, it had aspects of reality which had been too long ignored by the women novelists.

Another feminist novel-writer who drew upon herself a storm of protest was Mary Hays (1760-1843). Without Mary Wollstonecraft's greatness of mind, she appears, like her, to have been obsessed by painful aspects of life. But whereas Mary Wollstonecraft dwelt on unhappy episodes in her life and made them the starting point for a wider feminist protest, Mary Hays appears to have suffered from frustration. Her novels are case books of morbid psychology, and however much she dissociated herself from her first heroine, Emma Courtney, that she could ever have conceived such a character testifies to her own abnormal outlook. *The Memoirs of Emma Courtney* (1796) describe the predicament of a young woman who, having singled out a man whom she considers suitable to mate with one of her high powers, cannot induce him to marry her or even take her as his mistress. She pursues him with the most terrifying determination, but in vain, and she makes a marriage of convenience with a man to whom she is indifferent. Nevertheless, she still loves the first-chosen, and has the melancholy satisfaction of soothing his dying hours, a transaction which enrages her long-suffering husband. Emma resents her husband's attitude as unreasonable tyranny, and considers her morbid sufferings and the circumstances which cause them as 'the unnatural and odious result of a distempered and unnatural civilisation'. Mary Hays seemed unable to understand that the problem she presented had nothing to do with the state of society.

The Victim of Prejudice (1799) had, on the contrary, a reasonable thesis. The book does not, however, convey a reasonable impression partly because of the exaggeration of the story by which the thesis is to be proved, and partly because it is told in the manner of sensibility. This high-flown style of telling terrible truths is grotesque.

Mary, the heroine of the novel, is the daughter of a woman who, betrayed and abandoned by a man of fashion, falls into evil ways and dies on the scaffold.[16] Mary grows up under the benevolent care of a philosophic gentleman called Ramond, and is idyllically happy until she arrives at the age of love. Her beauty subjects her to the odious attentions of the profligate Sir Peter Osborne, but she is consoled by the respectful adoration of William Pelham, a young man of ancient family and ample fortune. Mary and William are deeply in love, but William's father, furious at the prospect of such a misalliance, orders his son to travel abroad for two years. He departs, but first solemnly promises Mary that they will marry when he returns. Mary is full of forebodings that 'he will imbibe the contagion of a distempered civilisation', and that he will, therefore, become *a man of the world* (a phrase always used in italics). No sooner is William safely out of the way than

16 This, like Mrs. Opie's *Brother and Sister*, was an echo of Agnes Primrose in Mrs. Inchbald's *Nature and Art*.

Sir Peter Osborne becomes more resolute than ever in his pursuit, particularly when Mary's guardian dies and she is left alone and helpless. He decoys her to his house and ruins her. She refuses all his offers of 'reparation', and rushes into the street. By a great coincidence she meets William, now returned from Paris, and long since become 'a man of the world'. He breaks the news that he has married another, and she refuses with the wildest indignation his suggestion that they forget everything except their love. In vain does William argue that she cannot now stand alone; in vain he 'hinted that society would, with inexorable malignity, hunt me from its privileges; that with a mind peerless and unstained, I should yet suffer all the penalties of guilt, without possible appeal or redress.' Mary's 'spirit still triumphs in conscious rectitude.'

She endeavours to find work, but soon discovers that her unfortunate story causes the women to condemn and the men to pursue her. Still, she refuses to change her name, since she is guilty of no crime. Her betrayer endeavours to ensnare her again. He has her imprisoned for debt, involves her in all kinds of miseries, deprives her of every comfort and refuge, but fails to secure his ends. At the conclusion of this novel, we leave her dying of consumption and hoping for death.

The myth of the betrayed woman conveniently dying of a decline had long persisted in fiction. Mary Hays tore it to pieces, and asserted the need for a single standard in morality. This was a theme which engaged the attention of Mrs. Inchbald and Mrs. Opie. Mary Hays's treatment destroyed the effectiveness of her argument for the woman innocent but ruined. That it had great artistic possibilities was superbly proved long afterwards in *Tess of the d'Urbervilles*

Mary Hays's high-flown exaggerations were sufficiently absurd to provoke a burlesque, which duly appeared as *Memoirs of Modern Philosophers* (1800).

In this amusing book Elizabeth Hamilton[17] set herself particularly to satirise Mary Hays, and seldom lost an opportunity of tilting also at Godwin. She has no quarrel with Mary Wollstonecraft, regretting only that she so much over-stated her case.

The company of modern philosophers has its leader in the arch-villain Vallaton, who poses as a French revolutionary of good family. He is really a gutter-rat reared in a stew of vice, and his most respectable avocation has been that of a barber. The disciples of this plausible rogue are Mr. Glib, the rascally chemist; the befuddled Mr. Myope; the Goddess of Reason, a French adventuress who has followed Vallaton from France, and Miss Bridgetina Botherim. Bridgetina, that dwarfish little egoist, that arrogant and absurd country bumpkin, is enchanted with the new philosophy and rants its pretentious jargon from morning till night, to the mingled admiration and misery of her unfortunate mother, whose pastry is so much better than her grammar. Bridgetina, though hideous, is particularly enthusiastic about the philosophic tenet by which a woman may pursue the man she loves—not simply await his approach supinely. She pursues two men with perfect safety, as her face is in itself a padlock to her virtue. Not so the unfortunate Julia, the beloved daughter of the invalid Captain Delmond. She is beguiled by Vallaton's sophistries, so that she revolts against her parents, considers herself victimised even by the mention of honourable suitors, and flees to London with Vallaton. In due time he deserts her. She is found by her friends, but she has taken poison and dies. Vallaton goes to France with the Goddess of Reason who, when she tires of him, betrays him to the guillotine. Bridgetina, who is present at Julia's death-bed, is galvanised into sanity and goes home with her

[17] Her other works of fiction were: *Translation of the Letters of a Hindoo Rajah* (1796) and *The Cottagers of Glenburnie* (1808). This latter work, which preceded *Waverley*, was written to inculcate in the working classes a love of industry and orderliness. To stress her didactic point, Mrs. Hamilton presents with grim realism the ignorance, squalor and misery too often found in the villages she knew. It is well worth noting that her rustic dialogues are in the Scottish vernacular.

mother, her reform being the more firmly established by a candid friend who informs her that only by her ugliness has she escaped Julia's fate.

This brief outline of the plot makes it clear that Elizabeth Hamilton employed two methods of discrediting the revolutionary philosophers. She began by heaping ridicule upon them, but soon engaged herself in serious contradiction of their arguments. At first she manipulated the plot merely to expose the evils which resulted from a practical application of such pernicious views. Her efforts to reconcile burlesque and explicit moral teaching are naturally unsuccessful, and the best parts of the story are those in which she appeals to our sense of humour. Her comic effects are greatly heightened by her malicious trick of putting into the mouths of her unreasonable characters the very words of Godwin and Mary Hays. Such theorists arouse her laughter by their lack of proportion and by their intense and declamatory style. Indeed she finds in their beliefs the crowning proof that they are humourless. Bridgetina says: 'The energies of philosophical authors are all expended in gloomy masses of tenebrific shade. The investigators of mind never condescend to make their readers laugh.'[18] Mrs. Hamilton's philosophers can never be cornered in argument. They always take refuge in such redoubtable phrases as 'infinite causation', 'perfectibility' and 'the fable of superstition'. They have no use for goodness unless it flows 'from a conviction of general utility pursued through the maze of abstract reasoning.' They constitute a Hottentotian Society which aims at leaving forever 'the corrupt wilderness of ill-constituted society, the rank and rotten soil from which every finer shrub draws poison as it grows.'[19] Life among the Hottentots is the ideal of these reformers. When Bridgetina is dunned by tradesmen she sighs to be where such vulgarians would not intrude upon her towering fancy, 'but each congenial Hottentot, energising in his self-built

18 Elizabeth Hamilton, *Memoirs of Modern Philosophers* (3rd. ed. 1801), ii, p. 77.

19 For this quotation Mrs. Hamilton wickedly appends the footnote 'See *Caleb Williams*.'

shed, would be too much engrossed by forming projects for general utility, to break in upon my repose.'[20]

Bridgetina is the splendidly idiotic heroine of this burlesque. Having imbibed Godwin's principles from the loose leaves that wrap up her mother's snuff, her 'ardent sensibility' led her back to novels.

> As I read each sweet, delicious tale, I reasoned, I investigated, I moralised. What! said I to myself, shall every heroine of all these numerous volumes have a lover, and shall I remain 'a comfortless, solitary, shivering wanderer in the dreary wilderness of human society?' I feel in myself the capacity of increasing the happiness of an individual; but where is he? Does he live in this town? Have I seen him? How shall I find him? Does his breast sympathise with mine? An idea of young Gubbles came across my mind. Yes, said I, it must be he! I heaved a convulsive struggling sigh. Tears half delicious, half agonising, gushed in torrents from my eyes. O Gubbles! Gubbles! cried I, my importunate sensibilities, my panting tenderness, are all reserved for thee![21]

Bridgetina, undeterred by torrential rain, went at once to the chemist's shop where Gubbles was employed. He was there 'looking into the mouth of an old woman who sat upon the floor to have a tooth pulled out. The attitude was charming; the scene was interesting; it was impressive, tender, melancholy, sublime. My suffocating sensibilities returned.' Bridgetina throws herself into a chair and bursts into tears. Gubbles, quite staggered at her peculiar behaviour, plies her with hartshorn. She believes that he is deeply moved. 'The tenderness of Gubbles inspired the most delightful hope. "The delicious poison circulated through every vein." I gave myself up to the ardent feelings of a morbid imagination.' Within a week Gubbles has married the young woman with whom he has been 'walking out'. Bridgetina transfers her tumultuous affections to Dr. Henry Sidney. She knows he loves her because once when she got stuck on a stile 'Henry sprung to my assistance, and with manly energetic fervour tore my petticoat from the stump in which it was entangled.' She perceives that it

20 Elizabeth Hamilton, *Memoirs of Modern Philosophers* (3rd. ed. 1801), iii, p. 143.
21 *Ibid.*, ii, p. 89.

is with his that her mind was formed to mingle and that he is henceforth the arbiter of her fate. But what is that mysterious reserve that seals his lips? She determines to pursue him more assiduously than ever.

This was Mrs. Hamilton at the top of her bent. The more one enjoys such a method of attack, the more one must regret that she did not sustain it throughout her novel. Julia's story is dull, and Mrs. Hamilton's direct moralising has really no place in a work of fiction.

In Godwin's group of philosophic enthusiasts was one woman who found it possible to be doctrinal without abating her femininity. This was the charming and gifted Elizabeth Inchbald. She subscribed to Rousseau's view of civilised society, but avoided the opinions of the extremists. The fact that she was a devout Catholic insulated her against those theories of sexual liberty by which other 'philosophesses' were held to have unsexed themselves, but, in any case, it was in her nature to maintain a moderate attitude. She had no ungovernable passions. She was not repressed. She had no grievance against men. On the contrary, she greatly enjoyed their admiration and she understood their outlook. It was Mrs. Inchbald's fortune to be beautiful and beloved, irreproachable, highly talented, and moderately well-off. Because she was a happy woman she was essentially sane and sweet-tempered. Indeed the converse would be equally true. And added to her charm and equability was a most engaging simplicity of manner. These traits characterised her not merely as a woman, but as a novelist. From the day when as Elizabeth Simpson, she had determined to become an actress, and ran away from her father's farm in Suffolk it had been necessary for her to support herself. An impediment in her speech made it impossible for her to make a success of the stage, but her good looks secured her engagements. She continued to act even after her marriage to Inchbald, a needy actor. Her husband's death two years later threw her completely on her own resources, and to eke out her slender earnings she took to writing plays. These were successful, but it is on her achievement as a novelist that her fame depends.

A Simple Story (1791)[22] was Mrs. Inchbald's first achievement in fiction—an achievement insufficiently praised in its own time and even since. By the very simplicity of its aim it avoided alike the hysterical and complicated plots of sensibility, and the unnatural adventures of the Gothic tale. It took for its theme the relations of a little group of people whose reactions create the real interest of the narrative. They are no paragons: 'They are human creatures who are meant to be pourtrayed . . . and where is the human creature who has not some good qualities to soften, if not to counterbalance his bad ones?'[23] In characterisation, in its directness, in the surprising modernity of its tone, this is an unusual novel. Its structure, however, is very faulty. The story consists of two parts separated by a lapse of seventeen years.

Miss Milner, a lovely, flighty but good-hearted girl, falls in love with Dorriforth, her guardian. When Dorriforth succeeds to the family title and becomes Lord Elmwood, he considers it his duty to marry. He knows nothing of Miss Milner's affection, and intends to marry (without any feeling but respect) a lady who has been suggested to him as a suitable wife, when Miss Woodley (the confidante of Miss Milner), grieved for her friend's secret misery, tells Dorriforth the truth. He realises that he loves Miss Milner and their marriage is arranged. But it is Miss Milner's fate that she must ever play with fire, and she cannot give up the fashionable amusements which Lord Elmwood condemns, or forbear arousing his jealousy. There are frequent quarrels and Lord Elmwood breaks the engagement and determines to travel abroad. At the last moment they are reconciled and married. For four years they are perfectly happy. A daughter is born. Then Elmwood

22 Written in 1777.

23 The words actually occur in *Nature and Art* (ch. viii), but they are more applicable to *A Simple Story*.

goes to inspect his estates in the West Indies. His return is delayed, and Lady Elmwood, doubting his love for her, and weary of waiting, returns to the frivolous life, and takes a lover. When Elmwood comes home, he casts off his wife and even his daughter Mathilda. After some years of repentance Lady Elmwood dies.

The second part of the story deals with the reconciliation of Lord Elmwood with his daughter. Mathilda falls in love with her cousin, Rushbrook, Lord Elmwood's heir. They succeed in winning Elmwood's consent to their marriage, and all ends happily.

By a moral introduced in the penultimate paragraph, Mrs. Inchbald proclaims that her object was didactic. She says that she wished to show that Miss Milner's misfortunes were the result of an improper education, and she contrasts the superior character of Mathilda who was reared in the 'school of prudence, through adversity'. Actually, however, the main narrative seems so free from a didactic intention that, if Mrs. Inchbald had such a purpose at the beginning, one would say that she lost sight of it when she was caught up by the human interest of her story. The inartistic addition of Mathilda's vicissitudes may have been inspired by the intention of establishing a didactic contrast. On the other hand, it may have arisen because Mrs. Inchbald did not know when to stop, or because she wished somehow to make a happy ending. One must remember that, simply because she failed in structure, there is an inartistic gap of fifteen years in *Nature and Art*. The general impression created by *A Simple Story* is that Mrs. Inchbald first wrote Miss Milner's part of the story, and then introduced the didactic purpose as an afterthought. Mrs. Inchbald represents that education at a boarding school was responsible for the faults in Miss Milner's character. In fact, Miss Milner's faults are those of temperament which education could scarcely change unless it could make her anew. Throughout the novel Mrs. Inchbald shows Miss Milner impulsively acting from the depths of her nature, not from some superficial stratum of worldliness or custom. Indeed, in many cases, her wilfulness and frivolity are defensive—either to cloak her real feelings, or because her real feelings sting her into a perverse defiance. When, for example, Lord Elmwood does not come to the opera, but spends the evening with Miss Fenton whom he contemplates marrying, Miss Milner allows the rake, Lord Frederick Lawnley, to escort her to her carriage—not because she likes him, but because she is 'piqued—heart-broken—full of resentment against the object of her uneasiness, and inattentive to all that passed'; because she 'thought this the moment to retaliate'. That is the sort of reaction, common to women and to men alike, with which education has nothing to do. Not only does Miss Milner not care for this particular rake; she has an aversion to all rakes: 'What! love a rake, a man of professed gallantry! impossible! To me a common rake is as odious as a common prostitute is to the man of the nicest feelings. Where can be the joy, the pride, of inspiring a passion which fifty others can equally inspire.' And yet Sir Frederick Lawnley is the very rake with whom Miss Milner, years later, was unfaithful to her husband. This heroine has many facets to her nature. She is affectionate, generous to an enemy, free from pettiness. Yet she is unwise in her impulses, and she runs 'a course full of perils, of hopes, of fears, of joy, and at the end of sorrows; all exquisite of their kind, for exquisite were the feelings of her susceptible heart.' She is indeed no paragon, but Mrs. Inchbald, although she stresses the necessity for prudence and self-control, has no use for paragons. Such a one is Miss Fenton, very evidently despised by Mrs. Inchbald because she has no heart. Mrs. Inchbald has courage enough to explode the fallacy that women felt love only after they had been solicited in marriage. Miss Milner, with no apparent hope of a return from Dorriforth, cries out: 'I love him with all the passion of a mistress, and with all the tenderness of a wife.'[24]

So excellently has Mrs. Inchbald mixed the elements in Miss Milner that we debate her character and motives

24 Elizabeth Inchbald, *A Simple Story* (ed. Routledge, 1893), p. 76.

as if she were (as she is to us) a living person. Mrs. Inchbald meant us to do this. She used in fiction the dramatic technique of presenting behaviour and allowing us to draw our own inferences. She says: 'The reader must form a judgment of the ward of Dorriforth by her actions—by all the round of great or trivial circumstances that shall be revealed.'[25]

Mrs. Inchbald shows her dramatic instinct in fiction, but she avoids melodrama. Only when Miss Milner, to prevent a duel, pretends to love Lawnley is there any exaggeration, and then it is deliberate. For the rest there are no high-flown ebullitions, no explosions of rhodomontade. When feelings are tense they relieve themselves in action, often of the most trivial kind. When Dorriforth imperiously forbids Miss Milner to keep her evening engagement there is a painful silence. Then 'Mrs. Horton rose from her chair—moved the decanters and fruit round the table—stirred the fire—and came back to her chair again before another word was uttered. Nor had this good woman's officious labours taken the least from the awkwardness of the silence, which, as soon as the bustle she had contrived was over, returned in its full force.'[26] By such touches (and there are many of them) Mrs. Inchbald shows her acute observation of life, and her familiarity with those 'bits of business' which would relieve such awkward moments on the stage.

The other characters in the Miss Milner's story are as interesting as she herself. Dorriforth is stern and gentle; slow to love; loving greatly when his heart is given; but his love betrayed turns to hatred. Despite his goodness there are in his nature 'shades of evil'. Sanford is a strange compound. In Miss Milner's frivolous days he sets himself to mortify her. Indeed he even seems to persecute her, but his intention is to destroy her vanity, and when at last he believes in her sincerity, he is generous. He it is who reunites Miss Milner and Dorriforth, and when Miss Milner has fallen from virtue he succours her. Miss Woodley is a complete departure

25 *Ibid.*, p. 16.
26 *Ibid.*, p. 30 f.

from the type of old maid which, up to that time, was a convention in fiction. Fielding and every other had presented an old maid as a thwarted fury oozing bitterness at her single state, and ever hoping to marry no matter whom. Miss Woodley is very plain and very good-natured—a loyal friend to beauty in distress. She could always discover a virtue 'although of the most diminutive kind', and, for all her meekness, she has courage enough for the most difficult situations.

In *Nature and Art* (1796) Mrs. Inchbald postulates that natural education is superior to formal education. To prove this contention she presents two brothers, Henry and William, who in character and fortunes are a complete contrast. Henry, who has a happy knack with the violin, fiddles his way into a livelihood and helps to support his brother who, unable to find employment, decides to continue his studies at a university. In due time a great man, delighted with Henry's fiddling, is induced to give William a living of £500 a year. William climbs to affluence, marries for money and position and becomes a heartless snob. He ignores Henry and Henry's plebeian wife. The brothers quarrel. Henry's wife dies shortly afterwards, and he goes abroad taking his son with him. He is captured by savages, but years later his son (also named Henry) escapes to England with a letter consigning him to the care of his uncle William. He is reared with his cousin (also named William). Again Mrs. Inchbald presents the contrast of simple good-nature and sophisticated self-seeking, and in this latter case her contention is more strongly enforced because the two youths have had a very different upbringing. The elder Henry and William do not really support Mrs. Inchbald's thesis at all, because they were reared and educated side by side until about the age of twenty. The wide divergence between their characters cannot be ascribed to William's sojourn at the university, since it was apparent before he went there. Mrs. Inchbald tells us that both were educated at a grammar school. She shows us that from the beginning William was moody, proud, selfish and ungrateful, and that Henry was sunny, affectionate, spontaneous and ingenuous. Had she reasoned out this part of the story, she would have been forced to admit that the contrast between William and Henry was due, not to education or environment, but to their very different dispositions. The younger Henry, however, reared without any formal education, is an excellent argument in favour of Rousseauism, and throughout he reasons remorselessly on the anomalies, shams, and abuses of the civilised society in which he comes to live. The younger William's mechanical acceptance of established conditions and his easy parroting of conclusions which he has never questioned appear cheap. His superficial religion and semblance of morality have no connection whatever with his daily life, which is governed entirely by self-interest and self-indulgence. Henry, on the contrary, learns with wonder that there is a God, and another world; and, untrammelled by social clap-trap, he applies these religious principles to the world without him and within. Henry's enquiring mind, directed to the social inequalities and injustices which prevail, gives Mrs. Inchbald a very good opportunity to flay the selfishness, the toad-eating and the supercilious patronage of the rich, and the defencelessness of the poor. In her view the poor are in much the same category as the natural man—both are free from the stale and pernicious ideas which pervert the rich.

For the purpose of social satire Mrs. Inchbald's style is really admirable. It is direct, terse, pithy and ironic. For example, it would be hard to better her description of the manner in which William, the purse-proud dean, received the news that Henry's wife is dead. William and his wife Lady Clementina have never recognised this honest creature's existence, but—

> If Henry's wife were not fit company for Lady Clementina, it is to be hoped that she was company for angels; she died within the first year of her marriage, a faithful, an affectionate wife, and a mother.
>
> When William heard of her death, he felt a sudden shock; and a kind of fleeting thought glanced across his mind, that—'Had he known she had been so near her dissolution, she might have been

introduced to Lady Clementina; and he himself would have called her sister.'

That is (if he had defined his fleeting idea), 'They would have had no objection to have met this poor woman for the *last time*; and would have descended to the familiarity of kindred in order to have wished her a good journey to the other world.'[27]

And again, this description of the relations between the dean and Lady Clementina:

> If the dean had loved his wife but moderately, seeing all her faults clearly as he did, he must frequently have quarrelled with her; if he had loved her with tenderness, he must have treated her with a degree of violence in the hope of amending her failings; but having neither personal nor mental affection towards her, sufficiently interesting to give himself the trouble to contradict her will in anything, he passed for one of the best husbands in the world.[28]

Mrs. Inchbald's use of dialogue is trenchant and sardonic. One almost commiserates the smug dean subjected to the pitiless inquisition of his young nephew. When Richard the coachman is turned away, Henry puzzles over his uncle's form of dismissal: 'You shall never drive me again.' The omniscient and superior cousin William elaborates: 'Richard is turned away; he is never to get upon our coach-box again, never to drive any of us any more.'

> 'And was it pleasure to drive us, cousin? I am sure I sometimes pitied him: it rained sometimes very hard when he was on the box; and sometimes Lady Clementina has kept him a whole hour at the door all in the cold and snow: was that pleasure?'
>
> 'No,' replied young William.
>
> 'Was it honour, cousin?'
>
> 'No,' exclaimed his cousin with a contemptuous smile.
>
> 'Then why did my uncle say to him, as a punishment, "he should never—" '

The dean hastily intervenes to explain the relations of rich and poor:

> 'The poor are born to serve the rich.'
>
> 'And what are the rich for?'

27 Elizabeth Inchbald, *Nature and Art* (1796), ch. vi.
28 *Ibid.*, ch. xv.

'To be served by the poor.'
'But suppose the poor would not serve them?'
'Then they must starve.'

But, when cornered, the dean says that the poor will be rewarded in the world to come, and reveals under further questioning that in the world to come all persons are equal.

'But cannot this world try to be as good as that?'
'In respect to placing all persons on a level, it is utterly impossible; God has ordained it otherwise.'
'How! Has God ordained a distinction to be made, and will not make any himself?'[29]

By far the best part of the novel deals with William's seduction and desertion of the cottage-girl, Agnes Primrose. His sensuality and heartlessness, her deep love, humility, weakness and self-torture are finely traced. To him it is a casual adventure broken off to contract an ambitious marriage. When eventually it is proved that he is the father of her child, it involves him in no censure. The suffering and disgrace are all hers, and everything conspires to degrade her further. Finally, after long years of misery and wrongdoing, she is arrested for robbery and on the day of her trial is brought before the learned judge—her seducer, William. Eighteen years, which have brought her to the depths, have raised him to his eminence. It is a scene which has been greatly praised and which is too well-known to need quotation. Its intensity of feeling, its sense of fate, its contrasts, its pathos, its restraint make this a memorable achievement in the history of English fiction. When William puts on the black cap to condemn to death the woman for whose mis-spent life he is responsible, this gesture is intended to represent the triumph of worldly corruption over untutored simplicity, of riches over poverty, of masculine privilege over woman's defencelessness. It is the coping stone of Mrs. Inchbald's didactic and artistic purpose.

29 *Ibid.*, ch. xiii.

Mrs. Amelia Opie (1769-1853) inherited her father's radical principles, and his active interest in such social works of mercy as visiting hospitals, workhouses and prisons. She was friendly with Horne Tooke and an admirer of Mary Wollstonecraft. Both Holcroft and Godwin had wished to marry her. She was also on very good terms with Mrs. Barbauld, Mrs. Siddons, the Duc d'Aiguillon and other French emigrants. By the time Mrs. Opie commenced author, the French Revolution had reached a stage which damped, if it did not entirely quench, the fervour of English sympathisers. Mrs. Opie's novels, written during this revulsion of feeling, are anti-Revolutionary. Her didactic purpose is primarily moral, and her interest in social questions is chiefly a prolongation of those earnest principles which eventually caused her to become a Quaker. She stresses the necessity of Christian education, condemns the slave-trade and opposes the outlawry of women fallen from virtue. She teaches through domestic portraiture, and her novels reflect her own generosity and gentle charm. She had a pleasant, simple narrative style, and was particularly praised in her own day for her pathos, but she had not a sure touch, and, by comparison with Maria Edgeworth, she appears mediocre.

Her first novel, *Father and Daughter*, appeared in 1801. The story begins well:

> The night was dark—the wind blew keenly over the frozen and rugged heath, when Agnes, pressing her moaning child to her bosom, was travelling on foot to her father's habitation.
>
> 'Would to God I have never left it!' she exclaimed, as home and all its enjoyments rose in fancy to her view.

This is Agnes Fitzhenry who a few years before had eloped with the fascinating villain, Captain Clifford. Marriage had never been his intention, but he deluded her with promises and intercepted her appeals to her father, so that she remained with him, and her dependence was all the greater when her child was born. When, however, she learns that Clifford has deliberately foiled her efforts at reconciliation with her father, she determines to return home. She finds that her father has gone mad through grief at her behaviour, and resolves that his restoration to reason and his forgiveness will be the sole object of her life. Braving public opinion, she settles down in her own town and earns her living by needlework. She wins respect from people of her own class whose friendship she had forfeited, and love from the poor who knew her charity and sympathy. In due time she makes a home for her father, but he recovers his reason only for a few moments before he dies. He pardons and blesses her, and, overwhelmed by the event, she dies a few hours later. They are buried in the same grave. Clifford, disappointed in a childless marriage, owns his son and makes him his heir. The moral is explicitly stated at the end:

> Peace to the memory of Agnes Fitzhenry!—and may the woman who, like her, has been the victim of artifice, self-confidence, and temptation, like her endeavour to regain the esteem of the world by patient suffering, and virtuous exertion; and look forward to the attainment of it with confidence! But may she whose innocence is yet secure . . . tremble with horror.[30]

Mrs. Opie followed up the success of *Father and Daughter* with *Adeline Mowbray ; or, the Mother and Daughter* (1804). This is the best of her novels. It is based on the life of Mary Wollstonecraft which it treats with sympathetic understanding. Considering the rigid morality of the age, the sex of the writer and the nature of her subject, it speaks well for Mrs. Opie that she recognised Mary Wollstonecraft's sincerity and her essential clean-mindedness. Adeline Mowbray's story differs in detail from Mary's, but in general outline it is meant to be the same. Adeline, reared by a theorising mother, puts into practice the false doctrines with which her brain has been filled. She falls in love with the revolutionary philosopher Glenmurray, and considers that marriage would be a betrayal of his principles and hers. He loves her sincerely and does not wish to expose her to public censure, but she insists on dispensing with

30 Elizabeth Opie, *Father and Daughter* (9th. ed. ,1824), p. 231 f.

a ceremony which she considers quite meaningless. They go to Lisbon and are happy for a time, but soon realise that ostracism must be the penalty of their illegal union. Glenmurray dies, and Adeline's miseries increase a hundred-fold. For the sake of her daughter, she marries Berrendale, as bad an argument for marriage as could well be. He is selfish, miserly and unfaithful, and constantly afflicts her with references to his generosity in marrying a 'kept woman'. Finally he deserts her. Mrs. Mowbray had, from the beginning, cast off Adeline not merely for her association with Glenmurray, but because Adeline had unfortunately attracted the attentions of a profligate who had (bigamously) married her foolish mother. Mrs. Mowbray, influenced alike by real horror at her daughter's repudiation of marriage and by jealousy, had vowed that she would never forgive her until she saw her disgraced and on her death-bed. She repents this vow, but when she does find Adeline, she *is* on her death-bed. The reconcilation is complete and Adeline consigns her child to her mother's care.

A good example of Mrs. Opie's simple pathos is the occasion when the dying Adeline, accompanied by her little daughter, returns to her old home. It seems to her that she will never live to see it, that she cannot endure the emotions which arise within her.

> At length, however, she did reach it! and the lawn before Mrs. Mowbray's white house, her hayfields, and the running stream at the bottom of it burst in all their beauty on her view—'And this is my mother's dwelling!' exclaimed Adeline; 'and there was I born; and near here—' shall I die, she would have added, but her voice failed her.
>
> 'Oh! What a pretty house and garden!' cried Editha in the unformed accents of childhood; 'how I should like to live there!' The artless remark awakened a thousand mixed and overpowering feelings in the bosom of Adeline; and after a pause of strong emotion, she exclaimed, catching the little prattler to her heart—'You *shall* live there, my child!—yes, yes, you *shall* live there!'
>
> 'But when?' resumed Editha.
>
> 'When I am in my grave,' answered Adeline.

'And when shall you be there,' replied the unconscious child, fondly caressing her: 'pray, mamma—pray be there soon!'[31]

But Mrs. Opie does not always achieve this simplicity. Although this novel is most sensible in outlook, there are many evidences that the melodramatic exaggerations of sensibility still survived. Adeline goes mad for six months after Glenmurray's death. When she fears lest she may infect her child with smallpox, she runs frenzied around the streets; is found by an acquaintance whom she does not recognise; is put to bed muttering incoherently, bled and drugged. She remains unconscious until the following morning. When Adeline hears that her mother inveterately hates her, she horrifies Glenmurray by shrieking frantically and continually: 'She detests me!'

There is in this novel a considerable ability in the presentation of the characters. On the whole, these are not individual, but Mrs. Opie draws on a fount of humanity or on a knowledge of human nature, so that we are constantly pleased with touches of reality which give these types a convincing appearance of life. Dr. Norberry, although he wipes away too many unobtrusive tears, is a creature of flesh and blood. He is good-natured, tactless, and faithful. He finds women a mass of contradictions and is nearly always defeated in his arguments with them, particularly by his wife and daughters.

The moral of the story is emphasised in Adeline's final retraction of all her mistaken views. Though her marriage has failed, she no more thinks that an argument against marriage 'than the accidental bursting of a musket would be for the total abolition of fire-arms.' She considers marriage a necessary contract, so that passion may give place to affection and affection may devote itself to the family. Through Dr. Norberry, Mrs. Opie repeatedly expresses her pity and admiration for the misguided Adeline—that is for the misguided Mary Wollstonecraft. Her opinion is summed up finely in the

31 Elizabeth Opie, *Adeline Mowbray, or, The Mother and Daughter* (ed. 1844), ch. xxii, p. 277.

words: 'What a glorious champion would this creature have been in the support of truth, when even error in her looks so like to virtue.'[32]

In *Adeline Mowbray* Mrs. Opie spoke out on such subjects as duelling and the slave-trade. In her subsequent works of fiction she concentrated chiefly on personal ethics. *Temper* (1812) is really a wretched novel. Every incident in the plot is framed so that a moral may be drawn from it, and the reader is never credited with ability to glean the moral for himself. The lesson is driven home endlessly with sledge-hammer sermonettes. *Temper* is a tract in three volumes showing the pernicious effects of this passion throughout three generations. The text is given in the front page: 'A horse not broken becometh headstrong, and a child left to himself will be wilful.' Mrs. Opie's other works consist mainly of short tales, unequal in quality.[33]

Hannah More was another of the women writers who strove by means of fiction to inculcate morality and to counteract subversive Jacobin doctrines. Since it cannot be said that she contributed anything to the art of fiction, and since her stories are nearer to direct pedagogy than to literature, it would serve no useful purpose to consider them in any detail. She and her sister, aided by private subscribers and by committees, published and circulated all over England an immense number of tracts and tales intended to disinfect the minds of the lower and middle classes from the disease of democratic thought. To aid the circulation of these propagandist works, they were sold at a price which undercut competitors. *Coelebs in search of a Wife, comprehending Observations on Domestic Habits and Manners, Religion and Morals* (1809) cannot be taken seriously. We are asked to contemplate this characterless prig, this sententious vacuum, while he scours England for one who might be worthy to marry

32 *Ibid.*, ch. xiv, p. 109.

33 i.e. *Simple Tales* (1801), *Temper, or Domestic Scenes* (1812), *Tales of Real Life* (1813), *Valentine's Eve* (1816), *New Tales* (1818), *Tales of the Hearth* (1820), *Madeline* (1822).

him. To endure his interviews with hopeful parents and marriageable daughters, one must laugh. The best of Hannah More's other works are *Tales for the Common People* and *Stories for Persons of the Middle Classes*, both published in 1818. These are characterised by shrewd commonsense, with an occasional glimpse of humour. Hannah More attracted a large reading public for which, as her tales and stories indicate, she provided specialised fare. Whether she succeeded in preventing the common people from perusing the fiction intended for their betters must remain a question.

Maria Edgeworth (1767-1849) was the greatest of the didactic moralists. She belonged to an English Protestant family which since the reign of Henry VIII had been landed proprietors in County Longford. Her father, Richard Lovell Edgeworth, was a broad-minded and kindly man whose imagination was as limited as his energies were immense. His greatest interest was in education (an earnestness which was fostered by his friendship with Thomas Day) but he also had a literary bent; amused himself with mechanical experiments; sat in the Irish House of Commons, where he spoke for the Union but voted against it; administered his estate with benevolence; married four wives and reared a huge family. Indeed the Edgeworth family were a happy and self-sufficient commonwealth, all apparently intent on being amiable and useful, and all loyally owning allegiance to their genial and self-assured parent. It would, one imagines, have been dashing to his vanity had he dreamt that only as a parent would he escape oblivion—only as the parent of Maria Edgeworth, who was hailed as one of the literary lions of her day.

Maria loved her father to the verge of idolatry. From him she inherited her literary powers, and it was he who directed their aim. It was his object that in her life and writings she should be 'amiable, prudent, and of *use*.' Whether Richard Edgeworth helped or hindered his daughter's development as a writer is a controverted point. If he was responsible for her extreme utilitarianism, if he was responsible for her neglect of her best fictional gift, then he certainly was her evil genius. But, after all, in determining responsibility, we must remember that Maria was not merely under his influence, she was of his blood. By heredity and training she appears to have become his second self—the extension of his own personality. His advice seems almost always to have coincided with her own views, and she tells us of the help he gave her in plot-construction—a point in which she was weak. His part in her work went far beyond mere encouragement. During his lifetime he actually supervised her writings. First he required a preliminary outline of the story.

> Then he would in his own words fill up my sketch, paint the description, or represent the character intended, with such life, that I was quite convinced he not only seized ideas, but that he saw with the prophetic eye of taste the utmost that could be made of them . . . When he thought that there was spirit in what was written, but that it required great correction, he would say, 'Leave that to me; it is my business to cut and correct—yours to write on.'[34]

It was not his business, but whether his interference aided or crippled her powers is a point very difficult to determine. For example, his decisions to kill off King Corny and to spare the life of the reformed Lady Delacour (in *Belinda*) were sad errors. Against them must be set his contributions to *Patronage* and to *Ormond*. But one cannot forget that although Maria agreed with his utilitarian view of fiction, she did once have the impulse to write 'for fun', and the resultant work (written without her father's supervision) was her best. Whether the impulse returned and was stifled by Richard Edgeworth's passion for didacticism we shall never know. Can genius be stifled? Does an eagle voluntarily fold its wings and walk?

From her youth Maria Edgeworth found her duty and her pleasure in teaching, whether it was the instruction

34 *Black Book*, p. 142.

of her little brothers and sisters or of the wider circle reached through her writings. Her first attempts at narrative, made at about the age of twenty, were the 'wee wee stories' which she wrote on a slate to please the younger children at Edgeworthstown. Soon she attained her first successes in print. *The Parent's Assistant* (1796-1800) and *Early Lessons* (1801-1815) were children's stories. *Moral Tales* (1801) were meant for young people of a more advanced age. In 1804 appeared *Popular Tales* specially written for middle-class readers. These volumes are the key to Maria Edgeworth's view of life and to her fictional technique. She evidently believed that God had ordained the differences in the social order, and that only by doing one's duty in one's appointed sphere could happiness be attained. Her tales and novels were simply fables by which to make palatable her moral teaching. She was so certain, for example, of the difference between the bourgeois and the upper-class mind that, like Hannah More, she considered it necessary to devise a suitable approach to each. Her *Popular Tales* are all unassuming cheerfulness and industry. *Fashionable Tales* expose unfeeling frivolity and extravagance, and stress the need for accepting the responsibilities of wealth and exalted station. Unlike Mrs. Inchbald, she never doubts the justice of the social order. When, for example, in *The Absentee* she shows a whole community groaning under the heel of oppression she appeals merely for a just exercise of power. She does not question that one man should have such power over the lives of others. Her own social position made such reflections impossible. Her views on morality are equally superficial, whether in her children's stories or in those intended for the grown-up. It is the child's duty to be good, amiable and useful. If he fulfils this duty he will be happy not only in avoiding the penalty of wrong-doing, but in the rewards invariably given to virtue. The naughty child can be reformed, but until reformation is achieved he must suffer not merely the penalty of disturbing the normal pattern of life, but active punishments also. So that the reader may not confuse good and evil, so that the issue may always be clear, there are no 'mixed characters' among the children of Miss Edgeworth's pen. Simple Susan is a really good little girl. Lazy Lawrence is undoubtedly a bad boy. Their behaviour makes happiness and reward as inevitable for the one as unhappiness and punishment are for the other. The Edgeworths evidently held that, since their tales for children were meant to instruct, this simplification was necessary. They were not concerned with amusing the young, and either discounted or were unaware of the child's wish to hear stories simply for the stories' sake—to read not of paragons and pariahs, but of children like himself; to find food for the imagination in tales of magic and wonder. Fairies were banned at Edgeworthstown because they could not enforce moral principles and did not admit of rational explanation. It was the Edgeworth principle that everything should be explained with complete thoroughness. After all, Richard Edgeworth had published in 1802 a monstrous little book entitled *Poetry Explained for Young People*. The same rational outlook which deprived children of fairies deprived adults of romance, of all that is mysterious and unpredictable in human existence. In the stories intended for mature people Maria Edgeworth still offers the same simplified pattern. She avoids 'mixed characters' with all the moral earnestness that drove her to reject Mrs. Inchbald's Rushbrook on the score that he told a lie. Since this simplification negated the knowledge and experience of maturity, it sinned grievously against art. To judge Maria's novels we must abandon the standards of reality and deliberately adopt the Edgeworth outlook. We must willingly become citizens of a world which we know does not exist—a schoolroom world where everything is reduced to clear, bright, cheerful sanity, where the good and industrious child wins the prize and the naughty, selfish child stands in the corner. To do Maria Edgeworth justice within the narrow limits of this her chosen myth we must at least suspend our disbelief.

When we do so, some really good qualities become apparent. It is true that her plots are weak not only because they are devised to point a moral, but even in resourcefulness. In this respect she tells us that she owed most to her father, and that, in fact, he invented the story of *Patronage* and told it aloud in instalments before she wrote it. Still, passing over the question of construction, there are aspects that deserve praise. She had the narrator's gift of securing interest. We read her shallow stories and swallow her specific for happiness as a hypochondriac might swallow quack medicine—not because we believe, but because it seems so easy and infallible. These obvious motives, these issues capable of only one interpretation, these natures which know themselves and which are never puzzled or thwarted by irreconcilable impulses—because they are presented with charm and wit we can find pleasure in watching this mimic show. There is often an exuberance, a vivacity which gives these puppets a convincing appearance of life. In the lower social strata we are always conscious that it is the benevolent lady of the manor who pulls the strings. No 'small farmer' ever talked like Farmer Grey, despite the letter of testimony which Maria appends as a footnote. But in her stories of fashionable life she is at her ease. It was a life with which she was familiar, and therefore in conversation and social behaviour there are no false notes. Indeed the conversation of her worldlings is unusually excellent in its suavity and in its delicate and malicious fencing. This was a higher social level than the world of Jane Austen's heroines, but, like Jane Austen, Maria quarrels with the heartless snobbery and manœuvring of such people. Maria, however, seriously sets herself to reform these worldlings. Jane simply laughs them out of existence. But Maria does poke fun at sensibility, notably in *Angelina, or l'amie inconnue*, in *Emilie de Coulanges*, and in *Patronage* where she tilts at Rosamund Percy. Maria is a votary of commonsense. So was Jane Austen, but Jane's commonsense and her instinct for the ludicrous could never have allowed her to reduce the whole of life to a tract. Jane's commonsense was the reasoning of a satiric genius; Maria's was the blind earnestness of a second-rate mind.

Maria Edgeworth was the first of the regional novelists. *Castle Rackrent*, *The Absentee*, *Ennui* and *Ormond* show that she was most successful in writing of the Irish life she knew. Nevertheless, since she never doubted the justice of the social order, it may be doubted whether she was qualified to become the national novelist of a country in which the social order was no natural growth, but an unnatural imposition. Ireland in the early nineteenth century was a dual Ireland locked in mutual and deadly opposition. It was entering on the last phase of that struggle which had continued down the ages. For centuries there had existed side by side two separate peoples, two separate racial traditions, two languages, two literatures, two codes of law, two ways of life and thought—all utterly irreconcilable. Time had resolved the struggle externally into a social system consisting of two strata, an alien system superimposed upon the native system. It had been possible to disrupt the Irish pattern of life, to break the sense of continuity with the past and to condemn the native Irish to a general level of poverty and illiteracy. Yet Irish remained the habitual speech of a very large number of the people and indeed was spoken up to the outskirts of Dublin city. Not only so, but there was still a remnant of the Gaelic school of writers. Out of that conflict had grown the Anglo-Irish dialect. The people who used it still conserved their ancient music, poetry and legends (transmitted by oral tradition), and their old customs, now dim in origin.

From these two classes, therefore—the Ascendancy class and the native Irish class—the Irish novelists of the nineteenth century must emerge, and their interpretation of that material would depend on their particular experience and point of view. One would expect two different kinds of Irish novel: that which dealt with Ascendancy life and with the peasants in relation to their masters; that which dealt with the life of the common people and with the masters in relation to the oppressed. In fact these two schools of fiction came into existence. The cultural advantage lay with the more educated class. Nevertheless, it was certain that the more Ascendancy the tone of the novel the more it would approximate to English life, since the higher the level of Irish society the fewer Irish characteristics were to be expected. But the descendants of the old Irish people were intensely themselves, and as such could not fail to be a rich source of inspiration to the novelist, an unworked mine of speech and behaviour. Yet who could write of the simple people of Ireland? Only those who were near enough to know them; if possible, one of themselves; someone who shared their daily life, their speech, their outlook, who realised their sources of action and re-action. Could such a man have the necessary equipment of education, and if he had not, what kind of novel would result? Time would tell. Meanwhile a writer emerged, as was most natural, from the class which had the greatest access to culture. Maria Edgeworth turned her eyes to the contemporary Irish scene.

Maria Edgeworth belonged to the Ascendancy class. There were other factors which diminished her opportunities of giving a true picture of Irish life. She came to Ireland at the age of sixteen. Since she had been reared in England, she brought to Ireland a set of values which could not apply in a very different state of society. In addition, her privileged social position did not help her to establish contact with that class of people which constituted the majority of the population. For these reasons she remained, despite her kindliness, an outsider. Yet the air she breathed was Irish air and she was impelled to write of Ireland. In 1800, the year of the Act of Union, there appeared her first novel, *Castle Rackrent*. This she wrote 'for fun' and without her father's supervision. It was her only work free from didacticism and her greatest achievement—facts which should have given her food for thought had she realised them.

Castle Rackrent records the annals of the old Irish family which, from one generation to another, pursues the rollicking way to perdition. It is told through the lips of an ancient retainer, Honest Thady—a character whom Maria draws from a steward on the Edgeworth estate. She says that she grew so accustomed to this steward's dialect that she could think and speak it without effort. That this was so is abundantly evident in the facility with which this vivid narrative flowed from her pen. The other three Irish novels contain much that is of value, much too that is worthless. The alternation between her natural bent and her deliberate didacticism is well seen in *Ormond*.[35] One moment we are in the wild domain of the Black Isles, observing with delight the uproarious nobility of King Corney; the next, there is Ormond snivelling (there is no other word for it) his repentance for having unwittingly intervened between Moriarty and his coquettish Peggy. It must truly be said, however, that Sir Ulick O'Shane is not merely a ruffian in black and white. Miss Edgeworth shows us that Sir Ulick justified to himself his own opportunism and knavery. His epitaph, spoken by one of the grave-diggers, represents her own view: 'There lies the makings of an excellent gentleman—but the cunning of his head spoiled the goodness of his heart.' As for King Corney, he was 'the true thing and never changed'. This hard-drinking, practical, daring, generous creature has about him something of the rugged splendour of those kings who won and retained power by their own strength. When he dies (killed by the intervention of Richard Edgeworth) the real interest of the story dies with him. He revenged his untimely end by dwarfing the rest of the characters and making the virtuous and sententious folk seem very mawkish.

35 In regard to Richard Edgeworth's contribution to this novel Maria writes: 'The following parts of *Ormond* were written for me by my dear father in his last illness: The death of King Corney . . . the whole of Moriarty's history of his escape from prison . . . . also the meeting between Moriarty and his wife, when he jumps out of the carriage the moment he hears her voice.' (*Black Book*, p. 229) These interpolations are certainly well written, but although they equal Maria's average writing, they are not comparable to the best of her Irish sketches.

But there are in Maria Edgeworth's novels curious evidences of myopia. In *Ennui* she uses the rebellion of '98 really as a means of relieving Lord Glenthorne's sense of futility. The plot of the United Irishmen (to make Glenthorne their leader or, alternatively, to kill him) would seem to indicate a degree of impulsiveness unusual even among the native Irish. And what are we to say to a writer who, having explained that the Clonbrony estate has been drained dry by the infamous agent, yet shows the incognito Lord Colambre being lavishly entertained in the cottage of the Widow O'Neill. He sups on bacon and eggs, potatoes, milk and butter; and there would have been a chicken had there been time to prepare it. He breakfasts on white bread, tea, cream, butter and eggs. Truly such hospitality is little calculated to show the evils of absenteeism.

Rebellion and famine, 'the state of the country'—of these Miss Edgeworth was aware. They did not induce her to change her chosen tone, but finally they caused her to give up writing of Ireland. In 1834, in a letter to her brother in India, explaining why *Helen* was not an Irish novel, Maria Edgeworth made this most illuminating remark: 'It is impossible to draw Ireland as she is now in a book of fiction—realities are too strong—party passions are too violent to bear to see, or care to look at their faces in the looking glass. The people would only break the glass and curse the fool who held the mirror up to nature.' One remembers that the Lady of Shallot could no longer spin when one glance at reality shivered her mirror to atoms. Even if Maria Edgeworth were not unable, it seems certain that she was unwilling to include in her novels any analysis of Irish life. The *Edinburgh Review* of 1831 says in regard to her Irish works: 'We are not sufficiently told the influence of circumstances upon the national character, nor what in each individual is natural and what the result of his position. There is a careful avoidance of political topics, the bearing of which upon Irish society is too marked and important to be altogether omitted.' In so far as politics represent the impact of history upon human life they could scarcely be omitted from the Irish novel. Unless the writer showed the causes which underlay rack-rents, evictions, tithe-proctors, hedge-schools and secret societies, then Irish figures in fiction would appear as meaningless as marionettes, acting without autonomy, out of no causation, dancing convulsively in response to the controlling finger. It was this cautious refusal to touch the roots of Irish life which led to the superficial growth of what may be called the Irish colonial novel. Its greatest exponents were the witty Lever and the farcical Lover.

The relation between Maria Edgeworth's picture of Irish life and the real life which surrounded her is essential to an estimate of her art, but her Irish stories carried conviction to those who did not fully know Ireland, and proved an inspiration to Scott[36] and to Turgeniev. Scott indeed had more claim to be styled a national novelist than had Maria Edgeworth, since he presented the people of his country as an integral whole, without that squinted vision which results from closing one eye. It was, of course, a simpler matter for him, because Scotland was not divided by an abnormal stratification.

A detailed examination of all Maria Edgeworth's fictional work is beyond the scope of this work, nor would such an examination add anything essential to the general criticisms we have offered. Still we may spare a little space for a brief outline of some of the stories which we have not already mentioned. These may all be loosely classified as tales of fashionable life. In 1801 appeared *Belinda*, which begins very interestingly after the manner of Fanny Burney, but soon dwindles into moral teaching and improbability. Belinda, like Evelina, makes her entrance into society under difficult circumstances. She is entrusted to the brilliant and worldly Lady Delacour who, in a negligent way, is her sponsor in the marriage market. Lady Delacour is a very unhappy woman who tries by perpetual gaiety, flirtation and social triumph to forget the failure of her married

36 See 'General Preface' to 1829 ed. of Scott's novels; also the original edition of *Waverley*.

life and the horror of being (as she erroneously believes) the victim of cancer. The locked room where she keeps her medicines excites her husband's jealousy, and leads to complications in which Belinda is involved. That gentle paragon[37] has fallen in love with Clarence Hervey who at first affronts her pride, more crudely indeed, but still in much the same way as Darcy offends Elizabeth Bennet. He comes to love her, but does not feel free to propose because a foundling whom he has reared according to Rousseauistic principles wishes to marry him out of gratitude. Belinda then imagines herself in love with a Creole, but these tangles, introduced to protract the course of true love, are unravelled in the end.

Lady Delacour is at her best in her moods of defiant brilliance. It is a theatrical brilliance, but it greatly impressed contemporary readers. A much-praised scene is that in which Lady Delacour, who believes herself dying, imagines even the faithful Belinda to be her enemy. But Lady Delacour redeemed and reunited to her husband does not hold our interest. Maria would have done better had she adhered to her first intention of making her die.

There is plenty of humour in this novel, and much excellent dialogue. Maria Edgeworth well knew the different varieties of fool, and she amuses herself with portraying the weak but good-natured Lord Delacour and the malicious numskull, Sir Philip Baddely. Sir Philip's proposal to Belinda, undertaken merely so as to make 'Clary look blue', is very diverting. It gives rise to such a rejection scene as previous novelists had described, and which was to become the climax of *Pride and Prejudice*. But Darcy and Elizabeth were deep in love and understanding. Between Sir Philip and Belinda there was only vanity and distaste.

Leonora (1806) was considered to be Maria Edgeworth's retort to Madame de Staël's *Delphine*. It is supposed

37 Maria Edgeworth herself speaks of 'the cold tameness of that stick or stone, Belinda'. Yet she continued to present such heroines, e.g. Grace Nugent, Helen, Miss Annaly.

to have been written with the hope of pleasing the Chevalier Edelcrantz, whose proposal of marriage Maria felt obliged to refuse. *Leonora* is a novel in letters, which resembles in subject Elizabeth Griffith's *The Delicate Distress*. In 1809 appeared the first series of *Tales of Fashionable Life*, comprising *Ennui*, *The Dun*, *Manoeuvring* and *Almeria*. The second series (which appeared in 1812) consisted of *Vivian*, *The Absentee*, *Madame Fleury* and *Emilie de Coulanges*. *Ennui* is a most wearisome book, relieved only by the amusing description of Lord Glenthorne's journey to his estate in the west of Ireland. The plot unrolls itself at first in so desultory a manner that it seems to be merely an essay on ennui relieved by anecdotes and slices of Baedeker. When the plot thickens it befuddles us with such improbabilities as the discovery that the humble Christy O'Donoghue is the real Lord Glenthorne. The question of absenteeism is prominently treated. *The Dun* is a homily on the injustice of not paying one's debts. *Manoeuvring* shows a cunning woman defeating by her deviousness the very aim she wishes to achieve. *Almeria* is the story of a vulgar heiress casting off the friends of her obscure days for fashionable people who sneer at her. Her social climbing brings upon her the heavy punishment of lonely spinsterhood. *Vivian*, which Scott greatly admired, is the life-story of a domestic Hamlet.[38] His vacillations involve himself and others in much misery. Evidently daunted by the difficulty of strengthening his will, Maria causes him to be killed in a duel.

The Absentee shows the injustice of landlords who live away from their estates on rents extorted from the harassed tenantry. In *Ennui* McLeod, the honest agent, is contrasted with the rascally agent Hardcastle. In *The Absentee* that pitiless schemer, Nick Gerraghty, is the villain of the piece. The Clonbronys live in London because Lady Clonbrony wishes to shine socially. She is willing to return to Ireland only when she is forced to realise that she is the butt of those fashionable people whom she has so abjectly tried to cultivate. Her

38 So Julia Kavenagh calls him (*English Women of Letters*, 1863, vol. ii, p. 159).

son Lord Colambre, who has seen for himself the misery of the people on the Clonbrony estate, persuades his parents that by living at home they will secure their own happiness and that of their tenants. Lord Colambre's sudden visit to Clonbrony is, despite its improbabilities, the most interesting part of the story. The scene where he reveals himself to his tenants and to the tyrannical Gerraghty has been compared by Macaulay to the recognition scene in the Odyssey. This might have been a really good Irish novel, but it is spoiled by its didacticism. The narrowness of Maria's moral code is but too apparent in the fact that, though Colambre loves Grace Nugent, he is prepared to abandon her because she is supposed to be illegitimate. But Grace Nugent is proved to have been born in wedlock, and her reward is marriage with Colambre and the privilege of spending her fortune in the rehabilitation of the Clonbrony estate. Another instance of Maria's wish to eat her cake and have it is that, although she wrote *Harrington* as a vindication of the Jews, she finds it necessary, at the last moment, to disclose that her heroine is not a Jewess, but 'a Christian—a Protestant'. She lacks the courage to abide by the consequence of her didactic thesis, and constantly disappoints us by dishonestly twisting the plot to escape the issue she has deliberately raised.

There is nothing much to be said of her remaining stories. *Patronage* has the same faults and the same good qualities as the other novels. It is shamelessly didactic and employs throughout the device of contrast which made her fiction so diagrammatic. *Madame Fleury* tells how a charitable lady is saved from the guillotine by those who have benefited by her benevolence. *Emilie de Coulanges* cleverly exposes the essential egoism in sensibility. *Helen*, written years after her father's death, shows a great falling off in power.

In summing up Maria Edgeworth's literary achievements one is forced to discount much of the praise assigned to her by over-generous critics. At every point she appears to have been incapable of the best. It is said that she excelled as a writer of children's stories and as a didactic novelist, and also that she showed much facility in the use of the short story form. The last claim only can one admit without reservation. The first depends on whether children prefer Frank and Rosamund to Brer Fox and Brer Rabbit or *Treasure Island*. The claim of didactic pre-eminence is in itself sufficient to range a novelist on a lower artistic level. The question of her Irish sketches remains. Her interest in local colour was secondary to her didactic purpose except in one single work—*Castle Rackrent*, on which must be based her surest claim as a novelist. Her greatest achievement lies in the fact that, although she had no clearly conceived intention and had imagined no corresponding artistic form, her novels did suggest the idea of regionalism to later writers.

A Scottish counterpart of Maria Edgeworth was Susan Ferrier (1782-1854). Like Scott, she had kept a half-written novel in a drawer for years, but *Waverley* was published four years before *Marriage* appeared. Susan Ferrier was not a follower of Scott. Her novels contain in general the same constituents as those of Maria Edgeworth. They are tales of fashionable life, blending a delineation of Scottish manners with a didactic purpose. But within this similarity there was a very considerable difference between the Irishwoman and her Scots sister of the quill. Susan Ferrier was much less didactic and had a far greater grasp of reality than Maria Edgeworth. She had a strong and satiric mind, but she lacked Maria Edgeworth's sympathetic tolerance. Both had plenty of wit and humour, but Maria's was mellow: Susan's was malicious and even pitiless. Maria presented 'characters', but despite their individual modes of thought and behaviour they are too essentially human to be called eccentric. Susan's 'characters' are a delight, but it must be admitted that they are often caricatures. In this she resembled Fanny Burney, as Maria resembled Fanny Burney in her portraits of the rich and noble.

Like Maria, Susan Ferrier was weak in plot-invention, but whereas Maria was led away chiefly by her didacticism, Susan (also digressing and dwindling into pedagogy) was becalmed by her intense pleasure in vivisecting her eccentrics. She holds up, indeed she frequently forgets, the plot while for her own diversion and ours she carefully oils her originals and as carefully disposes them on the gridiron for roasting.[39] They were originals in more senses than one. It was Susan Ferrier's method to draw such characters from the life, and this was evidently the reason why she delayed so long in publishing her first novel, and remained, even after her initial triumph, always rather hesitant in venturing into print.

Marriage (1818) grew from Susan's realisation of the rich harvest of humour to be gained by introducing an English society belle into the household of a Scottish laird. Since a frivolous butterfly like Lady Juliana would never voluntarily exile herself in a Scottish glen, Susan Ferrier invented circumstances which would force her to do so. Lady Juliana refuses to marry the wealthy old duke of her father's choice, and elopes with Harry Douglas who is dependent on his army pay. He is suspended for being absent without leave; she is disowned by her father, and nothing remains but to take refuge with Harry's father—the Laird of Glenfern. Everything goes badly from the moment of their arrival. Lady Juliana is merely a pettish child, who makes not the slightest effort to disguise her horror at the dreary residence and farouche manners of her new relations. There are three long-chinned spinster aunts: Miss Jacky, the sensible woman of the parish; Miss Grizzy, who is merely distinguishable from nothing; and Miss Nicky who as an individual is non-existent. There are also 'five awkward purple girls'—Harry's sisters, at the sight of whom his highbred wife 'gave way to the anguish that mocked control.' All these worthy creatures are quite unconscious that they are the abomination of

39 Saintsbury uses this amusing metaphor (*Essays in English Literature*, 1780-1860, 2nd. series, ed. 1895, p. 170).

desolation. They shower kindness on dear Harry's wife. When, as most frequently happens, she simulates a faint to express her nausea at her surroundings or at some Scottish phenomenon such as the pipes, the spinster ladies dose her with potent herbal brews, or revive her with a bowl of greasy cockie-leekie soup. Then again there is the terrific Lady MacLoughlin who speaks unvarnished truths and strides rough-shod over all mealy-mouthed efforts at politeness. Never is this more evident than when the ladies of Glenfern, accompanied by Lady Juliana, array themselves in their richest attire and set out for Lochmarlie Castle in acceptance of an invitation from Lady MacLoughlin. When they arrive they find they are not expected, and they are grimly received by Lady MacLoughlin who 'regarded the invaders with her usual marble aspect, and without moving either joint or muscle as they drew near.'

> 'I declare—I don't think you know us, Lady MacLoughlin,' said Miss Grizzy in a tone of affected vivacity, with which she strove to conceal her agitation.
>
> 'Know you!' repeated her friend—'humph! Who you are, I know very well; but what brings you here, I do *not* know. Do you know yourselves?'
>
> 'I declare—I can't conceive—' began Miss Grizzy; but her trepidation arrested her speech, and her sister therefore proceeded—
>
> 'Your ladyship's declaration is no less astonishing than incomprehensible. We have waited upon you by your own express invitation on the day appointed by yourself; and we have been received in a manner, I must say, we did not expect, considering this is the first visit of our niece, Lady Juliana Douglas.'
>
> 'I'll tell you what, girls,' replied their friend, as she still stood with her back to the fire, and her hands behind her; 'I'll tell you what—you are not yourselves—you are all lost—quite mad—that's all—humph!'[40]

A violent quarrel ensues, but the matter is cleared up when Lady MacLoughlin says that though she may have mentioned Tuesday in her letter she really meant Thursday. When Miss Grizzy meekly says that Tuesday was the day she read in Lady MacLoughlin's letter,

40 Susan Ferrier, *Marriage* (ed. 1881), i, p. 191.

that redoubtable woman closes the subject by declaring: 'How could you be such a fool, my love, as to read it any such thing? Even if it had been written Tuesday, you might have had the sense to know it meant Thursday.'

But unfortunately for the reader, he is soon dragged away from these delights to starve on moralising. Following the usual didactic pattern, Miss Ferrier presents us with a strong contrast to the petulant Lady Juliana. In the person of Mrs. Douglas we are shown that an Englishwoman may be happy on a Scottish estate, and may find happiness in marriage, even though duty has forbidden her to marry the man of her own choice. Thence the scene shifts to London. Lady Juliana leaves in the care of Mrs. Douglas, Mary, one of her twin daughters, and takes with her Adelaide. Before long Lady Juliana's brainless behaviour ruins her husband's prospects, and he goes on foreign service. She and Adelaide find refuge in her brother's home. After a lapse of years we are presented with the contrast between Mary and Adelaide; the one a most wearying miracle of sententiousness and sensibility, the other a languid young worldling. The didactic purpose works itself out to a suitable conclusion, but there is no dearth of amusing characters, and in addition we make the acquaintance of the inimitable Mrs. Macshake and Dr. Redgill.

Susan Ferrier's second novel, *The Inheritance* (1824), was far better than her first. Its plot is more skilfully devised, and we are again entertained with diverting character studies. The inheritance is the earldom and estates of Rossville to which the heroine, Gertrude St. Clair, comes as heiress presumptive. In due time she succeeds, but soon an American imposter called Lewiston claims that she is really his daughter. She finds it impossible to refute his lying assertions, but the loss of the title and property rids her at least of her false lover Colonel Delmour. She marries her true lover who later becomes Lord Rossville.

Amongst the many excellent characters in this novel the best of all is Miss Pratt:

> In the hum-drum society of a dull county, what a relief to the weary soul to have some person to be weary of! To have a sort of *bag-fox* to turn out, when fresh game cannot be had, is an enjoyment which many of my readers have doubtless experienced. Such was Miss Pratt—everybody wearied of her, or said they wearied of her, and everybody abused her, while yet she was more sought after and asked about, than she would have been had she possessed the wisdom of a More, or the benevolence of a Fry. She was, in fact, the very heart of the shire, and gave life and energy to all the pulses of the parish. She supplied it with streams of gossip and chit-chat in others and subject of ridicule in herself.[41]

Miss Pratt is the particular bête noire of the pompous and finical Lord Rossville, whose feelings she unwittingly lacerates by her every word and deed. The climax is reached when she arrives at his mansion in a hearse, the only convenience she can find to carry her through a snowstorm. Her nephew, Anthony White (whom she always quotes, but who never gives proof of his existence), seems to be the ancestor of Sarah Gamp. Miss Pratt is a character whom Jane Austen would have gladly owned. Another excellent personage is Uncle Adam, said to have been drawn from Susan Ferrier's father, but having, as Saintsbury suggests, prophetic touches of no less a person than Carlyle. Uncle Adam is related to Gertrude St. Clair through her mother—and this more plebeian side of the family offers such gems of characterisation as Lilly Black, and Major and Mrs. Waddell whose bridal tour can never be forgotten.

Miss Ferrier's third novel, *Destiny* (1831), shows an increasing power of plot-construction, but a falling off in vivacity. There is a greater seriousness in tone and a more marked didacticism, yet the old satiric spirit is still evident in such portraits as that of the odious McDow. *Destiny* was Susan Ferrier's last published work and though she could have continued to profit by her popularity as a writer, it speaks well for her strong critical sense that she knew when to retire. Her literary reputation stands in some respects lower than Maria Edgeworth's, in some respects higher. She made a

41 *The Inheritance* (ed. 1824), i, p. 102.

valuable contribution to Scottish fiction. Her power of satiric characterisation was great—great, that is to say, until we compare it with the artistic subtlety of Jane Austen.

CHAPTER VI

JANE AUSTEN

GENIUS should be judged only by its peers, and not merely by those of equal, but of similar powers. It is because such juridical conditions are impossible that literary criticism fails in proportion to a writer's greatness. How humbly then must critics of Jane Austen approach the mystery of her art, asking pardon (like the clumsy headsman) before proceeding to hack to pieces what they could never create. For when all has been said, when every tittle of evidence has been adduced, when her brain and her heart have been weighed and dissected, how far have we progressed towards the secret of her unique power? While we are fumbling through the post-mortem the elusive spirit mocks us where we cannot follow.

Jane Austen's genius was unique not merely in its peculiar essence, but in what one can only term its spontaneous maturity. Dispensing with the evolutionary stages of childhood, it sprang fully armed into the arena of letters. Although her artistic powers developed, her mental attitude at the age of fourteen is the same as it was at forty. There is evidence that at times her artistic balance was disturbed by the strength of her ethical convictions, but such waverings were only partial and momentary. They never caused a complete lack of poise, and they were always followed by a return to equilibrium so triumphant as to prove more than ever the insistence of her inspiration. Were she of a cold, impassive nature it would have been easier for her to maintain an invincible uniformity, but actually she was possessed of such intense energy as to make it impossible for her not to think and feel strongly. It is this energy of mind and heart which gives such vitality to her novels, and this force is all the more dynamic for being controlled and directed by an acute judgment. Jane Austen seems to have been born with a fine sense of values, and with an instinct for proportion which gave her mind its characteristic bent. 'To the soul is given intelligence and that delectation that cometh from the contemplation of truth.' This is the delectation which absorbed her life and which her articulateness offers to us with all the perfection of art. Truth, or sanity, or 'commonsense'—call it what you will—it was for this she hungered, for this that, even as a child, she felt impelled to reject all that was false in literary symbolism, and to forge for herself an appropriate technique. Jane Austen's 'commonsense' does not connote a bread-and-butter philosophy. Despite crass misunderstanding and reiteration, it does not mean the exclusion of beauty and romance from life, and the substitution of worldly wisdom. By 'commonsense' Jane Austen meant the repudiation of uncontrolled emotionalism, of grandiose clap-trap and melodrama, of hypocrisy and self-deception. It is a word which has been used so often in a narrow and utilitarian sense that we are disinclined to give it its positive value. Jane Austen's passion for 'commonsense' was a passion for reality—a mordant dissatisfaction with false standards of life. At first it was the falsity of novels which aroused her. Then, no longer content with showing the discrepancy between real life and literary misrepresentations, her attention was caught and held by the illusions and deceptions of human beings. A real world in which no one faced reality—in which each man spun for himself a cocoon of delusion; a world with no positive set of values since every mind was a separate kingdom; a world where bodily solitude and mental communion were equally impossible, where no man understood his neighbour nor even himself—a jostling, lonely, selfish, kindly, mean and noble world; a mad world—Jane Austen sharpened her quill.

Literature has grown out of the revolt against some aspect of life or of art. Emily Brontë was a rebel chained in the outer darkness of earthly life, trying to free herself by terrific convulsions of the spirit. Jane Austen was a rebel who freed herself by laughter, and, because she was not a fool, the laughter was ironic. The individual confronted by a majority holding an opposite opinion must either yield or resist. If he resists it cannot be merely a passive preference for his own view. It must be a direct negative, taking some tinge from the dissenter's feeling of isolation—an attitude of rebellion expressing itself in slashing attack, or more subtly transmuted into a feeling of superiority. It is the sense at once of rightness and of isolation which gives the ironic outlook.

Jane Austen was thus a dissenter. She did not subscribe to the delusions of life; neither could she tolerate literary flights from reality. The romanticists did not quarrel with the limitations of stunted minds and sordid aims. They simply took refuge in another world, and in fiction their efforts to express their romantic conceptions resulted in wild exaggeration. It was not in Jane Austen's nature to take fire from the Romantic Revival. She not merely evaded, but she deliberately repudiated it. Her interest was in human life as she knew it—an inexhaustible mine, and one very little worked. And it was not merely the romanticists' avowed flight from reality which she disowned, but the deplorable tradition of the Heroic Romance, which in itself had been sufficiently bad, but which, when vulgarised to suit middle-class tastes, had become quite shocking from an aesthetic point of view. The deification of emotionalism which evinced itself as sensibility was a further phenomenon of insincerity and lack of proportion. The novel which resulted from this blend of Heroic tradition, bourgeois taste and pseudo-introspection was a deplorable affair; the Gothic novel was a romantic illusion with sensibility as its plague-spot; the didactic novel was a prostitution of art. All ignored or distorted everyday life. No wonder that Jane Austen, with gales of ironic merriment, brought these pasteboard erections to the ground. Yet she owed them something. The characteristic outlook which led her to revolt was strengthened and clarified by these proofs of unreality taken to excess. On the other hand, these fictional exaggerations were partly responsible for the rigidity with which she denied herself emotional expression in her novels. She was like a sensitive woman in a house of mourning who, nauseated by noisy grief and melodramatic ebullitions, bites her lips and determines to show no emotion at all. 'I detest jargon of every kind [says Marianne in *Sense and Sensibility*] and sometimes I have kept my feelings to myself, because I could find no language to describe them in but what was worn and hackneyed out of all sense and meaning.'[1]

The attitude of amused detachment which was instinctive with Jane Austen (and which appears most strongly in those of her letters preserved by Cassandra) led her inevitably to fashion a corresponding technique. The ironic focus not only allowed, but necessitated the reticence of the author. However pleasing this reticence may have been when she set herself to expose exaggerated styles of fiction, she must have found it essential in the delineation of emotions and sentiments. It was a means of avoiding personal statements on subjects towards which her discretion, shyness, or her own personal experiences dictated an indirect approach. The aloofness thus secured by the ironic approach was reinforced by Jane Austen's use of the dramatic technique. But it must be said that although one may unravel the causes underlying her use of her particular technique, it is certain that she did not consciously reason out her choice of instruments, but instinctively fashioned the medium of story-telling most suited to her temperament. In a word, her sensitiveness sought the defence of irony, and irony gave to her mind a particular attitude which achieved its aim by characteristic means.

Jane Austen's use of the ironic focus, reinforced by the dramatic technique, involved a particular choice of material and certain manipulations of this subject-matter. One would expect the ironic mind to be mainly interested in human relationships, in the interplay of

1 *Sense and Sensibility*, ch. xviii.

motive and behaviour which constitutes the eternal comedy of life. Since Jane Austen was supremely an artist it followed that she would keep within the limits of her experience. They were narrow limits—a 'little bit (two inches wide) of ivory.' The daughter of a country parson at the end of the eighteenth century was almost entirely restricted not merely to her immediate surroundings, but to her own social class. Jane Austen did not feel cramped by such limitations. Indeed she says: 'Three or four families in a country village is the very thing to work on.'[2] In *Pride and Prejudice* she explains why such material is sufficient.

> 'I did not know before [says Bingley to Elizabeth] that you were a studier of character. It must be an amusing study.'
>
> 'Yes, but intricate characters are the *most* amusing. They have at least that advantage.'
>
> 'The country,' said Darcy, 'can in general supply but a few subjects for such study. In a country neighbourhood you move in a very confined and unvarying society.'
>
> 'But people themselves alter so much, that there is something new to be observed in them forever.'[3]

Jane Austen as a little girl rolling down the green slope at the back of Steventon rectory, Jane Austen the gay butterfly leading a cotillion, Jane Austen with but a month to live—at every stage there is evident her absorption in human behaviour and her minute dissection of motive and mannerism; at every stage she delivers judgment in tones that are gently mocking or coldly merciless. She has been too often blamed for the searing quality of her criticisms, which are adduced as proof that she had no heart. The truth seems to be that she had a heart which repudiated scornfully all that was evil, pretentious, hypocritical or poisonously silly. She had an ideal of inner harmony—to be achieved by honesty, sanity and self-control—and against those who fell short of these principles her judgments were launched with all the added impetus of feeling. But

2 *Letters of Jane Austen* (ed. Brabourne, 1884), ii, p. 321.
3 *Pride and Prejudice*, ch. ix.

good-natured foolishness she treated gently, as witness Mrs. Jennings and Miss Bates. It is not easy to reconcile the impulses of a sensitive heart and a relentless mind. Jane Austen had a mind which deprived itself of all the comforts of illusion, which obliged her to face the facts about herself and others, and to relate every word and action to the general sum of personality. As she says of Anne Elliot engaged in ruthless self-examination: 'One half of her should not always be so much wiser than the other half.' It was not merely that Jane Austen judged with pitiless justice. She observed with a selectivity, a minute realism and an analytic force which exactly served her dispassionate purpose. In her letters (which, as the direct account of actual events, are most valuable in this connection) there are many instances of her razor-keen perception. For example, in describing a ball, she says:

> There were very few beauties, and such as there were were not very handsome. Miss Iremonger did not look well, and Miss Blount was the only one much admired. She appeared exactly as she did in September with the same broad face, diamond bandeau, white shoes, pink husband, and fat neck. The two Miss Coxes were there: I traced in one the remains of the vulgar, broad-featured girl who danced at Enham eight years ago; the other is refined into a nice composed-looking girl, like Catherine Bigg. I looked at Sir Thomas Champneys and thought of poor Rosalie; I looked at his daughter and thought her a queer animal with a white neck.[4]

The words are mordant, but it is not the words which matter, but the kind of perception which they record. As the angle of vision or an effect of lighting makes a familiar object seem strange, so does Jane Austen's individual point of view find unending novelty in the human scene around her. She withdraws, viewing it from such a standpoint that the objects of her observation are no longer the people whose personal history and manners she knows by heart. In this perspective they take on new aspects—aspects as curious as that of Miss Champneys who suddenly appears sub-human—a queer animal with a white neck. The power that, by a trick of focus,

4 *Letters of Jane Austen* (ed. Brabourne, 1884), i, p. 242.

could find new appearances in solid bodies could never be at a loss for novelty in the instability of human behaviour, for it is true that 'Nobody ever feels or acts, suffers or enjoys, as one expects.'[5] Revolution and war, great movements, religious, social, political and literary—all the wider issues of life flowed by her, while she viewed under the microscope one single drop from a stagnant pool. Under the lens of her genius this drop became a microcosm teeming with the most varied and interesting forms of life.

The ironic technique[6] employed by Jane Austen narrowed her chosen field still further. As a satirist she was confronted not merely with the novelist's usual problem of presenting human life, but of presenting it in such a way as to imply critical comment. The satirist's first duty is to maintain the ironic tone throughout—a task which calls for the most impeccable artistry. To do so he must preserve what one may call the unity of satire, introducing only such characters as lend themselves to satiric treatment or at least serve to show others in a satiric light. He must be very sparing in the use of background, of nature, or of any other factor which might divert the attention from the human involvement which is being portrayed. He must avoid direct expressions of emotion which must be suggested by understatement rather than by exposition, by silence rather than by speech, by the hints offered in word and deed. Even behaviour should not often express a direct reaction, but rather, skipping a link or two, should represent a stage in the sequence of thought which must serve as a clue to the first cause. In a word, the ironic focus, working by undertone and understatement, requires subtlety from both author and reader, and this exigence partly explains why Jane Austen's novels have taken so long to come into their own, and why even now they tend to remain caviare to the general. They are works for the mental gymnast—a fact which she herself

5 *Ibid.*, i, p. 371.

6 See Lord David Cecil, *Jane Austen* (Camb. Univ. Press, 1935). This brilliant monograph is the finest dissection of Jane Austen's art which has appeared.

fully realised. She says: 'I do not write for such dull elves as have not a great deal of ingenuity themselves.' The necessity of securing the reader's active co-operation is rendered more acute by Jane Austen's use of the dramatic method. The ironic focus is not in itself a sufficient smoke-screen for the writer who wishes to keep his own views to himself. Ironic comment is a form of disguise easily penetrated by the reader, who has only to follow the satiric finger-post; but the dramatic method renders the author completely unobtrusive, and gives the characters an apparent autonomy. It involves still further subtlety, however, requiring from the writer the most carefully balanced relation between words and action, thought and speech. In dialogue especially it calls for the skill of a virtuoso. To succeed in a medium compounded of satiric and dramatic technique is to reach the highest peak of artistry in fiction. It calls for the most exquisite minuteness and forethought in planning and execution, for those tiny and perfect strokes by which so little seems achieved after the most patient and unwearying care. Such an aim had never before been projected, and, except perhaps by Flaubert, has never been fulfilled since. That Jane Austen evolved such a medium and succeeded in it sets her apart as the most consummate artist in English fiction. Her triumph was all the greater, and was all the less realised, because hers was the art which conceals art. To the unobservant, to those accustomed to a wider canvas and more lurid and sweeping brush-work this 'Chinese fidelity' this 'miniature delicacy'[7] appeared, as to Mme de Staël, 'vulgaire'. To Charlotte Brontë (whose great difference in temperament drove her to inimical comment) the Austen novels were merely 'an accurate daguerrotyped portrait of a commonplace face', but the judgment of succeeding generations may well be summed up in the saying of an excellent critic:[8] 'Jane Austen, Jane Austen and life, which of you two has copied the other?'

7 Expressions used by Charlotte Brontë.
8 Rev. Dr. Montague Summers. 'Jane Austen: An Appreciation', *Royal Soc of Lit. Transactions*, xxxvi, (1918), p. 33.

But although from the beginning Jane Austen saw the goal which she must reach, she achieved her purpose only by the most patient labour. Her youthful efforts and unfinished sketches serve to show the development of her art. This child had no particular educational advantages beyond what was usual among gentlefolk. Since her boarding-school period began at the age of seven and ended when she was nine, she could not have 'scrambled herself' into much learning, particularly as the school-mistress, Mrs. Latournelle, a jovial old lady with a cork leg, was chiefly occupied with giving out clothes for the wash, ordering dinner, and discoursing on play-acting and the private lives of actors. As the Rev. George Austen was a scholarly man, it would seem that Jane's real education was gained between the years of nine and sixteen which she spent under his care. But the time which Mr. Austen could spare from his duties as a clergyman was chiefly devoted to the education of his three sons and of such pupils as he took into his house. It does not seem probable that Jane and Cassandra could have received much deliberate instruction, but life at Steventon rectory was an education in itself. The Austens were a good-humoured, affectionate and lively race, inheriting from both sides of the family a tradition of culture and wit. They were omnivorous readers especially of novels and plays, very sociable, and on excellent terms with a large circle of relatives and friends. Steventon was emphatically not a place to rust the intellect, and a touch of cosmopolitan brilliance was introduced when the Comtesse de Feuillide, a niece to Mr. Austen, made frequent visits to Steventon and finally took refuge there when widowed by the French Revolution. In this exhilarating atmosphere the young Jane Austen found all that was needed for the growth of her particular mental powers. She seems to have read a good deal in an ill-regulated way, but certainly not as much and not with such clearly defined benefit as certain critics[9] would have us suppose. One cannot praise a school of criticism which believes that Jane

[9] Clara Linklater Thompson and R. Brimley Johnson.

Austen found her real inspiration in books and which observes in her plots and in her style resemblances to practically every author whom she is known to have read. It is impossible to agree with the statement that Jane Austen 'wrote books because she loved books, and for no other reason. She did not study human nature, but loved men and women; and her realism sprang from loyalty to her friends.'[10] One must regard with reserve the facility with which there are found in Jane Austen's novels imitations of Dr. Johnson's style and identifiable traces of Richardson and Fielding. Her debt to Fanny Burney has been magnified out of all proportion to the truth. Jane Austen loved Fanny Burney's novels, lavishing such praise on *Camilla* that only her obvious sincerity makes one take her seriously. Why she so greatly admired the worst of the Burney novels, when she might have chosen *Evelina*, is a mystery beyond solution. Jane Austen was attracted to Fanny Burney because the elder writer concentrated on themes of domestic life and manners. She purloined from *Cecilia* the three words 'Pride and Prejudice'. On the slight foundation of this trifling debt and of Jane Austen's generous praise there has been based a large and elaborate superstructure of obligation which she is supposed to owe to Fanny Burney. Similarities of speech and situation have been adduced to prove her indebtedness. It has even been found possible to recognise a fundamental likeness between the plot of *Cecilia* and of *Pride and Prejudice*, whereas none exists beyond the well-worn fact that high-born families dislike marrying outside their own caste. If the use of this theme establishes a debt, then Jane Austen is indebted to the hundreds of novelists who employed it before her. Human life can provide only a certain number of entanglements and juxtapositions; the English language can provide only a certain number of words in which to express them. These are the resources of the novelist, and his chance of originality is limited to the selection and arrangement of incidents,

10 R. Brimley Johnson, *A New Study of Jane Austen*, p. 4 (published in the same volume as *Jane Austen: A French Appreciation*, by Léonie Villard, 1924).

the individuality of his interpretation, and the form and style he chooses to employ. In all these essentials Jane Austen resembles Fanny Burney as much as a racehorse resembles a pony—no less and no more. It has been suggested that Jane Austen's sense of values 'might be described as Richardson's corrected by Fielding.'[11] With the first part of this statement one cannot agree. It is true that in *Mansfield Park* she departs from the ironic method to moralise directly—a fault in her art for which an admirer might wish to blame some outside influence. But the criticism is not made in a fault-finding sense. It maintains that '*Mansfield Park* is Richardsonian through and through; Sir Thomas Bertram has the unmistakable Grandisonian stamp. Darcy and Mr. Knightley, in other novels, show marks of the same origin. Richardson, admittedly, would never have drawn them as they stand; they are Richardsonian with radical differences.'[12] These differences are indeed so radical that they seem to negative Richardson's influence. His notion of morality was certainly not Jane Austen's, and his sensibility was precisely what her fastidious taste rejected with scorn. Neither can one really claim that 'she is like Richardson in her registration of the minutest details of mannerism and behaviour'. Richardson's was the realism of the bookish man—achieved by the sedulous accumulation of minutiæ. Jane Austen's was the realism of Crabbe, though not exerted on the subjects which absorbed Crabbe's interest. And again, though Jane Austen, like Richardson, is concerned with the 'annotation of the scarce perceptible, but significant and often decisive impulses of the heart', her conception of emotions and sentiments is not his, and her method of suggestion does not appear to owe him anything. For the rest, influenced perhaps by the epistolary vogue, or perhaps by the fact that Richardson and Fanny Burney had been its greatest exponents, Jane Austen twice essayed the letter-form. *Lady Susan* is a failure which she left unrevised and unexpanded. The first draft of *Elinor*

11 E. A. Baker, *H.E.N.*, vi, p. 64.
12 *Ibid.*, p. 63.

and Marianne was also in letters, but Jane Austen soon realised that through such a medium she could never express what she wished to convey, and she abandoned the epistolary form for ever. No more striking evidence can be adduced as to the essential difference in inspiration between Jane Austen and those writers to whom she is supposed to have owed so much. With Fielding she really had much in common—not his wide field, not his bold freedom of speech, but, to a most marked degree, his attitude. Allowing for the difference in sex, that is to say for the difference in scope and in experience, Jane Austen is the feminine counterpart of Fielding. Like him she is an ironic humourist, like him she curls her lip at everything spurious. In her writings, as in his, a depth of feeling gives force to the deliberate moderation of each measured word. Each rejoices in the endless variety of human nature, and finds in affectation 'the only source of the true ridiculous.'[13] Each finds his pleasure in marking 'the nice distinction between two persons actuated by the same vice or folly.' Each views the human tangle with detachment, and metes out justice according to a sense of values so profound as to ensure to their novels the abiding trait of universality.

Among the many opinions which Jane Austen shared with Fielding was the view that 'true nature is as difficult to be met with in authors, as the Bayonne ham and Bologna sausage is to be found in the shops.'[14] Jane Austen appears to have held this conviction from the time when she was old enough to read a novel. Instead of the imitations which are usually the young author's stock-in-trade, her early writings are rollicking burlesques of every type of contemporary fiction. With complete nonchalance this girl not yet fifteen points an unerring finger at all the improbabilities and absurdities which marred the novels of her day. It begs the question to say that *Love and Friendship* is 'a criticism and

13 Henry Fielding, Introduction to *Joseph Andrews*.
14 Henry Fielding, *Tom Jones*, bk. i, chap. i.

reproduction, of art—not of life.'[15] It is a criticism of art by comparison with life, and that involves a judgment of the standard applied. G. K. Chesterton called *Love and Friendship* 'a satire on the fable of the fainting lady'. Like all the rest of Jane Austen's precocious efforts, it is much more than this, attacking as it does not only sensibility, but also the Gothic tale, and especially such survivals of the old Romantic tradition as still contributed to the unreality of fiction. Laura, as a heroine of sensibility, must have a mysterious or highly complicated origin: 'My Father was a native of Ireland and an inhabitant of Wales; my Mother was the natural daughter of a Scotch Peer by an Italian Opera-girl—I was born in Spain and received my Education in France.' She describes, in the style of the romantic novelette, that in her mind 'every Virtue that could adorn it was centred; it was the rendez-vous of every good Quality and of every noble sentiment.' One can picture the wicked glee of the youthful satirist as she twists the stale jargon: 'A sensibility too tremblingly alive to every affliction of my friends, my Acquaintance and particularly to every affliction of my own, was my only fault, if a fault it could be called.' Isobel is an excruciating example of that self-conscious prudery which believes the whole world scheming against female virtue:

> Isobel had seen the world. She had passed 2 years at one of the first Boarding schools in London; had spent a fortnight in Bath and had supped one night in Southampton.
>
> Beware my Laura (she would often say) Beware of the insipid Vanities and idle Dissipations of the Metropolis of England; Beware of the unmeaning Luxuries of Bath and of the striking fish of Southampton.

The hero typically preserves an unmeaning incognito. He is one Lindsay, whose name for particular reasons must be concealed under the name of Talbot. Here Jane hits off excellently the moth-eaten situation of cruel father and love-lorn son:

15 R. Brimley Johnson, *A New Study of Jane Austen*, p. 37 (published in the same volume as *Jane Austen : A French Appreciation* by Léonie Villard, 1924).

> 'My father, seduced by the false glare of Fortune and the Deluding Pomp of Title, insisted on my giving my hand to Lady Dorothea. No never exclaimed I. Lady Dorothea is lovely and engaging; I prefer no woman to her; but know Sir, that I scorn to marry her in compliance with your wishes. No! never shall it be said that I obliged my Father.'
>
> We all admired the noble Manliness of his reply.

Sir Edward's comment is Jane's: 'Where Edward in the name of wonder (said he) did you pick up this unmeaning gibberish? you must have been studying novels, I suspect.'

The dependence on unnecessary change of scene for diversifying the novel, and a suggestion of the picaresque element are not forgotten. Edward Lindsay quits his father's house in Bedfordshire for his aunt's in Middlesex, and though he is a tolerable proficient in geography, finds himself in South Wales. After his immediate marriage to Laura, he sets off with his bride to Middlesex. No sooner have they arrived there than the unrelenting father is announced, and the defiant couple flee to M—, the seat of Edward's dearest friend, Augustus. They come just in time to witness the arrest of Augustus for the theft of money which, before his marriage to Sophia, he has 'gracefully purloined from his unworthy father's Escritoire'. Edward goes to comfort his friend in prison, and Laura and Sophia, alarmed at his prolonged absence, order a carriage and set out for London at breakneck speed, inquiring of every decent-looking person they pass 'if they had seen my Edward', but driving too rapidly to permit of any reply. Sophia flinches at the prospect of visiting Augustus in prison; they return to Wales, and then decide to go to Scotland. It is an echo of a thousand romantic wanderings, and is scarcely more unreasoning

The recognition scene, a *sine qua non* of the ink-spattering novelist and an important ingredient even in the works of Fielding and the better writers, provided Jane Austen with an excellent target. Laura and Sophia are about to set off on another stage of their frantic Odyssey when 'a coroneted coach and 4' enters the inn-yard, and an old gentleman descends. 'At his first appearance my sensibility was wonderfully affected and e'er I had gazed a 2nd time, an instinctive sympathy whispered to my heart, that he was my Grandfather.' No sooner have they embraced than the venerable peer catches sight of Sophia and exclaims 'Another Grand-daughter'. A moment later a beautiful young man appears, and 'Lord St. Clair started and retreating back a few paces, with uplifted hands, said, "Another Grand-child! What an unexpected Happiness is this! to discover in the space of 3 minutes, as many of my Descendants" '—whereupon a fourth enters and Lord St. Clair hastily retreats before this flood of relatives.

Every aspect of sensibility is travestied. Laura finds Dorothea lacking in 'interesting Sensibility' and 'amiable simpathy' because, when they meet for the first time, Dorothea does not confide any of her secret thoughts, or ask for similar confidences. The meeting of Edward and Augustus is so affecting that Sophia and Laura faint alternately on a sofa. All records are exceeded when these sensitive females come unexpectedly upon their husbands 'elegantly attired but weltering in their blood'. Sophia shrieks and faints upon the ground. Laura screams and instantly runs mad.

> Beware of fainting fits [says the expiring Sophia] . . . Though at the time they may be refreshing and agreeable yet believe me they will in the end, if too often repeated, prove destructive to the Constitution. . . . Beware of swoons Dear Laura . . . a frenzy fit is not one quarter so pernicious; it is an exercise to the Body and if not too violent, is I dare say conducive to the Health in its consequences—Run mad as often as you chuse; but do not faint.

Jane Austen parodies Fanny Burney's affected superlatives in *The Young Philosopher*, which is stuffed with such phrases as 'softness the most bewitching' and 'vivacity the most striking'. The ravings of Laura sound suspiciously like Cecilia's frenzy fit: 'Talk not to me of Phaetons . . . Give me a violin . . . Beware ye gentle nymphs of Cupid's Thunderbolts, avoid the piercing shafts of Jupiter . . . They told me Edward was not Dead;

but they deceived me—they took him for a cucumber—' There is a very clever distinction between the self-dramatisation which impels Sophia to post to Newgate, and the selfishness which makes her decide at the last moment not to overpower her delicacy by the sight of Augustus in durance. The Radcliffian cult of scenery is mocked in that passage which describes the place chosen by Laura and Sophia for meditation: 'A grove of full-grown Elms sheltered us from the east—. A Bed of full-grown Nettles from the West—. Before us ran the murmuring brook and behind us ran the turn-pike road.' And the use of nature to echo and exacerbate the anguished mood is inimitably caricatured when Sophia is unable to endure the summer sky because it reminds her of her Augustus's blue satin waistcoat striped with white. The other sketches in Jane Austen's *Juvenilia* carry on this exuberant burlesque of fiction. Melodrama, improbability and emotional flaccidity are stressed throughout. Nothing is forgotten—not even the blank-verse prose of the sentimental school:

> 'Yes I'm in love I feel it now
> And Henrietta Halton has undone me.'

Sometimes one can distinguish the very novel which she has in mind. Miss Jane's story (second letter) is plainly reminiscent of Susannah Gunning's *Memoirs of Mary*. But some of these early writings are interesting not merely because they reveal the assured aptness of Jane Austen's critical judgment, but also because they present in embryo situations and characters which later she incorporated in her novels. When Lady Greville arrogantly summons Maria Williams to the door of her coach where, despite a cold wind, she interrogates her, we have a foretaste of Lady Catherine de Burgh and Elizabeth Bennet. In the description of Maria chaperoned to her first dance and patronised by the *élite* there is a hint of *The Watsons*.

Another early work which shows Jane Austen as an experimenter is *Lady Susan*, supposed to have been written between 1792 and 1796. It is the story of an adventuress told in letters, without comment ironic or otherwise. Since we are completely admitted into Lady Susan's unscrupulous plans, there is no suspense and no subtlety. The only benefit which might be derived from such treatment—the reader's satisfaction in knowing more than the victims of Lady Susan's schemes—is negatived in this case, because Lady Susan has such a bad reputation that, without understanding precisely what is afoot, all the other characters agree in expecting the worst. They exchange letters recounting their various impressions, and some variety is achieved by this changing of focus, but it is all flat-footed and overdrawn. Lady Susan's delight in describing her wicked intentions reminds one of the moustached villain exultantly flicking his boots with a riding-crop. The burlesques of Jane Austen's early teens are in direct line with her mature method, since broad satire may be refined by sublety. *Lady Susan* lacks satire and wit, and serves to show how undistinguished a writer Jane Austen might have been had she continued to dispense with these essentials of her art. But, in fact, she was so conscious of the ineffectiveness of this method that she brought *Lady Susan* to a hastily conceived conclusion, and made no effort to polish it for publication. It appeared in print only in 1871, when Austen-Leigh made it an addition to his memoir of his aunt.

It is not easy to trace in Jane Austen's novels the exact sequence of her development as a writer, since they were not published in the order in which they were written and since she was continually revising the manuscripts which accumulated for want of a publisher. By about 1795 she read aloud to the family at Steventon a story in letters called *Elinor and Marianne*. From this she turned to *Pride and Prejudice*, which she began in October, 1796, and completed in August, 1797—a period of ten months. The title she first intended for the novel was *First Impressions*. She was then twenty-one years of age. In November, 1797, *First Impressions* was offered to Cadell by the Rev. George Austen and refused by return of post. Within that same month Jane began to rewrite *Elinor and Marianne* in its present form, and later decided to call it *Sense and Sensibility*. *Northanger Abbey* was certainly first composed in 1798. It was originally known to Jane Austen's family as *Susan*; then it became, by the changing of the heroine's name, *Miss Catherine*, and owes its permanent title to Henry Austen who arranged for its posthumous publication. Although no consistent line of artistic differentiation can be drawn in the period of her mature creativeness, it is convenient to consider her activities in relation to her various places of residence; and certain breaks in output due to migrations or experiences seem to sanction this superficial division. In what we may call the first phase Jane Austen, working at Steventon, accomplished that amount of literary composition to which we have just referred. In the spring of 1801, she removed with her family to Bath. Her unhappiness at leaving her old home was increased that summer when, during a holiday in Devonshire, she was romantically involved with a young man who died shortly afterwards. It was a blow with which the loving Cassandra could all the more fully sympathise since her own fiancé had died in San Domingo in 1797. During the three years of the Austens' residence at Bath, Jane revised *Northanger Abbey* which was offered to Crosby and Sons of London in 1803. The manuscript was purchased for £10, and put into a drawer where it remained until it was bought back some years later.

The period between 1803 and 1811 is generally regarded as a gap in Jane Austen's creativeness, and, despite some argument as to her activity during this time, one cannot deny that it shows a great slackening in productiveness at least, if not in effort. Since *Northanger Abbey* had already been written in full, the work of revision cannot have been great. *The Watsons*, possibly also written during these years, is only a partial outline of a novel, and even if, as has been suggested, *Lady Susan* also belongs to this period, it is too brief and too unsatisfactory to be worth serious consideration. The manuscript of *The Watsons*, which contains many erasures and alterations, has in some parts the watermark ' 1803 ' and in others ' 1804 ' — evidence which seems to establish the time of composition. The manuscript of *Lady Susan* bears the watermark '1805' but, as it is beautifully written, the probability is that it is merely a fair copy of some earlier effort. This view is reinforced by the quality of the work which ranges it with the *Juvenilia*. Whether because of uncongenial surroundings, or of depression still further accentuated by the death of the beloved Mrs. Lefroy in December, 1804, and of the Rev. George Austen in January, 1805, it seems clear that between 1803 and 1811 Jane Austen virtually laid down her pen.

In 1805 the Austens removed to Southampton. In 1809, Edward, the second son (who had inherited the property of a distant relative, and had taken his family name of Knight), offered a home to his mother and sisters, and thenceforward they lived in the little cottage at Chawton which was to see the second spring of Jane's creative power. Here, in the security of a settled background, she wrote, between February, 1811, and August, 1816, *Mansfield Park*, *Emma* and *Persuasion*. She also began, but never finished, *Sanditon*. Before undertaking these new subjects, however, she set herself to revise *Sense and Sensibility*, which was published by Egerton at the author's own financial risk. It was by no means a sensational success, but that it had at last seen the light was sufficient stimulus to renewed effort, and Jane turned to the revision of *Pride and Prejudice*, which appeared in 1813. Thereafter it was easy to secure publication and *Mansfield Park* came out in 1814, to be followed in 1816 by *Emma*. Her other writings appeared only after her death.

Since *Sense and Sensibility* was Jane Austen's first mature work, it is helpful to consider it before the more brilliant novels which succeeded it. It has excellences equal to her greatest writings and faults which appeared again in her weakest—*Mansfield Park*. It would be unprofitable to seek, like some of Jane Austen's critics,[16] for parallels between the characters and situations in Jane Austen's novels and her human experience. They exist, but are not so close as to allow more than a few identifications of detail, and no possible identification of character or circumstance. This is a great solace to those who claim for her the highest level of creativeness, and not merely the reproductive imagination of, for example, a Charlotte Brontë. But although Jane Austen transmuted her experience, one would expect to find among her characters some recurring symbol of her own personality and some echo of her own life. These may be guessed in *Sense and Sensibility*, as in some of the other novels, but they may never be established.

Sense and Sensibility is to some extent a diagrammatic story with a forthright moral, which somewhat disturbs the fine balance of satire. It is a blow aimed at once against a literary fashion and against the self-indulgent emotionalism which that literary fashion deified. It was Jane Austen's intention to show that self-control was the basis of that harmony which self-indulgence destroyed. At this stage, at least, she seems to have had a view of living which, though it coincided with Christian ethics, need not necessarily have been identified with it. She had a high and even an austere standard of human behaviour, but in this earlier period it appears to have been more concerned with aesthetics than with theology. If one were to formulate the impressions gained from the majority of her writings, one would say that to her life was a bitter fruit with a sweet kernel, a thorn-thicket enclosing a green dell, a noisy tumult through which one could win to an inner peace. In her view the bitterness, the wounds and the confusion of life are due to a lack of sanity—to a fecund illusion which throughout man's days never ceases to bring forth a brood as fatal to his own happiness as it is to that of the world. It is the illusion of self-importance which so warps the judgment that either man can never see

16 e.g. Clara Linklater Thompson, whose volume on Jane Austen is permeated with such attempted proofs and parallels.

reality, or if for a moment he should glimpse it, must frantically spin some veil to obscure it if possible from his own eyes, but particularly from his neighbours. In *Sense and Sensibility* Elinor stands for clear-eyed sanity, and when self becomes insistent she steadily maintains the just proportion between the importance of her personal trials and the general scheme of things. This cannot be done without exertion, and that is why exertion is the basis of Jane Austen's creed. Once we cease to exert control over our egoism it spins a web which blinds and fetters us, and ends by isolating us from the power or even the wish to see the truth. This were to live in a false twilight instead of in the unequivocal light of day. If one must suffer through the delusions of others (and one must), at least, says Jane Austen, let us be free from self-delusion: let there be peace and harmony within. But not all of man's evasions are harmful. Many are indeed merely foolish and sometimes so naïve as to be lovable. The serious framework of Jane Austen's novels is forged from such deceptions as threaten happiness; the humour depends on the clash of foibles and on those misunderstandings which arise from the irreconcilable preoccupations of the various characters. Both aspects of Jane Austen's conception are clearly shown in *Sense and Sensibility*.

The love affairs of Marianne and of Elinor are both based on deception. Willoughby engages the affection of Marianne without a thought of returning it—through 'selfish vanity', in fact. He deceives Mrs. Smith on whom his worldly expectations depend and, when the necessity for decision arises, he abandons Marianne. She, on the other hand, despite the fact that Willoughby never makes a declaration and that his conduct is entirely equivocal, cherishes the happy delusion that he intends to marry her. Elinor, not knowing that Edward Ferrars is secretly engaged to Lucy Steele, permits herself to find in his attentions sufficient promise to allow her love of him to grow unchecked. In one respect there is not much to choose between Edward Ferrars and Willoughby, although Jane Austen seems to justify the one and rigorously condemns the other. Edward Ferrars's interest in Elinor was so marked as to secure to her the jealous dislike of his mother and sister. If he was not a deliberate deceiver, it is certain that he was not behaving like an engaged man. His general character was unstained by such behaviour as Willoughby's towards Brandon's ward, but his integrity and his sedate manner made his unwarranted interest in Elinor all the more dangerous to her peace of mind, since from him such attentions were far more credible than those of the volatile Willoughby. Elinor was deluded as to Edward Ferrars's freedom, but not as to his love for her. Marianne was deluded as to Willoughby's love, but he was bound by no prior engagement—only by his own avarice. In his weak way he seems to have grown to care for Marianne, yet he savagely repudiates her claims and marries a wealthy shrew. Edward Ferrars does not care a jot for Lucy Steele, yet he prefers to be disinherited rather than to break his honourable engagement. Jane Austen is careful to mark these differences, and that we may not blame Edward for outgrowing his love for Lucy Steele, she is shown as a mean opportunist who has been actuated throughout only by a determination to make a brilliant marriage.

The difference between Elinor and Marianne is shown in the way in which each reacts to her unhappy love affair. Marianne luxuriates in her agony. Her sufferings involve all those who love her in great unhappiness, and also in the deepest embarrassment, since she makes not the slightest effort to hide her feelings. Her prostration drives such warm-hearted friends as Mrs. Jennings to conclude that Willoughby had engaged himself to marry her, and Elinor, who considers it necessary to clear him of having broken his word, has the added misery of explaining that Marianne has never been engaged. The high-flown tradition by which lovelorn maidens fall into a decline is deliberately shattered by Jane Austen's careful explanation that Marianne's illness has resulted from a careless indifference to wet shoes.

Against the foolishness of the one sister is set the sensitive self-respect and balanced sincerity of the other. Elinor always endeavours to be just, to admit the claims of others and to conceal her own misery. She is supported by those fundamentals, 'good principles and good sense'. Never turning from fact even when it is most painful, she can be surgically truthful, as when she sets herself to show Marianne the exact value of Willoughby's confession. 'Fancy must not be led astray by tenderness'; Marianne, in forgiving Willoughby, must not be softened into loving him again, or into preserving an idealised memory of him which might lessen her hopes of happiness with Brandon. Willoughby's charm must not obscure his selfishness, and his abject confession must not be attributed to real contrition with a purpose of amendment. 'At present,' says Elinor, 'he regrets what he has done. And why does he regret it? Because he finds it has not answered towards himself. It has not made him happy.' Marianne's lips quiver, but she sees all that has happened in its true light, and she resolves to amend those faults of her own which have been largely responsible for the whole wretched business. Her resolutions are fully expressed in chapter 43 — a chapter which is too didactically explicit.

The balance between Elinor's judgment and her emotions is well preserved. Her feelings, however repressed, surge up with a force of which the reader is all the more conscious because of the restrained narrative. When Edward, whom she believes married to Lucy Steele, is seen coming up the garden path, Elinor moves away and sits down. 'He comes from Mr. Pratt's purposely to see us. I *will* be calm; I *will* be mistress of myself.' The family waits in silence until he enters. He explains. Elinor hears that Lucy Steele has married Edward's brother. 'Elinor could sit it no longer. She almost ran out of the room, and as soon as the door was closed, burst into tears of joy.'

So perfectly are the other characters drawn that each deserves a most detailed examination. Space, however, allows only a brief and general treatment. In this novel we find the first of Jane Austen's inimitable portraits of fools. Mrs. Dashwood is a charming and faulty creature—one of those foolish mothers who are presented with such skill. Good-natured, emotional and undiscriminating, she is an older Marianne. She is well-bred, and although she delights in sentimental dreams for her children, she is incapable of the brazen manœuvring of the thick-skinned Mrs. Bennet. Mrs. Jennings at first appears merely a common and comfortable woman, but she soon wins the heart by her warm-hearted generosity. Her matter-of-fact philosophy is summed-up in her efforts to soothe Marianne's broken heart with a glass of Constantia wine. The elder Miss Steele is a vulgar and stupid upstart whose garrulous revelations nullify the cautious scheming of her sister. Lucy Steele is a crafty and heartless climber. She fears Elinor's power over Edward Ferrars, and shrewdly appeals to those very qualities of honour and magnanimity which she herself lacks. The interview with Elinor in the shrubbery is a triumph of subtlety and self-control on both sides. No example of the ironic situation in which Jane Austen delighted can surpass the dinner-party at the house of Mrs. Ferrars. This arrogant dowager and her daughter set themselves to freeze and to ignore Elinor who, they believe, is secretly engaged to Edward. For Edward nothing will satisfy them but a great match with, for example, the much discussed Miss Morton whose superlativeness is summed up in the words: 'Miss Morton is Lord Morton's daughter.' To mark their coldness to Elinor the Ferrars ladies shower attentions on Lucy Steele, unconscious of her secret claim to be treated as a prospective relative. Lucy Steele rejoices in her success with Mrs. Ferrars, thinking that it will pave the way to her happy reception into the family and little dreaming that, when her engagement comes to light a few days later, she will be abused until she faints, and turned out of the house. Meanwhile she hugs herself not merely at being singled out for preference, but because she is delighted at Elinor's humiliation. The complexities of the unwitting Mrs. Ferrars, confronted with two potential daughters-in-law, and choosing to be gracious to the more dangerous and more unsuitable is high comedy with a sharp sting of retribution at the tail. It is characteristic of Elinor that she is not unhappy or agitated at the behaviour of these mean-spirited people. She merely despises them. It is a scene in which every character unconsciously reveals himself. The famous conversation between John Dashwood and his wife as to the provision that might be made for Mrs. Dashwood and her daughters is another splendid example of dramatic self-revelation. Each maintains to himself and to the other a semblance of generous consideration for the widow, while Jane Austen mercilessly directs our gaze into their selfish and penurious hearts.

Jane Austen has often been accused of stressing too much the theme of husband-hunting. A realist could scarcely have avoided such an aspect at a period when matrimony was not merely a woman's choice, but, practically speaking, her only profitable career. 'Single women have a dreadful propensity for being poor, which is one very strong argument in favour of matrimony.'[17] *Pride and Prejudice*, more than any other Austen novel, is concerned with matrimonial scheming. The circumstances of the Bennet family are admirably planned to emphasise the importance of this issue. Five portionless girls must make some provision for their future before their father's small property will pass by the law of entail to their cousin, Mr. Collins. If they do not realise the urgency of getting married, their mother realises it for them, and applies herself to husband-catching with a blatancy which almost defeats her ambition. That power of conserving family resemblances for which Jane Austen has been praised is nowhere more strikingly exercised than in her portrayal of the Bennets. Elizabeth and Jane are their father's daughters; Lydia and Kitty are their mother's. The negligible Mary seems a blend of her father's sobriety and her mother's stupidity. She

17 *The Letters of Jane Austen* (ed. Brabourne, 1884), ii, p. 296.

is a sententious dullard—a development of the moralising Julia Millar.[18] Mr. and Mrs. Bennet might be considered an elaboration of the slightly-sketched Palmers, if one could imagine Mr. Palmer ceasing to snub his vacuous wife, allowing her to take command and withdrawing into a cynical passivity. It is certain, at any rate, that Mr. Bennet's cynicism, like Mr. Palmer's rudeness, arises from a defeated sense of being unequally yoked. Mr. Elton (in *Emma*) suffers no change of disposition, although his wife is not merely silly but also a spiteful and underbred snob. This is because Elton is the male equivalent of Mrs. Elton, and he requires no defence-mechanism to get through his life with her. Mr. Bennet, having married a pretty face, finds himself saddled until death with a garrulous and insensible vulgarian. He has sufficient detachment to see this joke at his own expense and, to lessen his feeling of failure, he generalises that the world is simply a large home for the feeble-minded in which a few sane people suffer for their lack of conformity. Because he sensitively continues to feel ashamed of his wife's lack of sense he sometimes directs at her sarcasms of which she can make neither head nor tail. It is not because Mrs. Bennet's people were in trade that she is vulgar. Her brother, Mr. Gardiner, is 'a sensible, gentlemanlike man'. Mrs. Bennet is vulgar for the same reason as Lady Catherine de Burgh—because she has a coarse-grained mind. Jane Austen never meant to show vulgarity as the stigma of any particular class. It seems to have been her view that vulgarity is like the wind which bloweth where it listeth. The predicament of the two elder Misses Bennet resembles, without the disadvantage of caricature, the predicament of Evelina. Their eligible suitors become faint-hearted at the sight and sound of Mrs. Bennet and her hoydenish younger daughters. It is perhaps to widen the gap between Elizabeth and her lover that Jane Austen made Mrs. Bennet so impossible and Darcy so proudly fastidious. But he is not merely fastidious; he is

18 See *The Female Philosopher* (*Love and Freindship*, ed. G. K. Chesterton, 1922).

arrogant and a snob, and this makes him a distasteful character—to the present writer at least. He begins by being abominably rude to Elizabeth, and becomes conscious of her attractions only because she treats him with cool and sparkling scorn. He falls in love against his will, a backhanded compliment which testifies at once to Elizabeth's charm and unsuitability. Perhaps the strongest proof of her love for him was that she brought herself to forgive the implied insult. It was very clever of Jane Austen to arrange that Darcy's sister should have intended to run away with Wickham, and so provide Darcy with an excellent reason for not holding Elizabeth disgraced by Lydia's behaviour. Darcy is too concerned with cautious considerations to be likable. He is too self-assured, too invulnerable in his pride, rank and wealth. The measure of our resentment against this Cophetua is the satisfaction with which we watch Elizabeth refuse his proposal in terms which humble him to the dust. True, it is not his former attitude towards her which brings upon him her vehement condemnation. For a long time there has rankled within her a deep resentment of his open scorn for the less creditable members of her family. She knows their faults, but they are nevertheless her own flesh and blood. Such feelings, however, are as nothing compared to her anger at the sufferings which Darcy's interference has inflicted on Jane. And indeed the more one thinks of Darcy's unhesitating decision to prevent Bingley's proposal to Jane, and of Bingley's lap-dog acquiescence, the more one is assured that these reluctant lovers needed more castigation than they ever got. Elizabeth has been criticised for having too sharp and ready a tongue. Those who hold this view have evidently made no attempt to fill in the details of intonation and look which the dramatic method can only hint. If one accepts Jane Austen's words as to Elizabeth's way of neutralising her spirited sallies, one can be in no doubt of her inescapable charm: 'There was a mixture of sweetness and archness in her manner which made it difficult for her to affront anybody; and Darcy had never been bewitched by any woman as he was by her.'[19] Elizabeth's circumstances made it necessary for her to be perpetually *en garde*, and the brilliant deftness of her parries and ripostes was due not only to her quick-silver temperament, but because she was fighting, not indeed for her life, but for her happiness and self-respect. Never is her nervous skill so curiously displayed as when she takes the field against the lumbering Lady de Burgh —the young David trying to find a vulnerable spot in an extremely pachydermatous Goliath. With what power does Jane Austen make us feel the inequality of these combatants—on the one side rank, arrogance, and brutal stupidity, on the other worldly insignificance and all the indomitable spirit of a cool brain and a stout heart.

In regard to Lydia Bennet a critic has said: 'The whole treatment of Lydia conclusively removes Jane Austen from the modern realists. She is neither oppressed by ethics nor determined upon naked truth. The episode never develops into a problem.'[20] It does not become a problem, because there was nothing in the least mystifying in Lydia's elopement, which Jane Austen treated with her usual sense of proportion. Lydia's condemnation by those characters whom Jane Austen presents as the most valuable is entirely in accordance with sound ethical principles. Lydia is shown throughout as a brainless little animal, and so we can scarcely feel surprised when through a lack of training, her sensuality gets the upper hand. When Wickham refuses to marry her she is quite satisfied to remain with him without benefit of clergy. When he is bribed into marrying her, she comes flaunting home to queen it over her sisters, generously offering to get husbands for them all before the winter is over. 'I thank you for my share of the favour,' said Elizabeth, 'but I do not particularly like your way of getting husbands.' Mrs. Bennet, forgetting the method in the accomplished fact, is overjoyed at having a daughter

19 *Pride and Prejudice*, ch. 10.
20 R.Brimley Johnson *A New Study of Jane Austen*, p. 40 (published in the same volume as *Jane Austen: A French Appreciation* by Léonie Villard, 1924).

married, and especially that daughter whom she best understands. There is no problem in Jane Austen's shrewd but incidental treatment of Lydia Bennet. The treatment is incidental because Lydia is a minor character in the plot; because in any case her fate is not in the least tragic. She had lost nothing that she valued. She was not even immoral—she was amoral. Why should one use a two-handed sword to decapitate a butterfly?

The immortal Mr. Collins is so well-known as to need merely a passing glance. In him the delusion of self-importance is a monomania, and yet he is as craven a sycophant as ever drew breath. One can reconcile these contradictions only by recalling that he had spent the greater part of his life under the guidance of an illiterate and miserly father. This subjection had left in him an instinct to cower to those in authority over him, or to those who derived their importance from sources which, because he had always lacked them, he regarded with awe. Wealth and power could always secure the subservience of Mr. Collins. Because he had been used to nothing, his moderate success in life went to his weak head and 'made him altogether a mixture of pride and obsequiousness, self-importance and humility.' He marries, as he does everything else, to please his patroness. It is no mean achievement of Jane Austen's that she makes it possible to retain our respect and liking for Charlotte Lucas after she became Mrs. Collins. Poor plain Charlotte must find her security in this bumptious oaf. No wonder Elizabeth cries out in horrified amazement. And Charlotte sums up her reasons in the words: 'I am not romantic, you know; I never was. I only ask a comfortable home.' When Elizabeth visits her at Hunsford she finds that Charlotte's comfort consists in seeing as little as possible of her husband. For the most part we are too busy laughing at Mr. Collins to bother much as to whether a sound heart may not, after all, be his. We feel that we have not undervalued him when we come to his spiteful letter on Lydia Bennet's elopement. Still, he is a harmless creature in comparison with Bingley's sisters, those nettles in the path of Elizabeth and Jane Bennet.

Pride and Prejudice is, in every respect, a masterpiece. Its closely woven plot, the *élan* of its development and the minute perfection of its characterisation show nowhere an unsure touch. Whatever it may have owed to the author's later revision, there is not the slightest evidence of patching. Indeed the sustained brilliance and energy of this novel leave no room to doubt that it was composed in one creative outburst, and owed to second thoughts merely the polishing of its wit. That Jane Austen realised her own *tour de force* is evident in her words of pretended self-depreciation:

> The work is rather too light, and bright, and sparkling; it wants shade; it wants to be stretched out here and there with a long chapter of sense if it could be had; if not, of solemn specious nonsense, about something quite unconnected with the story; an essay on writing, a critique on Walter Scott, or the history of Buonaparté, or something that would form a contrast, and bring the reader with increased delight to the playfulness and epigrammatism of the general style.[21]

Pride and Prejudice was to Jane Austen her 'own darling child', and she rightly considered Elizabeth Bennet 'as delightful a creature as ever appeared in print.'[22]

Northanger Abbey, like *Sense and Sensibility*, suffers somewhat from a double aim. It is not easy to maintain an even balance in a work which satirises a school of fiction and endeavours at the same time to present a faithful picture of human life. In *Northanger Abbey* the plot and, in one instance, the characterisation are so governed by the intention of burlesquing the Gothic romance[23] that there appears to be a lack of verisimilitude. Catherine Morland is sufficiently simple and credulous

21 J. E. Austen-Leigh, *Memoir of Jane Austen*, (1871). Letter to Cassandra from Chawton, Feb. 4. 1813.

22 *Ibid.*, letter dated Jan. 29, 1813.

23 In *Sense and Sensibility* Edward Ferrars opposes the Gothic notion of scenery: 'I like a fine prospect, but not on picturesque principles. I do not like crooked, twisted, blasted trees, I admire them more if they are tall, straight, and flourishing. I do not like ruined, tattered cottages. I am fond not of nettles, or thistles, or heath blossoms. I have more pleasure in a snug farmhouse than in a watch-tower—and a troop of tidy, happy villagers, please me better than the finest banditti in the world' (ch. 18).

to accept Gothic mysteries as gospel-truth, and to expect a Gothic building to enforce such circumstances as were inevitable in Gothic novels. Her intrusive curiosity, a parody of Mrs. Radcliffe's Emilys and Elleanas, is quite in keeping with her childishness, but General Tilney is really not convincing. He is made to behave outrageously because some Montoni must be provided for Catherine in her rôle of Emily. Since his behaviour must spring from some circumstance which links it with the normal plot, it is explained as being due to the discovery that Catherine, after all, is only a penniless nobody. But however great his disappointment and however vile his temper, it does not seem probable that he would turn a young girl out of his house at a moment's notice, and make it necessary for her to return home unprotected in the common stage-coach. At that period the necessity for chaperonage would make such an enforced journey an outrage against the conventions. It was an improbable outrage, but it was the best Jane Austen could do in subjecting Catherine to a tyranny which would establish a parallel with Gothicism and which, at the same time, would seem to arise out of the everyday life portrayed.

Elizabeth Bennet's commonsense and self-reliance, her pleasure in long, muddy walks, set her apart from the heroine of romance. Catherine Morland establishes an even greater contrast. The first chapter of *Northanger Abbey*[24] is really a sardonic essay on the absurdities of the conventional heroine. It vigorously presents all the reasons which would make it impossible that anything of the slightest importance could happen to this insignificant young creature. She is the child of ordinary, respectable parents. In her earlier years she was very plain, and even when she begins to curl her hair and to gain some colour and plumpness her looks are not at all above the average. 'She could never learn or understand anything before she was taught, and sometimes not even then.' She has not the slightest ability in music

24 In regard to the consistency of Jane Austen's mental attitude, it is interesting to compare this chapter with *Love and Freindship* and again with her *Plan of the Novel* written in 1816 (included in J. E. Austen-Leigh's *Memoir of Jane Austen*, ed. Oxford, 1926).

or drawing, and up to the age of fifteen 'loved nothing so well in the world as rolling down the green slope at the back of the house.' She is a most unpromising focus for romance. At the age of fifteen her love of dirt and romping gave way to an inclination for finery. 'From fifteen to seventeen she was in training for a heroine; she read all such works as heroines must read to supply their memories with those quotations which are so serviceable and so soothing in the vicissitudes of their eventful lives.' Alas! the parish contained not one lord, not one foundling, not one man of unknown origin. 'But when a young lady is to be a heroine, the perverseness of forty surrounding families cannot prevent. Something must and will happen to throw a hero in her way.'

In choosing Henry Tilney as the hero for such a heroine Jane Austen showed her usual sense of fitness. He is an attractive and sensible young clergyman, wise and kind enough to see her honest worth, not too brilliant for her timid inexperience. He marries her because he has grown sincerely attached to her, but 'I must confess that his affection originated in nothing better than gratitude; or, in other words, that a persuasion of her partiality for him had been the only cause of giving her a serious thought. It is a new circumstance in romance, I acknowledge, and dreadfully derogatory of a heroine's dignity; but if it be as new in common life, the credit of a wild imagination will be at least all my own.'[25]

The lets and hindrances which impede this dénouement are very skilfully devised. There are no real dangers; indeed there are no real difficulties, but only such a concatenation of circumstances as would seem difficult to a young girl who has left home for the first time. That Catherine's chaperon, Mrs. Allen, should be kind, but rather self-engrossed is a good stroke, because it deprives her of that helpful support which would

25 *Northanger Abbey*, ch. xxx.

have blown away her troubles like thistledown. It is Catherine's ingenuousness which makes a little tangle seem a complicated web; and it is because of her ingenuousness that this tangle falls apart. She weaves no counter-plots; she watches each encompassing strand with troubled eyes, and because she is so simple and trusting Henry Tilney becomes the hero that she imagined him to be. For her he faces that dragon, the General, and this heroine without beauty, or brains, but with an unassuming charm which is very lovable—lives happily ever after. The success of her entire lack of strategy is in strong contrast to the failure of Isabella Thorpe's selfish manœuvring.

Mansfield Park was the first of those novels written in Jane Austen's later period. When she commenced it (in 1811) she was nearing her forties, and she had remained comparatively inactive for eight years. Of her actual experiences during that interval we know a little. Of her mental reactions we know practically nothing. One can only say that in *Mansfield Park* there is an unaccustomed sobriety and a temporary change of focus. The extent of this difference can best be judged by comparing *Mansfield Park* with the preceding novels—not merely with the exuberance of *Pride and Prejudice*, but also with the spirited irony of *Northanger Abbey* and *Sense and Sensibility*. This latter novel had shown Jane Austen not yet arrived at perfect equilibrium, wavering at times towards didacticism, but, by relaxing into her instinctive attitude, finding her true poise. In *Mansfield Park* this ironic poise is lost almost entirely. It is exerted only in the portrayal of the minor characters, such as Mrs. Norris and Lady Bertram. The plot and the main dramatis personæ are fashioned and directed from the standpoint of moral earnestness. Nor is this the only surprise in Jane Austen's fourth novel. She offers to us in Fanny Price very much the sort of heroine whom she had formerly derided. Fanny Price is a young woman of exquisite sensibility who alienates our sympathies from the first. She is too much of a 'creep-mouse'; she is too prim and juridical; she is too completely the sweet, suffering saint. Her physical delicacy is almost as extreme as her mental delicacy. She is above all things unfitted to be a poor dependent. She must have a horse because walking exercise tires her. If she pulls roses or walks a mile or so in the sun, she becomes so prostrated that she needs to be revived with a glass of wine. She has no vivacity, no youthful spirits. She is slighted and overlooked by the Bertram family, but not with deliberate unkindness. It seems as if her meekness at least as much as her dependence causes her to be set at naught. Even a poor relation need not have been so colourless. She might have been many times more cheerful than she was without overstepping the bounds beyond which poor relations may not presume. Indeed so thin-skinned and frail a poor relation could not fail to arouse in her wealthy connections an unsalutary sense of power, and to incur more bullying than might otherwise have been her share. In fact, except for Mrs. Norris who was a mean and cowardly oppressor, the others at Mansfield Park were not so much unkind as self-engrossed. They were not a whit more self-engrossed than Sir Walter Elliot and his eldest daughter Elizabeth, nor was Fanny much more ignored and ill-used than Anne Elliot. 'Anne, with an elegance of mind and sweetness of character, which must have placed her high with any people of real understanding, was nobody with either father or sister; her word had no weight, her convenience was always to give way—she was only Anne.' Fanny Price, by her uncle's ruse sent back for a while to her home in Portsmouth, is a sore trial. She finds her mother 'a partial, ill-judging parent, a dawdle, a slattern, who neither taught nor restrained her children.' Her father is a coarse man given to tippling and swearing. The children are boisterous and unmanageable. Every time the door bangs Fanny's temples ache. She pines for Mansfield. 'After being nursed up at Mansfield, it was too late in the day to be hardened at Portsmouth.' She cannot eat hash and pudding with half-cleaned knives and forks, and is constrained to defer her heartiest meal till she can send her brothers in the evening for biscuits and buns. One cannot be expected to have much patience with a girl who droops in luxurious surroundings because she is a dependent, and who, in the equality of her own home, recoils in fastidious horror at its crudities—and still droops. It does not increase our respect for her that at Portsmouth 'the men appeared to her all coarse, the women pert, everybody underbred.' It is to be feared that she was not merely a snob, but a self-righteous prig. Her strictures on private theatricals are staggering to the modern mind, particularly when we remember that there were private theatricals at Steventon. Fanny's moral reflections on every situation pall upon us, and in one instance they appear unfeeling. When Tom Bertram is very ill and threatened with consumption, her sorrow is exceeded by her perturbation at his spiritual unpreparedness: 'Without any particular affection for her eldest cousin, her tenderness of heart made her feel that she could not spare him, and the purity of her principles added a keener solicitude, when she considered how little useful, how little self-denying his life had (apparently) been.'

Throughout the novel Fanny and the earnest Edmund drive home every moral explicitly. Maria and Julia Bertram are foils for Fanny. Their selfishness, flamboyance and ungoverned passions provide a strong contrast with Fanny's selflessness, unobtrusiveness and quiet firmness. We foresee that Maria will wreck her marriage, but Julia's elopement is ill-judged on Jane Austen's part. It is improbable that the two sisters should elope at the same time, and still more improbable that Julia should elope with Yates, who is merely a chattering monkey. At Mansfield, during the week of the theatricals, she had not shown any marks of favour that would prepare us for such a violent preference later. Yates at Mansfield provides some very amusing comedy and is the necessary agent for the introduction of the play-acting virus, but it can only have been through Jane Austen's desire to limit the number of her characters that he is shown as the partner of Julia's flight. Julia

Bertram was a fine-looking girl with a large fortune. Failing to secure Crawford, she had really no reason to go from the sublime to the ridiculous. She is made to elope so as to mark the evil fruit of that indulgence which the lethargic Lady Bertram and the adoring Mrs. Norris have accorded to the sisters. But, in fact, Maria's behaviour is presented so direfully that we cannot be expected to feel further shock at the second elopement.

The characters of Mary and Henry Crawford do not seem to be consistent. They are a worldly, frivolous and fascinating pair. We are told at the beginning that their principles are not sound. Mary Crawford, however, is so good-natured that she makes a point of being attentive and comforting to Fanny when that meek creature is snubbed by Mrs. Norris. She does not show herself capable of bad taste and even her slighting observations on clergymen are made before she is aware that Edmund intends to take orders. It is very surprising, therefore, towards the end of the story to find her behaving with an insensibility that is really shocking. When Tom Bertram is supposed to be dangerously ill, Mary Crawford writes to Fanny to inquire whether she can rely on Tom Bertram's being in a decline, and to hint broadly that nothing could be more fortunate because then Edmund would inherit, and she could marry Edmund without relinquishing her intention of making a wealthy marriage. Referring to Tom Bertram's grave condition she says:

> I need not say how rejoiced I shall be to hear there has been any mistake, but the report is so prevalent, that I confess I cannot help trembling. To have such a fine young man cut off in the flower of his days, is most melancholy. Poor Sir Thomas will feel it dreadfully. I really am quite agitated on the subject. Fanny, Fanny, I see you smile and look cunning, but upon my honour I never bribed a physician in my life. Poor young man! If he is to die, there will be *two* poor young men less in the world; and with a fearless face and bold voice would I say to anyone, that wealth and consequence could fall into no hands more deserving of them.[26]

How could such a perceptive young woman have supposed that the loyal and conscientious Fanny could

26 *Mansfield Park*, ch. xiv.

smile and look cunning over the imminent death of a young man with whom she had been reared, and to whose family she owed everything? Mary Crawford could certainly have hoped for Tom Bertram's death, but her worldly sense could not have allowed her to express such hopes to a member of the Bertram family.

Henry Crawford's character seems to fluctuate unconvincingly. At first we see him as a vain and rather unscrupulous philanderer. Then, when Fanny's indifference piques him, his sole happiness seems to depend on making her his wife. Her poverty and her unpresentable family do not deter him, and when he visits Portsmouth he is as determined as ever to persevere in his suit. Nevertheless, the next thing we hear is that he has eloped with Maria (now Rushworth's wife). Had he ever had a serious feeling for Maria, one could imagine that Fanny's coldness might make him yield to the temptation of Maria's accessibility, but Jane Austen explicitly states that while flirting with both of the Bertram sisters, he concentrated on Maria only because, as she was then engaged, he need not be supposed to have any intentions. Even when he elopes with Maria he still loves Fanny. If Jane Austen meant to convey that Maria had for him a physical attraction to which he yielded, she should have made this clear. Or rather, since she had a strong objection to such themes, she should have formed some other motive. To state the circumstances and avoid the explanation merely lays her open to the charge of inconsistent characterisation.

These are the faults of *Mansfield Park*. It has many compensatory aspects. Mrs. Norris's self-justifying meanness is inimitably sketched. There are some well-managed descriptions of background, as, for example, the economy and vividness with which Jane Austen makes us visualise the ever-changing hues of the sea at Portsmouth. We hear the waves dashing against the ramparts. We smell the salt. Her power of minute realism is forever established in the much-quoted passage which describes the sordid home of the

Prices.[27] But Fanny's prim eulogy on the evergreen[28] is a bad lapse, and her rhapsody on the beauty of night[29] is even worse. Such outbursts of lyrical feeling are precluded by the ironic focus, which, although much neglected in this novel, is still sufficiently in use to render such emotional expression out of place.

Mansfield Park was, on the whole, a departure from Jane Austen's characteristic outlook and method. In *Emma* she returns triumphantly to the same level of achievement as *Pride and Prejudice*. With a resilience all the more surprising in a woman of thirty-nine, she regains not the extraordinary vivacity of *Pride and Prejudice*, but a sufficient degree of high spirits to restore her to her normal sense of proportion. She had always had strong moral principles firmly governed by the exigencies of her art. In *Sense and Sensibility* the governance was not fully established. In *Mansfield Park* it was in partial abeyance, due to some experience which so increased her moral earnestness as to impel her to that direct expression which her particular technique could not sanction. *Emma* shows her again in the full mastery of her powers.

Fanny Price was a heroine so dear to Jane Austen that she even calls her in the context 'My Fanny'. She does not seem to have doubted Fanny's claim to a favourable reception. On the other hand, she believed that Emma was a heroine whom nobody but herself would like very much. In one sense, perhaps this is true. Many critics have voiced their disapproval of Emma's self-assurance and snobbery. But the temperament of the critic can never be discounted in his criticisms, and some there are who find Emma far more lovable than Fanny. Fanny was humble, but she was convinced that her judgments were sound; and, of course, they *were* sound because they were based on unimpeachable moral principles. Emma was self-opinionated, and she was convinced that

27 *Mansfield Park*, ch. xlvi. The passage begins: 'She was deep in other musing . . .'
28 *Ibid.*, ch. xxii.
29 *Ibid.*, ch. xi.

her judgments were sound, but they were completely mistaken in every case, because they were based only on inexperience and intolerance. This difference is the key to our strong preference for Emma. If we must have youthful infallibility—always a grievous affliction to the less assured adult—then we prefer an infallibility at which we can laugh. We can not only endure, but hugely enjoy Emma's vaunting cock-sureness because we know that her house of cards will come crashing about her. Fanny's impregnable fortress is founded on a rock, and that is not likely to endear her to poor wandering mortals who bide the pelting of the pitiless storm. We love Emma because she is not wise, because we know that her blundering progress will bring her to a salutary realisation of her own shortcomings. We cannot love Fanny because she is too wise. It is perhaps unjust, or perhaps merely in keeping with some law of compensation, that in this world wisdom must be its own reward, and that we reserve our love for the foolish and the faulty.

Emma is in structure probably the most perfect of the Austen novels. An excellent critic has summed up the substance of this work in the words: 'The heroine in her wrong-headed folly spins six separate, interlacing, circles of delusion. On this highly formalised base the characters move to and fro with a naturalness that defies description.'[30] Emma's insistence on organising the lives of those around her is the mainspring of the action, and the humour lies in the comparison of Emma's misconceptions with the characters and circumstances as they really exist. Never did Jane Austen present with such unerring skill reality and delusion, and it required no little ingenuity to weave together such people and such events as might move towards their own aims without shattering too soon the fantasy which Emma has based on them. There are points at which illusion and reality impinge upon each other. Poor simple Harriet is forced to realise that the eligible suitors designed for her by Emma have other plans. Emma is forced to

30 Elizabeth Jenkins, *Jane Austen* (1939), p. 248 f.

realise that Mr. Elton has mistaken her efforts to secure him for Harriet, as efforts on her own behalf, and again that Frank Churchill's sedulous attentions to her were designed merely to cloak his secret engagement to Jane Fairfax. If these discoveries caused real suffering, we should be unable to see Emma's delusions in a comic light, but Jane Austen is careful to emphasise that the good-natured Harriet has so indefinite a character that she is ready to love any kind and personable man, and does not suffer unduly in transferring her affections. Emma is insulated against Frank Churchill's charm by her unrealised love for Mr. Knightley. It is beyond doubt, however, that if Harriet is too simple and trusting to resent Emma's interference in her life, we are much inclined to resent it for her. Jane Austen provided for this attitude by giving it an outlet in Mr. Knightley. Mr. Knightley's sanity is throughout offered as the antidote to Emma's irrational perverseness, and he never hesitates to reprove her as strongly as she deserves. But though he sees her faults very clearly, he loves her for her essential goodness of heart. He knows that her arrogance and intolerance will eventually be corrected by experience, that they arise from a hasty lack of judgment, and not from a lack of generosity. Emma's attitude to the Martins really *is* very distasteful. She scorns them because they belong to the farming class—too low for her intimacy and too high for her patronage. With the whole weight of her own prestige and personality she crushes Harriet's obvious wish to marry Robert Martin, and forces her to repay the kindness of his mother and sisters with the most unfeeling rudeness and ingratitude. Emma's attitude is that of her class and period. That she should have imposed it on Harriet was shocking from every point of view; because Harriet was a weak character, and became merely the instrument of Emma's snobbish cruelty; because Harriet was illegitimate and therefore, as Knightley points out, really the inferior of Robert Martin; because Harriet had only a pretty face to recommend her, and almost completely lacked personality and intelligence—circumstances which made it highly desirable that she should gain the protection of some honest man as soon as possible. But Emma comes to repent her behaviour sincerely, and it is an ironic comment on human nature that she begins to realise the enormity of her mistake only when it affects herself. Misinterpreting Emma's mysterious hints that a far more eligible suitor will console her for Elton's contempt, Harriet directs her ready affections towards Mr. Knightley. Then and only then does Emma see the absurdity of those pretensions with which she has inspired her simpleton protégée. Then she is only too glad to hear that Harriet will willingly turn to the rejected Robert Martin, and withholds her former threat that such a misalliance must cut her off from Hartfield for ever. Other shocks help to explode her opinionation. She finds that from the first she has misjudged everyone and misunderstood every happening—these blind stupidities recoiling upon her and stinging into life her dormant commonsense. She has put herself in a false position with Elton, whose resentment at her refusal of his proposal causes him to marry at once. Emma must show to the upstart Mrs. Elton more courtesy than she otherwise would, lest the Eltons should suppose that her coldness was due to envious disappointment. She must even, as an unmarried lady, give precedence to Mrs. Elton in company. She has flirted with Frank Churchill. Now she must bear the sympathy of those who believed her in love with him. She has confided to Frank Churchill humorous suggestions that Jane Fairfax's mysterious depression is due to the fact that she is in love with a married man. Now she finds that Frank Churchill and Jane Fairfax share a confidence from which she has been excluded, and that he has enjoyed a humorous aspect of which she was unconscious. She now realises that her hints as to Jane Fairfax's love-sickness were in the worst of taste. In a fit of nervous instability, brought on by the jarring moods and ominous silences of the unhappy picnic party, she was flippantly rude to the humble and kindly Miss Bates. Mr. Knightley's authoritative reprimand sends her in shame to make her peace. It is characteristi of Emma that, once she realises her mistakes, she feel them deeply and tries at once to make reparation.

Dramatic dialogue is so much the substance of th Austen novels that it would be invidious to single ou for praise any particular passages, but the use o dramatic monologue to forward the action is well wort noting. On the occasion of the strawberry party a Donwell, the garrulous Miss Bates, in a disjointed strea of remarks, expresses what the rest of the party migh be taken as saying if they had not been too busied i eating fruit. Again, at the ball Miss Bates, by he spontaneous flood of comments, gives us a lively pictur of the arriving guests, their greetings, their small-talk and all the stir and bustle of circulating refreshments She bridges the gap between the arrival of the first comers and the opening of the ball. In *Persuasion*,[31] Admiral Croft, walking through the streets of Bath wit Anne Elliot, is made to achieve the same purpose.

The lesser characters in *Emma* repay as full consider ation as that afforded to the heroine. Frank Churchil who seems, but is not, boyishly ingenuous; Jane Fairfa who seems not, but who is, sensitively upright; th valitudinarian Mr. Woodhouse and his true daughte Isabella; the gentle and motherly Mrs. Weston, th pushing Eltons — all live as vividly and as completel as if they were our nearest neighbours, all revea themselves so surely that, if they were silent, we coul invent speeches for them. We could predict how the would act in any situation. Is there, after all, a highe criterion of the art of fiction?

Jane Austen's heroines are the victims of some soci or financial disadvantage. Emma, the rich and conse quential heiress, is the victim of her own illusions, an is shown thoroughly humbled at the end. In *Persuasio* the heroine is at a disadvantage which, because it seem almost insuperable, arouses from the first our anxiou sympathy. It is not poverty, or obscurity or a flaw i

31 *Persuasion*, ch. xviii.

character which deprives Anne Elliot of happiness. It is because of one mistaken decision in the past that her future seems devoid of hope. When, years before the story opens, Anne refused to marry Wentworth, it was due not to a want of love, but because she feared lest an early marriage might impede his career. She was influenced by the over-persuasion of Lady Russell, who altogether disapproved of a union which seemed to offer nothing but poverty. When it is too late, Anne realises the undying quality of her love. 'She had been forced into prudence in her youth, she learned romance as she grew older.' The return of Captain Wentworth, rich, distinguished, and apparently quite indifferent, accentuates her love, her pain and her consciousness of having irrevocably ruined her life. Loneliness and isolation are the keynote to *Persuasion*. It is an autumnal symphony which, above the monotone of waning beauty, weaves every moment of pain and longing with the *motif* of endurance. There is a great deal of endurance in Jane Austen's novels—silent, polite, well-bred endurance, that patience which, she says, is synonymous with hope. Endurance can wait for better times, or even survive without them. Even at the worst, suffering wears itself out and that *is* hope, however forlorn. Anne Elliot, like Jane Austen's other heroines, cannot have the luxury of grieving alone. Indeed not only is such withdrawal considered a selfish indulgence, but we are told that human society offers the kind of solitude most suitable to a disturbed mind. Anne's 'spirits wanted the solitude and silence which only numbers can give.'[32]

Of all Jane Austen's novels none contains the intensity of emotion which pulses through *Persuasion*. It is expressed by indirection, by short dramatic sentences, by staccato repetitions, by sudden phrases or gestures which reveal only in such momentary release the crescendo of feeling that has been silently growing. When Wentworth, after the eight years' parting, enters the crowded breakfast-room at Kellynch, only a bow and a curtsey pass between the former lovers. When the

32 *Persuasion*, ch. x.

room has emptied and Anne is alone: '"It is over! It is over!" she repeated to herself again and again, in nervous gratitude. "The worst is over."' When she hears that Wentworth is freed by Louisa Musgrave's marriage to Captain Benwick, 'she had some feelings which she was ashamed to investigate. They were too much like joy, senseless joy!' In Bath, when she meets Wentworth unexpectedly in the street, he shows confusion because by that time he has begun to love her anew. She is less agitated because she has so long been accustomed to loving him secretly, and because already she suspects, even more than he, that the miracle has been performed and that his heart has returned to its allegiance. 'She had the advantage of him in the preparation of the last few moments. All the overpowering, blinding, bewildering, first effects of strong surprise were over with her. Still, however, she had enough to feel! It was agitation, pain, and pleasure; a something between delight and misery.'[33]

The stages by which Wentworth passes from coldness to love are excellently planned. At first he has a heart for any pleasing young woman who can catch it, but Anne Elliot is not out of his thoughts when he more seriously describes his ideal of womanhood as being 'A strong mind, with sweetness of manner.' After the first meeting she has the humiliation of hearing that he found her so much altered that he would not have known her again. Still, he is hyper-sensitive to her presence. He shows in various ways a desire to spare her annoyance or fatigue. The conversation in the nut-hedge proves that he is inwardly dwelling with puzzled resentment upon the past. At Lyme the fresh breeze gives bloom to her cheek and a glow to her eyes; she is stared at by a gentleman who seems to admire her exceedingly. 'Captain Wentworth looked round at her instantly in a way which showed his noticing of it. He gave her a momentary glance, a glance of brightness, which seemed to say: "That man is struck with you, and even I, at this moment,

33 *Ibid.*, ch. xix.

see something like Anne Elliot again.'"[34] Thereafter fate conspires for Anne. She secures his admiration by her behaviour on the Cobb, but since the shrewd Jane Austen doubted man's willingness to worship an ideal woman with a faded face, she gives to Anne Elliot 'a second spring of youth and beauty' and two admirers, the more dangerous of whom arouses in Wentworth a fine rage of jealousy. Thenceforward the outcome is inevitable.

In this, as in all Jane Austen's other works, she avoids describing the lovers' *éclaircissement*. Such scenes could not fail to be very emotional and could not be treated by her reticent method. In the first draft of *Persuasion* she showed Anne and Wentworth coming together in an actual interview. Then, dissatisfied with what she had written, she planned a far more subtle method of reunion. In the famous scene with Captain Harville, Anne in discussing Captain Benwick's engagement, reveals her own heartfelt convictions on the eternal constancy of women, their way 'of loving longest, when existence or when hope is gone.' Wentworth overhears, and answers her in a letter which declares his fervent devotion. It is perhaps the supreme example of Jane Austen's triumph over the difficulty imposed upon her by her art.

The softer tone of *Persuasion* has led some critics to suggest that, had Jane Austen lived, she would have brought to her writings less irony and more heart. One can only say that *Sanditon*, left unfinished at her death, is a return to her more characteristic mood of brilliant satire. In her beginning was her end.

* * * *

The chronicler of women's achievement in fiction must pause somewhere, and nowhere perhaps more fittingly than with Jane Austen. It would, perhaps have been more satisfying to go on and to show that

34 *Ibid.*, ch. xii.

what Jane Austen left unsaid about the passions Emily Brontë expressed with terrifying power—thus proving that women may claim not only the highest artistic level in fiction, but also the most profound depth and the most unshackled freedom of conception. These two women, each supplying what was deficient in the other, are the true apex of English fiction. Nobody has ever reached, much less surpassed, the perfection of Jane Austen's art; nobody has ever crossed the threshold of Emily Brontë's genius.

But one cannot rest on such an apotheosis without a backward glance, without hailing that vast army who, through some hunger of the body or of the spirit, enlisted under the tattered banner of the female pen. They come, brave and hardy as ever out of the past, pushing aside the cerecloths of time and prejudice and obloquy which have shut them from men's eyes. They press around, showing their scars and their achievements, crying like George Sand riding madly through the storm: 'Here we are! Here we are! It is our turn to be judged!' Who can doubt in surveying that great multitude, who can doubt in weighing their varied campaigns and victories, that these were no sporadic camp-followers but a united army advancing doggedly towards their objective. We have stressed their disabilities so that their feats may appear in their true light. These were women who not merely contributed to the development of English fiction, but who had to fight for their right to contribute. We have judged them not in relation to their opportunities, but by the standard which men, with every advantage on their side, established. It is because this standard of judgment had to be applied, that this book[35] traces as background the fictional movement as a whole, and considers, sometimes even in detail, the men's contribution. If this background, this scaffolding, were neglected the work of the women novelists would appear merely as an occasional

35 This final summing-up refers to the entire work *The Female Pen* which, owing to the exigencies of war-time, it was impossible to publish in one volume. The first part of *The Female Pen* appeared in 1944 under the title *Women Writers: their Contribution to the English Novel*, 1621-1744.

phenomenon, and not, as it was, an inevitable, sequential and highly characteristic movement, tending always to the moment when, having discarded the male standards by which at first they were governed, the women would choose their own canvas, their own point of view and their own technique. They can claim to have attempted almost every genre of fiction, to have enriched many and to have initiated some of the most important. They can boast that the nearer fiction came towards their characteristic outlook and subject-matter the nearer it came to reality. And they can add that it was women who were largely responsible for giving fiction this orientation, since only thus could they ever hope to make their own peculiar contribution. Fighting then on their own home territory, who could withstand them, when the long tradition of courage and genius culminated in an Austen and a Brontë? To the memory of that great band of women who contributed to the development of English fiction, a woman and a lover of English fiction, humbly offers this record of the female pen.

BIBLIOGRAPHY

Abbreviations : D.N.B.=Dictionary of National Biography ; H.E.N.= Dr. E. A. Baker's *The History of the English Novel.*

Unless otherwise stated, London is the place of publication.

An Index to the biographical and obituary notices in the Gentleman's Magazine, 1731—1780. 1891.

Biographical Dictionary of Living Authors. 1816.

Cambridge History of English Literature. 14 vols. 1907-16.

Dictionary of National Biography. 1885 ff.

Halkett and Laing. *A Dictionary of anonymous and pseudonymous Literature.* Edinburgh. 1882-8.

Julleville, L. Petit de. *Histoire de la langue et de la littérature française.* Paris. 1896-9.

Manuel de bibliographie biographique et d'iconographie des Femmes célèbres ..... par un vieux bibliophile. Turin. Paris. 1892.

Watts, R. *Bibliotheca Brittanica.* 1824.

Adams, O. F. *The Story of Jane Austen's Life.* Chicago. 1891.

Apperson, G. L. *A Jane Austen Dictionary.* 1932.

d'Arnaud, Baculard. *Les Amans malhereux, ou le Comte de Comminge.* Paris. 1766.
Euphémie. Paris. 1768.

Austen-Leigh, J. E. *Memoir of Jane Austen.* Oxford. 1926.

Austen-Leigh, M. A. *Personal Aspects of Jane Austen.* 1920.

Bailey, John C. *The Continuity of Letters.* Oxford. 1923.
Introduction to Jane Austen. Oxford. 1931.

Baker, E. A. *The History of the English Novel.* 10 vols. 1924-39.
Ed. *Aphra Behn's Novels.* 1905.

Baker, E. A. and Packman, James. *A Guide to the best Fiction, English and American, including Translations from Foreign Languages.* 3rd ed. 1932.

Baker, Reed and Jones. *Biographia dramatica.* 1812.

Ballard, George. *Memoirs of Several Ladies of Great Britain.* Oxford. 1752.

Barry, F. V. *Maria Edgeworth, Chosen Letters*, with an introduction by F. V. Barry. 1931.

Bassi, Emelia. *La Vita e Opere di Jane Austen e George Eliot : studi inglesi.* undated.

Beer, H. A. *English Romanticism.* 1899.

Bell, H. W. Ed. *Letters of a Portuguese Nun.* 1901.

Bernbaum, Ernest. ' Mrs. Behn's *Oronooko* ' (*Kittredge Anniversary Papers*, 1913).

' Mrs. Behn's Biography a Fiction ' (*Modern Language Association of America.* xxviii. 1913).

The Mary Carleton Narratives, 1663-1673 ; *a missing chapter in the history of the English Novel.* 1914.

' The Drama of Sensibility : a sketch of the history of English sentimental comedy and tragedy, 1696-1780' (*Harvard Studies in English.* 3. 1915.)

A Guide through the Romantic Movement. 1930.

Birkhead, E. ' Sentiment and Sensibility in the eighteenth century Novel' (*Essays and Studies of the English Association.* vol. xi. 1925).

The Tale of Terror ; *a Study in Gothic Romance.* 1921.

Bissell, F. O. ' Fielding's Theory of the Novel ' (*Cornell Studies in English.* 22. Ithaca, New York. 1933).

Block, Andrew. *The English Novel*, 1740-1850 ; *a Catalogue including Prose Romances, Short Stories and Translations of foreign Fiction.* 1939.

Boas, F. S. ' Richardson's Novels and their Influence ' (*Essays and Studies of the English Association.* vol. 2. 1911).

Bonnell, H. H. *Charlotte Bronte, George Eliot, Jane Austen.* 1902.

Brabourne, Lord. Ed. *Letters of Jane Austen.* 2 vols. 1884.

Bradley, A. C. ' Jane Austen ' (*Essays and Studies of the English Association.* vol. 2. 1911).

Brown, Rev. Stephen J. *Ireland in Fiction.* Dublin. 1916.

Buchan, John. ' The Novel and the Fairy Tale ' (*English Association Pamphlet.* 1931).

Burton, R. E. *Masters of the English Novel.* New York. 1909.

Butler, Harriet J. and Edgeworth, H. *The Black Book of Edgeworthstown and other Edgeworth Memoirs*, 1585-1817. 1927.

Canby, H. S. *The Short Story in English.* New York. 1909.

Cecil, Lord David. *Jane Austen.* Cambridge. 1935.

Early Victorian Novelists. 1934.

Chesterton, G. K. *The Victorian Age in Literature* (Home University Series).

Church, Richard. *Mary Wollstonecraft Shelley.* (Representative Women). 1928.

Cibber, Theophilus. *Lives of the Poets of Great Britain and Ireland.* 5 vols. 1753.

Collins, A. S. *Authorship in the Age of Johnson, being a Study of the relation between Author, Patron, Publisher and Public*, 1726-1780, 1927.

' The Growth of the English Reading Public in the eighteenth century ' (*Review of English Studies.* July-Oct. 1926).

The Profession of Letters : a Study of the Relation of Author to Patron, Publisher and Public, 1780-1832. 1928.

Conant, M. P. *The Oriental Tale in England in the eighteenth century.* New York. 1908.

Cornish, F. W. *Jane Austen* (English Men of Letters). 1913.
Crosse, W. L. *The Development of the English Novel.* New York. 1899.
The Life and Times of Laurence Sterne. 3rd ed. New Haven. 1929.
Dawson, W. J. *The Makers of English Fiction.* 1905.
Disraeli, Isaac. *Curiosities of Literature.* 3 vols. 1849.
Dobson, Austin. *Eighteenth Century Vignettes* (3 series) 1892-96.
Samuel Richardson. 1902.
Fanny Burney (English Men of Letters). 1903.
Ed. *The Diary and Letters of Madame d'Arblay.* 2 vols.
Ed. *Evelina.* 1904.
Dowden, E. *Studies in Literature,* 1789-1817. 1878.
New Studies in Literature. 1895.
Downes, John. *Roscius Anglicanus.* 1709.
Doyle, J. A. *Memoir and Correspondence of Susan Ferrier.* 1898.
Drew, E. A. *The Modern Novel: some Aspects of Contemporary Fiction.* 1926.
Dunlop, J. C. *History of Prose Fiction* (revised ed.). 1896.
Ellis, A. R. Critical prefaces to: *Early Diary of Frances Burney,* 1768-1778 (ed. Bohn. 2 vols. 1907); *Cecilia* (ed. 1882); *Evelina* (ed. 1881).
Elswood, Mrs. *Memoirs of the Literary Ladies of England.* 2 vols. 1843.
Elton, O. *A Survey of English Literature.* 6 vols. 1912-28.
The Augustan Age. 1899.
Ernle, Lord. *The Light Reading of our Ancestors; Chapters in the Growth of the English Novel.* Oxford. 1921.
Esdaile, Arundell. *A List of English Tales and Prose Romances printed before* 1740. 1912.
Fairchild, Hoxie Neale. *The Noble Savage: a Study in Romantic Naturalism.* 1928.
Firth, C. H. Ed. *Memoirs of Colonel Hutchinson.* 1885.
Ed. *Life of William Cavendish.* 1886.
Forster, E. M. *Aspects of the Novel.* 1927.
Foster, James R. 'The Abbé Prévost and the English Novel' (*Publ. of The Modern Language Association of America.* xlii. 1927).
Garnett, R. *The Age of Dryden.* 1895.
Gates, L. E. *Studies and Appreciations.* New York. 1900.
Gates, W. B. 'An Unpublished Burney Letter' (*Journal of English Lit. History.* Dec. 1938).
Genest, John. *Some Account of the English Stage.* 10 vols. Bath. 1832.
George, W. L. *The Intelligence of Woman.* 1917.
A Novelist on Novels. 1918.
Gerwig, G. W. *The Art of the Short Story. New York.* 1909.
Gildon's Langbaine. *The Lives of the Poets.* 1699.
Gosse, Edmund. *Seventeenth Century Studies* (2nd revised ed.). 1885.

Ed. Thomas Nash's *The Unfortunate Traveller*. 1892.
'A Nun's Love Letters' (*Fortnightly Review*. 43. 1888).
Grabo, C. H. *The Technique of the Novel*. New York. 1928.
Grainger, J. *Biographical History of England* (3rd ed.). 1779.
Gregory, Allene. *The French Revolution and the English Novel*. 1915.
Grierson, H. J. C. *The First Half of the Seventeenth Century*. 1906.
Gryll, M. R. G. *Mary Wollstonecraft Shelley*. 1938.
Hamelius, Dr. Paul. 'The Source of Southern's *Fatal Marriage*' (*Modern Language Review*, iv, 1909).
Hamilton, C. M. *Materials and Methods of Fiction*. New York. 1909.
Hamilton, Catherine J. *Women Writers : their Works and Ways*. 1893.
Hare, Augustus. *The Life and Letters of Maria Edgeworth*. 2 vols. 1894.
Harrington, G. *Nugae Antiquae*. 3 vols. 1779.
Harrison, F. *Studies in Early Victorian Literature*. 1895.
Hazard, Paul. *L'Abbé Prévost et l'Angleterre* : *étude critique sur* '*Manon Lescaut*.' Paris. 1929.
Hazlitt, William. *Lectures on the English Comic Writers* (3rd ed.) 1841.
Review of Fanny Burney's *Memoirs of Dr. Burney* (*Edinburgh Review*. 24 Feb. 1815).
Heine, Heinrich. *Prose Writings*. 1887.
Hentch, Alice A. *De la Littérature didactique du moyen age s'adressant spécialement aux femmes*. Cahors. 1903.
Hill, Constance. *Jane Austen, her Homes and her friends*. (3rd ed.) 1923.
Maria Edgeworth and her Circle in the Days of Bonaparte and Bourbon. 1910.
The House in St. Martin's Street. 1907.
Juniper Hall. 1904.
Fanny Burney at the Court of Queen Charlotte. 1912.
Horner, Joyce. 'Women Novelists, 1688-1797' (*Smith College Studies in Modern Languages*. xi. nos. 1-3).
Hunt, Leigh. *Men, Women and Books*. 1847.
Hutchinson, Rev. Julius. *The Memoirs of Colonel Hutchinson*. 1810.
Jack, A. A. *Essays on the Novel as illustrated by Scott and Jane Austen*. 1897.
Jacobs, Joseph. *Literary Studies*. 1895.
James, Henry. *Partial Portraits*. 1888.
Jeaffreson, J. C. *Novels and Novelists from Elizabeth to Victoria*. 1858.
Jenkins, E. *The Cavalier and his Lady*. 1872.
Jenkins, Elizabeth. *Jane Austen*. 1938.
Jerrold, W. and C. *Five Queer Women*. 1929.
Johnson, R. Brimley. *The Women Novelists*. 1918.
Novelists on Novels. 1928.
Jane Austen : her Life and Critics. 1930.
Fanny Burney and the Burneys. 1926.

Jusserand, J. J. *Literary History of the English People* (new ed.). 1926.
The English Novel in the time of Shakespeare. 1890.
Kavenagh, Julia. *English Women of Letters.* 2 vols. 1863.
Killen, Alice M. *Le roman terrifiant ou le roman noir de Walpole a Ann Radcliffe, et son influence sur la littérature française jusqu'en* 1840. Paris. 1924.
Krutch, J. W. *Five Masters: Boccaccio, Cervantes, Richardson, Stendhal, Proust.* 1931.
Lang, Andrew. *History of English Literature from Beowulf to Swinburne.* 1912.
Langbaine, Gerard. *An Account of the English Dramatic Poets.* Oxford. 1691.
Lanier, S. *The English Novel and the Principles of its Development.* New York. 1891.
Lasserre, Pierre. *Le Romantisme français: essai sur la révolution dans les sentiments et dans les idées au XIXe siècle.* 1919.
Lathrop, H. B. *The Art of the Novelist.* 1921.
Lawless, Emily. *Maria Edgeworth* (English Men of Letters). 1904.
Leavis, Q. D. *Fiction and the Reading Public.* 1932.
Lloyd, Christopher. *Fanny Burney.* 1936.
Lodge, E. *Portraits of Illustrious Personages of Great Britain.* 12 vols. 1835.
Longueville, T. *The First Duke of Newcastle-on-Tyne.* 1910.
Lovatt, Robert and Hughes, Helen. *The History of the Novel in England.* 1933.
Lower, M. A. Ed. *Lives of the Duke and Duchess of Newcastle.* 1872.
Lubbock, P. *The Craft of Fiction.* 1921.
Lussky, A. E. *German Romanticism.* 1932. (Translation of *Deutsche Romantik* by Oskar Walzel. 2 vols. 1918).
Macaulay, Thomas Babington. *Critical and Historical Essays.*
McIntyre, C. F. *Ann Radcliffe in relation to her time.* New Haven. 1920.
Horace Walpole and the English Novel, 1764-1820. 1934.
Mais, S. P. B. *Books and their Styles.* 1920.
Malden, S. F. *Jane Austen* (Famous Women). 1889.
Marshall, Julian. *Life and Letters of Mary Wollstonecraft Shelley.* 2 vols. 1889.
Masefield, Muriel. *Women Novelists from Fanny Burney to George Eliot* (University Extension Series). 1934.
Masson, David. *English Novelists and their Styles.* Cambridge. 1859.
Mathias, Thomas J. *The Pursuits of Literature.* 1798.
May, Marcel. *La Jeunesse de William Beckford, et la genèse de son 'Vathek.'* 1928.
Meakin, A. M. B. *Hannah More* (Eminent Women). 1911.
Meres, Francis. *Palladis Tamia.* 1598.
Mitton, G. E. *Jane Austen and her Times.* 1905.
Moore, F. F. *The Keeper of the Robes.* 1912.
Moore, Virginia. *Distinguished Women Writers.* New York. 1934.

More, Paul Elmer. *The Drift of Romanticism.* 1913.

Morgan, C. E. *The Rise of the Novel of Manners : Fiction between* 1600 *and* 1740. New York. 1911.

Morley, Edith. ' Fanny Burney ' (*Essays and Studies of the English Association.* no. 60. April. 1925).

Nicol, J. R. Allardyce. *Restoration Drama*, 1660-1700. (2nd ed.) 1928.

Nichols, John. *Illustrations of the Literary History of the Eighteenth Century.* 1817.

Overton, G. M. *The Philosophy of Fiction.* New York. 1928.

Painter, William. *The Palace of Pleasure* (ed. Jacobs. 3 vols. 1890).

Parrish, M. L. *Victorian Lady Novelists.* 1933.

Paterson, A. H. *The Edgeworths* (Univ. Tutorial Press). 1914.

Patterson, Richard Ferrar. *Six Centuries of English Literature.* 6 vols. 1933.

Perry, B. *Study of Prose Fiction.* New York. 1902.

Phelps, W. L. *Essays on Modern Novelists.* New York. 1910.

Pollock, W. H. *Jane Austen, her Contemporaries and herself.* 1899.

Praz, Mario. *The Romantic Agony* (Translated). 1933.

Prestage, E. Ed. *Letters of a Portuguese Nun.* 1903.

Railo, Eino. *The Haunted Castle : a Study of the Elements of English Romanticism.* 1927.

Raleigh, Sir Walter. *The English Novel.* 1894.

Rawlence, Guy. *Jane Austen* (Great Lives). 1934.

Reeve, Clara. *The Progress of Romance.* 1785.

Reynaud, Louis. *Le Romantisme ; ses origines anglo-germaniques.* 1926.

Rhydderch, David. *Jane Austen : her Life and Art.* 1932.

Rickert, Edith. Translator of *Lays of Marie de France* (ed. Nutt. 1901).

Roquefort, J. B. de. Ed. *Works of Marie de France.* 2 vols.

Rossetti, Lucy Madox. *Mrs. Shelley* (Eminent Women). 1890.

Sackville-West, V. *Aphra Behn*, 1640-1689. 1927.

Sadleir, Michael. ' The Northanger Novels ; a Footnote to Jane Austen ' (*Essays and Studies of the English Association.* no. 68. Nov. 1927).

Introduction to 1927 ed. of *The Heroine* by Eaton Stannard Barrett.

Saintsbury, George. *The English Novel.* 1913.

A History of Criticism and Literary Taste in Europe. Edinburgh. 1900.

A Short History of French Literature. Oxford. 1882.

A History of the French Novel. 1917.

A History of Elizabethan Literature. 1887.

A History of Nineteenth Century Literature, 1780-1895. 1896.

Scott, Sir Walter. *Lives of Eminent Novelists and Dramatists.* 1835.

Ed. *Mrs. Radcliffe's Novels* (Ballantyne). 1824.

Seeley, L. B. *Fanny Burney and her Friends.* 1890.
Sheavyn, Phoebe. *The Literary Profession in the Elizabethan Age.* Manchester. 1909.
Simonds, W. E. *Introduction to the Study of English Fiction.* New York. 1911.
Singer, G. F. *The Epistolary Novel : its origin, development, decline and residuary influences.* 1933.
Small, Miriam R. *Charlotte Ramsay Lennox.* Yale Univ. Press. 1935.
Smith, G. B. *Poets and Novelists.* 1875.
Smith, Goldwin. *Life of Jane Austen* (Great Writers). 1890.
Soet, Frans de. *Cavalier and Puritan in the seventeenth century.* Delft. 1932.
Stephens, Sir Leslie. *English Literature and Society in the Eighteenth Century.* 1904.
A History of English Thought in the Eighteenth Century. 2 vols. 1876.
Hours in a Library. 1874.
Stoddart, F. H. *The Evolution of the English Novel.* New York. 1900.
Stokoe, F. W. *German Influence in the English Romantic Period,* 1788-1816. 1926.
Summers, Montague. ' A Great Mistress of Romance : Ann Radcliffe, 1764-1823 ' (*Royal Society of Literature.* vol. xxxv.)
Ed. *Works of Aphra Behn.* 1915.
'The Source of Southern's " The Fatal Marriage" ' (*Modern Language Review.* April. 1916).
' Jane Austen : an Appreciation ' (*Royal Society of Literature Transactions.* xxxvi. 1918).
Thackeray, W. M. *The English Humorists of the Eighteenth Century.* 1853.
Thomson, Clara L. *Jane Austen : a Survey.* 1929.
Tieje, A. J. ' The Theory of Characterisation in Prose Fiction prior to 1740 ' (*University of Minnesota Studies in Language and Literature.* 1916).
Tinker, C. B. *Dr. Johnson and Fanny Burney.* 1912.
Tompkins, J. M. S. *The Popular Novel in England,* 1770-1800. 1932.
' Ramond de Carbonnières, Grosley and Mrs. Radcliffe ' (*Review of English Studies.* July. 1929.)
Tourtellot, A. B. *Be Loved no More.* 1938.
Trahard, Pierre. *Les maitres de la sensibilité française au XVIIIe siècle.* 2 vols. 1931-32.
Tucker, T. G. *The Foreign Debt of English Literature.* 1907.
Tuckerman, B. *A History of English Prose Fiction.* New York. 1891.
Turberville, A. S. *English Men and Manners in the Eighteenth Century : an illustrated narrative.* 1926.
Upham, A. H. ' Lucy Hutchinson and the Duchess of Newcastle ' (*Anglia.* xxxvi. 1912).

Verschoyle, Derek. *The English Novelists.* 1937.

Villard, Léonie. *Jane Austen : a French Appreciation* (Translated). 1924.

Walford, L. B. *Twelve English Authoresses.* 1892.

Walker, H. *The Literature of the Victorian Era.* Cambridge. 1910.

Walpole, Horatio. *A Catalogue of the Royal and Noble Writers of England* (ed. Parks. 5 vols. 1806).

Works. 5 vols. 1798.

Ward, A. W. *History of English Dramatic Literature.* 3 vols. 1899.

Warren, F. M. *The History of the Novel previous to the Seventeenth Century.* New York. 1911.

Warren, George. *Impartial Description of Surinam.* 1667.

Wharton, Edith. *The Writing of Fiction.* 1925.

Whincop, Thomas. *Scanderbeg* (with appended list of dramatic authors covering period until 1747).

Whitmore, Clara. *Women's Work in Fiction from the Restoration to the Mid-Victorian Period.* New York. 1910.

Wicher, George F. *Life and Romances of Mrs. Eliza Haywood.* New York. 1915.

Wieten, A. A. S. *Mrs. Radcliffe : her relation towards Romanticism ; with an appendix on the novels falsely ascribed to her.* Amsterdam. 1926.

Wilson, F. P. Ed. *The Bachelor's Banquet* by Dekker, 1929.

Wright, James. *Historia Histrionica.* 1699.

Woolf, Virginia. *The Common Reader.* 2 vols. 1925.

Zimmern. *Maria Edgeworth* (Eminent Women). 1883.

INDEX

The references are to pages; (n) signifies a footnote.